EMBRACING THE SUPERNATURAL IN JUDAISM

Signs from Our Deceased Loved Ones and Stories About the World-to-Come

Stephen A. Karol

Amazon

D1503092

Excerpts from A Passover Haggadah, Revised Edition, 1994 by Central Conference of American Rabbis; B'chol L'vavcha: With All Your Heart, 1976 by Central Conference of American Rabbis; Gates of Shabbat, 1991 by Central Conference of American Rabbis; Mishkan HaNefesh, 2015 by Central Conference of American Rabbis; Mishkan T'filah, 2007 by Central Conference of American Rabbis; The Torah: A Modern Commentary, 2005, by Central Conference of American Rabbis; and The Torah: A Women's Commentary, 2008, by Central Conference of American Rabbis and Women of Reform Judaism. Used by permission of the Central Conference of American Rabbis. All rights reserved.

Permission granted for excerpts From Major Trends in Jewish Mysticism, Gershon Scholem, 1995, Penguin Random House.

Excerpt From The Hebrew Alphabet: A Mystical Journey, ©1998 Edward Hoffman. Illustrations by Karen Silver.
Used with Permission from Chronicle Books, LLC.
Visit www.ChronicleBooks.com.

Excerpt From The Hand on the Mirror: A True Story of Life Beyond Death by Janis Heaphy Durham, copyright ©2015. Reprinted by permission of Grand Central Publishing, an imprint of Hachette Book Group, Inc.

Excerpts from The Everything Kabbalah Book by Mark Elber, Copyright ©2006, Simon & Schuster, Inc.
Reprinted by permission of Adams Media, an imprint of Simon & Schuster, Inc. All rights reserved.

Excerpts from The Jewish Book of Why, Alfred J. Kolatch, 1981, The Second Jewish Book of Why, Alfred J. Kolatch, 1985, and The Jewish Mourner's Book of Why, 1993--Reproduced by arrangement with Jonathan David Publishers, Inc. www.jdbooks.com.

Permission provided by the University of Nebraska Press for excerpts from

This book is dedicated to:

My wife Donna, whose faith in undying love has inspired me to change my beliefs and write this book;

My parents Joseph and Ruth Karol, whose lives ended too soon but whose spirits continue to motivate me;

My friend Gary Kamen, whose personal kindness and editorial expertise have enriched my journey as an author.

CONTENTS

INTRODUCTION: LINKS BETWEEN
THE LIVING AND THE DEAD

A song from the 1960s, a mysterious peanut, an inconspicuous rubber band and an ice cream truck…you may wonder what these diverse items have to do with life-after-death experiences. Allow me to explain.

When the Covid-19 coronavirus pandemic reached Long Island in March of 2020 and New York Governor Andrew Cuomo announced stay-at-home regulations, I had some doubts about how I was going to spend my free time. Although I'm retired, I had a full schedule of classes to take and classes to teach out in the pre-pandemic world. Previously, when my wife Donna—who is a music teacher at a private school and a piano teacher with her own studio—and I would talk about our days, I would usually have a lot to say about how I'd spent my mornings and afternoons. Faced with the prospect of going nowhere and doing nothing, I became concerned that she would get bored with me. While she thought I was kidding, I was truly concerned. We were sitting at the kitchen table when, all of a sudden, music began to play on my iPad. My iTunes app hadn't been selected and the song hadn't been cued up or played recently. It was an oldie from the Sixties by the "Turtles", called "I Know She'd Rather Be with Me." We searched and searched for a reason why this particular song would be playing so randomly and without either one of us initiating it. We were shocked and confused, and then we smiled. I got the message!

Some months ago, Donna and I were discussing her relationships with her mother and grandmother, both of whom had died. She was telling me a story to be included in this book that contained negative references to both women. Donna decided to take a break from our conversation, and she went outside to the deck of our apartment. Glancing down at the floor, she found a peanut. I eat peanut butter, but not peanuts. Neither one of us eats on the deck. We live on the second floor of our building, so it couldn't have been dropped there by someone else. Our cleaning woman is the only other person who comes into our apartment, and she doesn't bring peanuts with her. Its appearance was a mystery—except that, when Donna found the nut, she had a flashback to her late grandmother who, whenever she left the house, would always take a piece of bread and a peanut with her. Overcome with emotion, Donna threw the nut over the railing to the grass below. When we went downstairs to find the peanut in the dark, something else happened: we smelled the distinctive, sweet fragrance of Donna's late mother's perfume. There was no one else around, and the windows and sliding doors of the apartments on the first floor were all closed. The fragrance didn't seem to have a source, but it was pervasive. By the way, I found the peanut the next day and deleted any negative references to her mother and grandmother from my manuscript.

Last year, I was asked to conduct a funeral for a man I didn't know. This isn't unusual for me as a retired rabbi, and this service was like many others that begin at a funeral home and conclude at a cemetery. The widow and her two children delivered the eulogies, and each one of them spoke about their husband and father as having been "the fix-it man." They all agreed that he would fix things in the house with rubber bands, paper clips, and duct tape. Their reminiscing brought smiles to the faces of family and friends—especially when one of them remarked that this was his way of making everything okay. As I left the funeral home and headed to my car, I looked down at the small patch of grass between the door and the parking lot. There, hidden among the leaves of grass, was a rubber band. I did a double take, picked it up, put it on my wrist, and concluded that this was a "sign" from the deceased. When we all got together at the grave, I walked up to the wife before I started the service, handed her the rubber band, and said: "I found this outside the funeral home. I think it's a message from your husband that everything is going to be okay." She and her children teared up, nodded, and thanked me.

I did a number of funerals during the beginning of the pandemic (while wearing a mask and social distancing). They were all graveside ceremonies with a limited number of people. At one of them—for the first time in more than 40 years of my conducting funerals—the mourners brought a bottle of gin and some cups to toast the deceased. They described her as a woman who loved life, and I found out that she loved to drink gin and have ice cream every night. Shortly after the service concluded and they were all enjoying their tribute to her with more than a sip of gin, I heard a familiar sound coming from one of the streets that runs parallel to the cemetery. The sound was the music from a Mister Softee truck—one of the deceased's favorite brands of ice cream. The mourners and I were convinced that it was a "sign" from their Mom/Grandma.

Many people will be cynical about these experiences. Skeptics will certainly ask a number of pertinent questions: Can't the playing of the song be explained logically rather than seeing some supernatural[1] significance in it? How can you possibly think that a peanut could have any meaning at all? Wasn't it just coincidence that you hear about the man who used rubber bands and then you see one on the grass? Isn't it just random rather than purposeful that a Mister Softee truck would be passing by a cemetery at a time when a woman who had loved ice cream was being buried?

I've asked questions like these for most of my life. I always believed in logic and pure coincidence. Even though I have been a spiritual leader, I did not agree with the spiritual interpretation that some of my congregants and friends attached to seemingly random occurrences. While I have always believed that "God works in mysterious ways," I was convinced that there was no reasonable explanation for random occurrences other than co-incidence or dumb luck. I had been trained by my parents, by my teachers, and at rabbinical school to use intellect and logic to analyze why and how things happened in the world. I believed the supernatural should be viewed symbolically and metaphor-ically, a representation of an idea but not reality itself.

The "appearance" of Elijah on Passover is an example of that. What is important is the hope that Elijah represents, ra-ther than a too-literal contention that someone who didn't die could miraculously visit every house where a Seder is being held. Similarly, my co-religionists didn't pray for resurrection of the dead, as our more traditional friends did. We were taught that we achieve immortality through our deeds in life and in the memories of our loved ones and friends. When we would say that our souls would "return to God in the World-To-Come" when we died, I never thought that there could be any connec-tion between those who have died and those who are still alive.

When I began my voluntary early retirement in the summer of 2014, I embarked on a journey that had intellectual, social, and spiritual aspects. For the first year, I was predominantly a student at the Hebrew Union College-Jewish Institute of Reli-gion in New York City and in the Osher Lifelong Learning Insti-tute program (OLLI) at Stony Brook University, and I met a lot of great people. I had the opportunity to study with professors and instructors and encounter subjects to which I hadn't been exposed that much previously. Jewish beliefs about the afterlife and mysticism interested me the most, and I have been fascin-ated by what I have learned. In addition, I have talked with my wife, my rabbinic colleagues, friends, and acquaintances who have had experiences with "signs" from deceased relatives and friends. I have studied Jewish texts, such as the *Talmud, Pirkei Avot* (The Sayings of the Fathers), the *Tanakh* (the Hebrew Bible), the *Zohar* (the mystical Book of Enlightenment), and the *Midrash* (legend literature). And, I have discovered that there is a series of books called *GodWinks*, an area of psychology pertaining to coincidence but connected to God, and a large body of literature about "signs."

I've also found that many people who have experiences that they interpret as "signs" are reluctant to reveal them to others, including family members. They are afraid of being dismissed and disregarded and disrespected. When they find an attentive ear and a receptive spirit, though, they feel affirmed and re-assured and normal. And, what struck me the most about these people and their stories is that they are happy to have these experiences and to share them. They find comfort in believing and feeling that they still have a link to their deceased relatives and friends. They find joy. They find faith. All of this hap-pens because they are receptive to the possibility of contact from above, communication from beyond, and spirituality within. For many, it has strengthened their belief in God, eternal life, boundless love, and great hope.

As with my first book, *Finding Hope and Faith in the Face of Death: Insights of a Rabbi and Mourner*, this book is intended to bring hope and faith, knowledge and comfort to its readers—no matter what their religious background or lack of a background. There is much more in Jewish tradition about the links between the living and the dead than I ever thought possible. Too often, we Jews and Christians and Muslims tend to look to one text or one story to prove a point or establish a custom or belief. For example, the Book of First Samuel contains an incident in which King Saul goes to the "Witch" of Endor to bring the prophet Sam-uel back to life. She does, and the prophet yells at Saul for doing something that the Torah absolutely forbade. Suffice it to say that things don't end well for Saul. But there is more to Jewish belief through the generations than that story. I have tried to be as inclusive as possible in this book, while maintaining a deep re-spect for our tradition.

So, I invite you to go on an intellectual and spiritual journey with me now. Try to do so with an open mind, a gentle spirit, and a willing heart. We will go back to 4,000 years ago and confront the fear of idolatry and of "The Pit." We will see what the Rabbis in later centuries thought about voices from above and spirits in cemeteries and explore how supernatural phenomena made their way into prayers and customs. We will find out whether Judaism believes in "Heaven" and "Hell," and if not, how the afterlife is perceived. We will deal with the sense of cause and effect in our lives, and whether we have the power to make things happen through prayer or superstition to produce the results we want—or is it all just dumb luck and pure coincidence? We will go on a "magical mystery ride" with Jewish mysticism and Hasidic stories, and focus on one famous Jewish prayer that our tradition says has the power to affect the afterlife of the deceased. We will give voice to the testimony of the recipients of signs through dreams and a sense of their loved one's presence, through significant numbers repeating and coins appearing out of nowhere, and through music playing and lights flashing (or not) for no apparent reason. We will mention familiar shapes and persistent animals around us, meaningful objects cropping up, and lights in photos that weren't visible when the picture was taken. Finally, we will consider the possibility that, instead of being weird, delusional, silly, and ridiculous, the people who experience signs are the recipients and beneficiaries of blessings made possible by God. And when we are done, it is my hope and my faith that you will have gained knowledge and comfort, and that you will have a smile on your face. So, let's get started.

CHAPTER 1: WHEN THE "SUPERNATURAL" AND JUDAISM AGREE

In his book *Memories, Dreams, Reflections*, Carl Jung M.D. reported the following evidential ADC [After Death Communication]:

"One night I lay awake thinking of the sudden death of a friend whose funeral had taken place the day before. I was deeply concerned. Suddenly I felt that he was in the room. It seemed to me that he stood at the foot of my bed and was asking me to go with him. I did not have the feeling of an apparition; rather, it was an inner visual image of him, which I explained to myself as a fantasy.

Then I said to myself, 'Proof is neither here nor there! Instead of explaining him away as a fantasy, I might just as well give him the benefit of the doubt and for experiment's sake credit him with reality.' The moment I had that thought, he went to the door and beckoned me to follow him."[2]

You may be thinking that this book was written by a "true believer" or by someone who has had an incredible number of experiences involving "signs." If that's what you're thinking, you're wrong. I am married to a true believer, and I usually describe myself as a "convert" to her way of thinking and feeling about the connection between the living and the dead. As for experiences with signs, the number for me has been incredibly low. There are a couple of reasons for that—first, one has to be receptive to signs and acknowledge and identify them as such; and second, my experiences of receptivity and acknowledgment and identification have been relatively recent. As I said in the Introduction, I was raised to be intellectual and logical. The truth is, though, I was always fascinated by the supernatural and phenomena that defied logic—and that included "signs." Maybe it was because I wanted them to be true or that I simply was open to considering the possibility.

My earliest memory of this fascination comes from the Fifties when I was a pre-teen. I recall one of my friends telling me about a "neat" book called *The Search for Bridey Murphy*. Published in 1956, it was about a Colorado woman named Virginia Tighe who had undergone hypnotic regression and revealed to her hypnotist Morey Bernstein that she had been an Irish woman living in Cork in the early 1800's. During her sessions in 1952, she recalled specific details about her parents and her husband and her death—all related to Bernstein with an Irish brogue. Virginia was 29 at the time, was born and raised in the Midwest, and had never been to Ireland. When the story was conveyed in a series in the *Denver Post* in 1954, it led to the selling of the rights to a movie, which was produced by Paramount and starred Academy Award winner Teresa Wright.

Amazed by this story, I developed an interest in the supernatural and science fiction that was fed by my connection to television and my religion. I watched *The Twilight Zone* from 1959 to 1964 and *The Outer Limits* from 1963 to 1965—often with my parents and brother Larry (who became and still is a *Star Trek* fan). Then, I discovered in my teens that Orthodox Judaism believed in the resurrection of the dead so much that it was prayed for every day. We didn't do that in the Reform temple in which I grew up. When I began my rabbinical studies at the Hebrew Union College-Jewish Institute of Religion for a year in Jerusalem, and continued with that during four years in Cincinnati, I learned more about resurrection and then about *gilgul hanefesh* (the concept of reincarnation in Jewish mysticism). And, throughout my years in the rabbinate, I read and taught about two influential books: *The Death of Death: Resurrection and Immortality in Jewish Thought* by Neil Gillman, and *Does The Soul*

Survive? A Jewish Journey to Belief in Afterlife, Past Lives & Living with Purpose by Rabbi Elie Kaplan Spitz. The courses I have taught using those books have been among the most popular of my adult education offerings in more than 40 years. You'll read more about them in a subsequent chapter when I discuss the prevalence of "supernatural" phenomena in traditional Jewish thought and literature.

There is also a supernatural quality attached to Jewish marriage by some people. The Yiddish word *bashert* (also spelled *beshert)* is mentioned to describe how the couple met and fell in love. The word can appear as a noun, as in "she's my *bashert"*—my soul mate. It can also be an adjective, as in "our meeting and falling in love was *bashert"*—predestined, meant-to-be. I hear this over and over again from couples whose weddings I conduct, and my wife and I believe that's what happened with us. Whenever I hear someone mention this, it is clear to me that whoever says it sees it as a positive event and acknowledges that a force/Force above and beyond them or within them made it possible. For me, that falls into the category of what I call "supernatural." The individuals are the recipients rather than the instigators of their love and they are happy that it came to be. The implication is that God is involved as a *shadchan*—a matchmaker, or, more correctly, "The Matchmaker." That point is stressed in the Talmud:

"God takes single individuals and causes them to dwell in a house by properly matching a man to a woman. This is similar to the Exodus from Egypt, which culminated in the splitting of the Red Sea, where He released prisoners into prosperity....Forty days before an embryo is formed a Divine Voice issues forth and says: 'The daughter of so-and-so is destined to marry so-and-so; such-and-such a house is destined to be inhabited by so-and-so; such-and-such a field is destined to be farmed by so-and-so.'... This clearly states that these matters, including marriage, are decreed for a person even before he is formed."[3]

Sixteenth Century Rabbi Ovadia ben Jacob Sforno offers two pertinent commentaries on the story in Genesis about Abraham sending his servant back to his ancestral homeland to find a wife for his son Isaac. Setting up the requirements for the ideal woman who will be kind and compassionate, the servant says: "... let her be the wife **whom the Lord has decreed** for my master's son."[4] Sforno comments: "This recalls the statement in the Talmud Sotah 2 that already prior to birth a heavenly voice proclaims **which girl is destined to marry which young man. This was proof to me that all of this has been planned so by G'd.** [5] [Emphasis added] In verse 50, Laban and Bethuel [Abraham's nephew and great-nephew] declare: **"The matter was decreed by the Lord**; [Emphasis added] we cannot speak to you bad or good."[6] Sforno finishes the sentence for them: "...in order to neutralize His decree (or) to make His decree come true, seeing that He does not need our help in this respect."[7] And then, in verse 51, Laban and Bethuel agree to let Rebekah [Isaac's future wife] go with the servant, saying "take her and go, and let her be a wife to your master's son, **as the Lord has spoken.**" [Emphasis added][8] Sforno comments: "Since it is Hashem's will, you are able to take her even without our permission. Hashem declares who a person will marry and in this case He has given a clear sign of what He has decreed.[9]

So, going all the way back to the Book of Genesis, and moving forward to Sforno, it is apparent that there was some belief in God controlling what happens with humans on Earth. This doesn't mean that this has been a position officially taken by Judaism throughout the centuries. But it does mean that there is evidence to support the idea that what we may assume to be totally within the control of human beings may not be. It doesn't mean that God manipulates us or our emotions as if we were marionettes at the end of some strings. But it does mean that we should at least consider the possibility that God cares about us and what happens to us during our lives. I believe that our faith in God and our ongoing connection to our deceased family and friends can combine to enhance the quality of our lives, give us a sense of perspective about death, and sustain our love forever.

I see a connection between believing in past lives and acknowledging that our contact with those who have died can be continuous. Those who have either or both of these beliefs have told me that they hesitate to talk about them with friends or even with family because they will be regarded as being "weird." I know or have met many people who are reluctant to share their experiences with others due to a fear of being labeled negatively and stigmatized as someone to be avoided. When I have asked them to share their experiences with me, there is almost always a real or virtual sigh of relief that someone finally is interested in them and doesn't disapprove of their stories. When I tell them that their stories are similar to others I've collected, they are comforted as if they are part of a special and proud club. Their memories and experiences can stretch the limits of logic and intellect, but they can touch your heart and penetrate your soul.

In his well-known book *The Jewish Way in Death and Mourning*, Rabbi Maurice Lamm wrote:

"Man has had an abiding faith in a world beyond the grave. The conviction in a life after death, unprovable but unshakeable, has been cherished since the beginning of thinking man's life on earth...

The after-life has not been 'thought-up'; it is not a rational construction of a religious philosophy imposed on believing man. It has sprung from within the hearts of masses of men, a sort of *consensus gentium*, inside out, a hope beyond and above the rational, a longing for the warm sun of eternity.

The after-life is not a theory to be proven logically or demonstrated by rational analysis. It is axiomatic. It is to the soul what oxygen is to the lungs. There is little meaning to life, to God, to Man's constant strivings, to all of his achievements, unless there is a world beyond the grave."[10]

What happens in "a world beyond the grave?" What would we *like* to have happen in that world? And how would we want what happens in that world to affect what happens in this world? Are we eager for or afraid of a connection with "a world beyond the grave?" If we had such a connection, would it uplift us or depress us? These and other questions will be answered in the following chapters. Remember: the subject of "signs" is happy, positive, inspiring, and hopeful. It is not sad, negative, depressing, and hopeless. Since I believe that God plays a role in the experiences you will read about, I feel privileged to bring them to your attention in this book.

CHAPTER 2: IT ALL STARTS – BUT DOESN'T END – WITH THE BIBLE

"Like other peoples in the ancient Near East, the Israelites held various conceptions of a hereafter. The Tanach—the Torah, Prophets, and Writings—demonstrates an evolving understanding of life after death...Two basic ideas seemed to dominate biblical thinking on life after death: 1. God is life-affirming and the source of all goodness. One finds in the Hebrew Scriptures few speculations about life after death and little preoccupation with the hereafter. The ultimate purpose is to 'sanctify' life here on earth. 2. Death does not represent a total annihilation of the individual but a transition to a new kind of life, where people meet their own ancestors, continuing to live in a shadowy kind of existence."[11]

One of the questions I have been asked most often during my career as a rabbi is this: "Do Jews believe in Heaven and Hell?" My initial thought is to answer a question with other questions: Which Jews—Orthodox, Conservative, Reform, Reconstructionist, Renewal, secular? Do you mean "Heaven" as a place of reward? Do you mean "Heaven" up in the clouds somewhere? Do you mean "Hell" under the ground? Does it include the Devil/Satan/Lucifer? Do you mean now or in the past? And, if in the past, when—Biblical times, Rabbinic times, Medieval times? Are you asking me whether Judaism believes in an afterlife even though some Jews don't? Are you asking me whether Judaism believes in an afterlife but doesn't (anymore) use the terms "Heaven" and "Hell?"

All of those answers affirm the view that Jews often answer a question with another question. However, the question-answers are not meant to be annoying or evasive, because there is more than one answer to such a seemingly simple and straightforward question. Literally, the short answer is "No." There should be a follow-up question: "So, do Jews *not* believe in an afterlife?" The answer to that would be: "*some* Jews." Or it would be: "Judaism *now* does not believe in "Heaven" and "Hell," but *does* believe in an afterlife. Part of the problem is that Jews and Christians alike tend to view the Hebrew Bible as the main, if not the only, source for what Judaism believes. Nothing could be farther from the truth because Jewish beliefs have changed over the centuries.

Because Jewish history is both long and involved, here is a timeline for the Biblical period to provide you with some background context for the excerpts that follow:[12]

c. 1750 B.C. E. (Before the Common Era): Abraham migrates to Canaan

c. 1700-1600: The Israelites migrate from Canaan to Egypt

c. 1280: Exodus of Israel from Egypt

c. 1250-1200: Conquest of Canaan

c. 1200-1020: Period of the Judges

c. 1050: Samuel

c. 1020-1000: Saul

c. 1013-973: David

c. 973-933: Solomon

c. 930: Division of the Realm into the Kingdoms of Judah and Israel

c. 850: Elijah the Prophet

c. 722: Samaria falls [to the Assyrians], End of Israel

c. 586: Fall of Jerusalem; Babylonian Exile

c. 538: Cyrus grants permission to return

c. 520-515: Rebuilding of Temple

c. 500-450: Malachi [the last of the Hebrew Prophets}

What amazes me about the wording in the Hebrew Bible to describe death and the hint of an afterlife is that it is not much different from what the Jews I know believe today. The deaths of Abraham, Ishmael, Isaac, Aaron, and David are all described as being "gathered to his kin" or "people" or "fathers." In my opinion, this phrase implies that there is ultimately a connection between the living and the dead. It is an optimistic prospect, assuming that you actually want to be gathered to your people or family. You could say that it's like a family reunion. As a rabbi on Long Island for 19 years, I have heard many eulogies delivered by spouses and children and grandchildren who imagine that their deceased loved one is "up there" having a great time with relatives and friends who died before him or her. You can call this folklore or wishful thinking, and I wouldn't call it a theological statement. And yet, there is a sense of comfort expressed today that echoes the Biblical concept repeatedly quoted above.

That was the good news of Biblical belief. Here's the bad news: Sheol. Most people are familiar with the verse from Genesis 3 that we are dust and return to dust—most likely having heard it at a funeral. It is later in Genesis that Sheol is introduced. Rifat Sonsino and Daniel Syme tell us:

"The Bible refers to Sheol as 'the Ditch,' 'the Pit,' 'the realm of Death,' 'Perdition,' 'the Grave,' 'the Dust,' 'the torrents of Belial,' and 'the land of Darkness,' among other things... Sheol is a place located beneath the earth, a place to which one always 'goes down.' 'To go down to Sheol' in the Hebrew, means 'to die.'"[13]

Some of the references to Sheol in the Bible are: Jacob saying that he will end up there because of his mourning for Joseph (Genesis 37) and for Benjamin (Genesis 42); Dathan and Abiram going there because of their rebellion against Moses and God (Numbers 16); the prophet Samuel declaring that God has power over life and death (First Samuel 2); David charging Solomon to make sure that one of his old enemies goes there (First Kings 2); Isaiah speaking of it as the destination for sinners and the King of Babylon (Isaiah 5, 14 and 38); Ezekiel reminding people that the kingdom of Assyria died because of God's power over it (Ezekiel 31); Psalms identifying it as the place of depression and death (Psalms 30, 49, 88, and 139); Job acknowledging that hope doesn't exist there (Job 17); and Ecclesiastes saying that nothing good exists in Sheol (Ecclesiastes 9).

These citations make it clear that the Biblical view of life after death was bleak, that it was down and below, and dark and the Pit—a place bereft of God and hope and the joys of life. It was hell before there was a Hell, without a lot of details and without a figure such as the Devil or Satan or Lucifer. Sometimes, the answer to the question about what Jews believe is that Judaism has always emphasized life on earth rather than life after death. With Sheol as the inevitable destination after death, that emphasis shouldn't come as a surprise to anyone.

As if Sheol wasn't bad enough, the belief in Gehinnom arose much later in the Biblical period and became the subject of speculation among the Rabbis. Rabbi Or N. Rose—Associate Dean of the Rabbinical School of Hebrew College in Newton, Massachusetts—described this later Jewish view of the afterlife in an article for My Jewish Learning, entitled "Heaven and Hell in Jewish Tradition":

"The average person descends to a place of punishment and/or purification, generally referred to as *Gehinnom*. The name is taken from a valley *(Gei Hinnom)* just south of Jerusalem, once used for child sacrifice by the pagan nations of Canaan (II Kings 23:10) 'He [King Josiah] also defiled Topheth, which is in the Valley of Ben-hinnom, so that no one might consign his son or daughter to the fire of Molech.' Some view Gehinnom as a place of torture and punishment, fire and brimstone. Others imagine it less harshly, as a place where one reviews the actions of his/her life and repents for past misdeeds."[14]

By the way, the word for "valley" in Hebrew is *"gei"* and often this reference to this particular valley is called *Gei Ben-Hinnom*. It is mentioned in Joshua 15 in terms of its location, in Jeremiah 7 regarding the burning of children in fire, in Jeremiah 32 about the shrines to Baal and the sacrifices to Molech, and in II Chronicles 28 pertaining to one of the kings engaged in pagan practices.

My take on the *Gehinnom/Gehenna/Gei Ben-Hinnom* as a hell-ish place is three-fold.   First, the gods of idolaters were "competition" for *Yahweh* and forbidden by the Second Commandment. Second, the Third Commandment stated that our ancestors should not adopt the practices of idolaters. And third, from a very practical and emotional standpoint, killing your children kills your future. Many people today agree that the death of a child is the worst or one of the worst experiences that we can have. "Hell on Earth" is having to kill your child to make your god happy. It is a true, permanent, undeniable, and unimaginable sacrifice. *Gehinnom/Gei Ben-Hinnom/ Gehenna* rather than Sheol drew the attention of the Rabbis in the post-Biblical period. I will deal with that in more detail in a subsequent chapter. While Sheol is not part of Jewish belief anymore, the idea of a reunion with those who died before us continues to remain a possibility.

CHAPTER 3: MEDIUMS AT-LARGE

"You shall not practice divination or soothsaying."[15]

"Do not turn to ghosts and do not inquire of familiar spirits, to be defiled by them; I the Eternal am your God."[16]

"When you enter the land that the Eternal your God is giving you, you shall not learn to imitate the abhorrent practices of those nations. Let no one be found among you who consigns a son or daughter to the fire, or who is an augur, a soothsayer, a diviner, a sorcerer, one who casts spells, or one who consults ghosts or familiar spirits, or one who inquires of the dead.
For anyone who does such things is abhorrent to the Eternal, and it is because of these abhorrent things that the Eternal your God is dispossessing them before you. You must be wholehearted with the Eternal your God. Those nations that you are about to dispossess do indeed resort to soothsayers and augurs; to you, however, the Eternal your God has not assigned the like."[17]

For years I have believed in the "afterlife" and reincarnation. When I turned 50, I had what I would call my "spiritual awakening" where I finally was able to accept the gifts of being a psychic and medium (without worrying about what others would think). And I finally recognized that what I have referred to as "coincidence," "luck," or "G-d" has been a combination of all of these. I am a passionate person and I have accepted the gifts that I have received with a great deal of gratitude, compassion, and awe. I thank G-d, my spirit guides, and my guardian angel for allowing me to use these blessings, and I am grateful for their guidance when I do my work.

Jennifer, a Medium

Here we find two different views of having contact with the spirits of the deceased and whether or not it is allowed or encouraged, negative or positive, bad or good. The Torah is absolutely clear with its position in the Books of Leviticus and Deuteronomy, and in this chapter, I will provide some commentary about these verses and how the beliefs can be interpreted today. Mediums like Jennifer are also absolutely clear that they are individuals who are blessed with a gift and are not charlatans or fakes. I believe that the biblical tradition and commandments are the products of the time in which our ancestors lived when all around them were people who practiced what our ancestors regarded as "abominations." And I believe that there are individuals who—blessed with the ability to convey touching and positive messages from our deceased family and friends to we who still love them—are not "abominations," but "gifts."

Let's go back to that first quote: "You shall not practice divination or soothsaying." It is important to note that this verse appears in Chapter 19 of Leviticus in a section referred to as "The Holiness Code." You might think that it's all about the priests and sacrifices and praying and "other holy stuff." But, for the most part, it deals with being holy through our actions in our personal lives and in business. What impresses me is how it starts: "You shall be holy, for I the Eternal your God, am holy."[18] The "you" is stated in the plural and is addressed to the entire community—male and female, rich and poor, adult and child. We are commanded to strive to be God-like in our lives. It switches to singular in some of the verses, and I think that makes it more personal and attainable. The famous "You shall love your neighbor as yourself" is in the Holiness Code, and there are many scholars who have proposed that the chapter is a restatement of the Ten Commandments. Some behavior is commanded because it enables us to draw closer to what God would want us to do and be, and some is commanded because we should consider it to be the right and natural thing to do. Examples of that are: loving your neighbor, revering your parents, showing deference to the aged, caring for the poor and the stranger, judging others fairly, and being honest in business. And some behavior is commanded because it enables us to avoid the bad behavior of others. Examples of that are: not turning to idols, being greedy, being deceitful, stealing from friends and employees, holding a grudge, making your daughter a harlot, and relying on sketchy ways of determining the future and supernatural ways of linking with the past.

Just in case you're not familiar with "divination or soothsaying," here is how a few commentators explain them:

"The diviner would examine the shapes made by insoluble liquids, such as oil in water."[19]

"All we know from the Bible about the manner of pronouncing incantations [i.e., divination] is that goblets were used in the process...The forms of clouds, their times of appearance, their movements and positions, and the heavenly bodies they obscure were all factors in interpreting omens."[20]

"Ancient life, whether in Egypt, Canaan, or Mesopotamia, was crushed under an intolerable weight of enchantment, magic, and demonology. The Israelite was freed from the incubus of superstition by these prohibitions, which constitute one of the great negations of Judaism." [21]

"Ancient peoples had a variety of techniques for discovering the future. The Bible does not suggest that they are ineffective or fraudulent, but it bans them as idolatrous. In Israel, knowledge of the future could be sought legitimately only through prophets, through dreams, or through the sacred lot of Urim and Thummim (I Sam. 28:6)."[22]

The shapes of liquids in goblets, the form of clouds, and the movement of heavenly bodies were the ways to interpret the future in other societies. And it's probable that some Israelites were attracted to the magical but superstitious nature of these practices. The commandment to not engage in them may have been promulgated in order to stop Jews from doing that. Or, it may have been made because there was no reason for Jews to rely on these unreliable methods when they had God, the prophets, dreams, and the amazing *Urim* and *Thummim* available to them. [The *Urim* and *Thummim* date back to the Exodus and were used by the High Priest to consult with God]. Yes, they were "one of the great negations of Judaism," but they were considered to be minor-league methods that could not compare to the major-league methods of Judaism. Why depend on superstition when you have your faith? Why turn to them when you have a combination of God, prophets, dreams, and the *Urim* and *Thummim*?

The second verse focuses on being defiled by "ghosts" and "familiar spirits." We may have our own ideas of what a ghost is, and it doesn't have to pertain just to Halloween. There is a scary aspect to ghosts that we would all love to avoid—probably because we have been "spooked" by portrayals in literature and films. They usually hang around haunted houses and dark graveyards, which would not be our choice unless we *want* to be scared. Encountering a friendly ghost is something we would prefer but wouldn't imagine that we would always experience. And the term "familiar spirits" for us today conjures up the practice of communicating with the dead through a séance or a Ouija board. The problem with ghosts in the time of the Torah, or even later when it was edited and written down, is that they often became substitutes for the Divine. That was a concept and a reality that our ancestors didn't need, and that God and the prophets didn't want. It is followed in the verse by a not-so-subtle reminder that the Eternal your God is there for you and that you shouldn't turn to anything else. If you do, you will become "defiled"—dirty, polluted, unholy. There is a push-me, pull-me aspect to this verse: "I love you and will provide you with what you need," and "don't you dare give in to temptation because it will defile you."

There is a historical background to all of this:

"From remote antiquity people have turned for guidance to the spirits of the dead, and mediums still do a thriving business in supposedly civilized countries. Such practices were well known to the ancient Israelites; though banned by the Torah, they had their devotees (I Sam. 28; Isa. 8:19f). The term 'familiar spirit' means what present-day mediums call a "control," that is, a ghost with which they can readily communicate and so make contact with other persons who have died."[23]

"There is archaeological and textual evidence that ancient Israelites engaged in ancestor veneration, i.e., worship at the site of the tombs of known relations."[24]

"The English word 'familiar' here means 'attendant.' The wizard professes to know through the spirit attendant upon him, or residing within him, what is hidden from the ordinary person."[25]

I'm interested here in the use of words that connote a point of view expressed by the commentators, like "supposedly civilized countries" and "wizard professes to know." There is no denying that there was at the very least definite skepticism, if not downright disapproval, of these other methods of communication. They took the power away from God and from God's representatives. They were based on the act of seeking by the family or friends of the deceased. You would think that a Jewish leader would know better. But the chief offender of what the Torah commanded was the first king of the Jewish people, Saul.

You need to know something about him from what we read in the First Book of Samuel before you form an opinion of him. Samuel is a prophet of God and judge who appoints his sons to succeed him. Unfortunately, they are selfish, corrupt, and unjust, and the elders of Israel come to Samuel and ask him to anoint a king to rule over them just like all the other nations have. (I have often said that this reminds me of when a child approaches a parent and says he or she wants something because everyone else has one). The prophet is upset, feeling that God should be enough of a King for them, and that copying what their neighbors do is not a good idea. Samuel prays for guidance and is told that it is God against Whom the people are rebelling and that he shouldn't take it personally. God basically communicates to the prophet that if it's a king they want, it's a king they'll get—with all that may involve, whether good or bad—and it's almost *totally* bad. The man chosen for the job is Saul—"an excellent young man; no one among the Israelites was handsomer than he; he was a head taller than any of the people."[26] Saul may look the part, but he is prone to sudden fits of anger, disobeying God, becoming terrified by an evil spirit sent from God, belittling David, and then feeling threatened by his success. He deteriorates by demanding an outrageous bride-price for David to have the privilege of marrying Saul's younger daughter Michal, then throwing a spear at him, and turning David into an outlaw. The evil spirit overtakes Saul, and we find him taking off all of his clothes and speaking in ecstasy, resenting his son Jonathan's close relationship with David and cursing him out, ordering David's allies among the priests to be slaughtered, and being humiliated by David in front of all of his soldiers.

What Saul does next, though, seals his doom and catapults him to the heights (or depths) of infamy. Samuel is dead, Saul no longer has a connection to God, he is preparing to go out and fight the Philistines, and he is scared to death. He asks God for help but doesn't get an answer in any form, not from dreams or the *Urim* or prophets. Saul has expressly forbidden any turning to ghosts and familiar spirits (in keeping with the laws of the Torah), and then does exactly the opposite. He tells his courtiers to find a woman who consults ghosts so that he can hypocritically do what he himself has forbidden, and there happens to be a woman in *En-dor* who can help him. Saul puts on a disguise and goes to her during the night and asks her to divine a ghost for him. She replies that the king has banned the practice of her profession and she accuses him of laying a trap for her and trying to get her killed. He assures her that she won't get into trouble. When she inquires who she is supposed to bring up, he asks her to summon Samuel. She recognizes Saul, but he tells her not to be afraid and asks her what she sees. It is definitely Samuel, who screams at Saul about having been disturbed from his rest, and who warns Saul that he will die the next day in battle because of his disobedience. The Philistines attack the Israelites and pursue them to Mount Gilboa, where Saul sees his three sons die in front of him. He orders his arms-bearer to kill him, but he can't do it, so Saul literally falls on his own sword. I will not go into the gory details of how the Philistines deal with Saul's body; suffice it to say that it's savage and cruel.

I know some people who believe that Saul died solely because of his patronizing the woman at *En-dor,* sometimes called "the witch of *En-dor.*" As a result, they contend that any attempt to contact the spirits of the deceased today is not only explicitly forbidden by the Bible, but also carries with it a terrible penalty. That then morphs into a blanket condemnation of mediums, who are viewed as doing "the Devil's work," or at least participating in an idolatrous practice that goes against what God wants. Saul's death, however, was the result of an accumulation of bad decisions brought on by a terribly damaged psyche. In my opinion, Saul suffered from some sort of malady that caused mood swings, fits of anger, and paranoia. Perhaps the consulting of spirits was the straw that broke the camel's back, so to speak. But some people I know won't even consider that connection with a spirit can be a good thing—especially if it is initiated by the living. I will deal more with that later.

You could easily protest that Saul shouldn't have been punished so severely for breaking one rule of the Torah contained in one verse—even though he did exactly what he commanded his subjects not to do. His dressing up in a disguise and showing up in the dark of night reveal something about him knowing consciously or subconsciously that he was doing something that he shouldn't do. You could argue that taking one verse from the Bible and attributing so much significance to it is an example of "proof-texting"—essentially, "cherry-picking" a verse to prove a point. But your protest and your argument would be wrong because there is a second source in the Torah that prohibits these practices. It is in the Book of Deuteronomy, which in many ways serves as a summary and elaboration of laws that appear previously in other books of the Torah. Characterized as Moses' final, long speech to his people before he dies, Deuteronomy's texts remind the people about what was commanded before and urge the people to follow those commandments since Moses won't be there to remind them. Saul should have been well-aware of these words that appeared at the beginning of the chapter, along with an addition:

"When you enter the land that the Eternal your God is giving you, you shall not learn to imitate the abhorrent practices of those nations. Let no one be found among you who consigns a son or daughter to the fire, or who is an augur, a soothsayer, a diviner, a sorcerer, one who casts spells, or one who consults ghosts or familiar spirits, or one who inquires of the dead.

For anyone who does such things is abhorrent to the Eternal, and it is because of these abhorrent things that the Eternal your God is dispossessing them before you. You must be whole-hearted with the Eternal your God. Those nations that you are about to dispossess do indeed resort to soothsayers and augurs; to you, however, the Eternal your God has not assigned the like..."

"I will raise up a prophet for them from among their own people, like yourself [Moses]: I will put My words in his mouth and he will speak to them all that I command him; and if anybody fails to heed the words he speaks in My name, I Myself will call him to account."[27]

The commentators recognize the power of this section:

"To Deuteronomy the prophet is the most important and authoritative leader. In contrast to the king, whose power has its limits, Deuteronomy strengthens the authority of the prophet. It affirms that he is the successor of Moses, the highest authority during the desert period (v. 15) ...The reason Israel is to heed prophets is that they are God's messengers and spokes-men. Hence, following them is an expression of loyalty to God, whereas following diviners and sorcerers is an attempt to circumvent Him."[28]

"Deuteronomy takes for granted that either females or males might perform the types of divination listed here...These practices are abhorrent to God not because they are ineffective, but because they call upon powers other than God, thereby undermining monotheistic belief."[29]

"'Wholehearted'—The [Hebrew] word *tamim* means 'whole,' 'without blemish.' The idea in context is that you cannot serve God and yet keep one foot in the pagan realm by having recourse to necromancy and divinations."[30]

God's messengers. Powers other than God. Being wholehearted. The common thread here seems to be that serving God and engaging in "pagan" practices is mutually exclusive. You are either for God or against God. You are either observing the laws of the Torah or violating them. But what if Jewish mediums today believe that they have the *God-given ability* to connect us with the spirits of our deceased family and friends? What if someone is not actively pursuing contact with a "familiar spirit," but is given the opportunity to do so by someone that they know and trust? What if the unsolicited "signs" that people receive can no longer be accurately identified as being paganism? What if God has a hand, so to speak, in that communication that we would regard as supernatural?

One of the quotations with which this chapter began was from a Jewish medium by the name of Jennifer—a friend and a congregant of the synagogue where I served as Rabbi for twelve years and have been Rabbi Emeritus for seven years. She is a proud Jew, a loving wife, a devoted mother, and an excellent teacher. In addition, she is well-aware of traditional Judaism's disapproval of mediums (based on the Torah texts), general skepticism of the gifts that mediums have, and the validity of their messages. Here is what she has experienced:

"I am 51 years old, happily married, and my husband and I have three children ranging from ages 19 to 22. I hold a bachelor's degree in Family Counseling, a Masters' degree in Elementary School Education, and an advanced certificate in teaching English as a Second Language K-12. I am currently teaching kindergarten, first, and second grades in a nearby town.

When I turned 50, I had what I would call my "spiritual awakening" where I finally was able to accept the gifts of being a psychic and medium (without worrying about what others would think), and finally recognized that what I have referred to as coincidence, luck or G-d has been a combination of all of these. I am a passionate person and I have accepted the gifts that I have received with a great deal of gratitude, compassion, and awe. I thank G-d, my spirit guides, and my guardian angel for allowing me to use these blessings, and I am grateful for their guidance when I do my work.

My first memory of an experience with recognizing spirituality was when I was ten years old. I was sitting outside of my house and thinking: "I'm only ten years old but there are things that I know that I can't explain how I know." It was at that moment that I recognized that I have been on the Earth before, and that I knew things that a ten-year-old couldn't possibly know, and yet I didn't understand what that meant. As I now reflect as an adult, it just meant that I was a soul that has been on the Earth before this life. It's an understanding that I have and, no matter what religious beliefs or doubts others may have, I know this as sure as I live and breathe.

A few years ago, I was sitting outside by our pool speaking to my son, and we were having a very calm and beautiful conversation. I was joking with him, telling him how I felt because, last year at this time when we opened the pool, ducks flew into the pool and swam around. I then said out loud: "I wish some ducks would come and swim in our pool!" Immediately following that statement, to my and my son's utter amazement, a duck flew over my head and landed in our pool. I'm not sure who was listening, but I thanked G-d and my

Spirit guides for the duck.

Last summer, I decided to read a book that was recommended to me called Angelspeake: How to Talk With Your Angels. *When I walked into the library, the first thing I saw there—where I have been going for over 15 years—was a stained-glass picture of an Angel. Obviously, this beautiful window has been there for years, but it just never drew my attention. From reading the book, I learned that, if we pay close attention, we get messages from angels. After completing it, I heard a whispering in my right ear that told me to go upstairs and look for a message. The last chapter of the book had specifically stated that if you asked a question, the Angels would answer you. I climbed the stairs looking for the response to the question I asked, which was "Can you hear me?" I felt I was directed to a specific location in the stack of books. I took a picture of the book where they sent me (because I, too, have my very logical side). The name of the book I was sent to was* I Hear You, *by Donny Ebenstein. I had a wave of chills running up and down my back and arms, which is my typical sign for validation that this was real. I left the library both in shock and joy and was thankful for the message. A few months after reading the book, I kept seeing the numbers 555. I would wake up at exactly 5:55, or my car mileage would have 555 in it, or I would see it on a license plate. I looked up the meaning of "555" and found out that 555 is considered to be "angel number symbolism" that a positive change is happening soon. I learned to accept angels as real helpers of G-d that day.*

One day, when I was 32, I was sitting with my friend Mary, whom I had met while living in Tampa, Florida. Mary was telling me how concerned she was in her present relationship and was wondering if she would ever meet her husband. It was at that moment that I was provided with information and shared it with Mary. I "saw" (it's a vision I can equate to when you have a daydream) her wearing a blue, button-down blouse and a white pearl necklace while she was meeting a man with dark hair and piercing blue/green eyes. Approximately three years after that conversation, I received a phone call from Mary reminding me of the day that we had spoken and the details that I had provided. I truly had remembered a little bit of it, yet Mary reminded me of all the details. One of the details that I had forgotten was that it was going to be a family friend that Mary had known for years. Mary was calling to tell me that she was wearing a blue, button-down blouse and had on a white pearl necklace when she met a family friend who had dark hair and piercing blue eyes. This man is now her husband and is named Matt. They are happily married and have two beautiful daughters. At the time, I had no idea how I received this information, but I was open to it and willingly accepted it. I at the time did not imagine that this would come to fruition, but I am grateful that it did.

Two years ago, after the unexpected death of our friend Roger (name changed), my husband and I were sitting in the temple when, unexpectedly, I received a message from our deceased friend. We were sitting a few rows back from his widow and he told me to give her the message: "Kitty." I told Roger ("mediumistically") that I would give his wife the message. When the service was over, his wife was crying so hysterically that I was unable to deliver it to her. The deceased husband telepathically sent me the message that he was disappointed that I did not deliver the message to his wife. Later, at 1 a.m., my husband and I awoke to a strange occurrence—a stick deodorant flew out of his medicine cabinet and turned on the sink's water faucet full blast! Upon hearing the first sound, I immediately woke up and said, "I'm sorry, Roger, for not delivering the message." I then felt—as an apology to Roger—that I should text his wife. My husband and I invited her for dinner and, a few months later, when we all met, I told her of this occurrence. My husband and I thought she was going to refer to a pet cat that she had at the time. To my surprise, she explained that the word made logical sense, since the message from her husband was impactful because he was buried next to her mother, whose name was Kitty!

At the end of the school day last year, while speaking to a colleague, I received a message from her deceased father. After realizing it was her dad, she told me her dad had died when she was a little girl. She asked me how old the sender of the message was when he died, and he showed me that he was 42. The teacher validated that her dad was, in fact, 42 when he died. Her dad wanted her to know that he had seen all of her accomplishments, including her educational degrees. He then kept showing me a yellow bird. When I asked the colleague if a yellow bird meant anything to her, she explained that he had bought her a yellow parakeet two days before his death. She knew it was her dad, and we hugged in the hallway.

The universe is a fascinating place, and the more I began to accept my psychic abilities and communicating (telepathically) with spirits, the more I have received. I prayed for a teacher, received the same teacher's name from my uncle in Florida as a new friend on Long Island, and knew it was not a coincidence. I am enrolled in his classes to enhance my abilities. I prayed for the opportunity to practice my psychic ability/skills as a medium and, while being advised about nutritional support, the nutritionist with whom I worked booked me my first professional client.

While in the nutritionist's office...I heard a gentleman say, "good morning...please tell him, I am ok." I asked the spirit if he would mind if I had my nutritional session first and, with the same personality he had while on the Earth, he chuckled and said, "sure... standing by!" The gentleman began to show me how he died in a motorcycle accident (leaving out the gory details... I don't want that information), and then showed me himself and a man (the nutritionist's fiance) "sneaking off when they were 15 and drinking beers in a rowboat." It turned out that this man was my nutritionist's fiancé's cousin/best friend who was killed in a motorcycle accident when he was only 19 years old. He wanted her fiancé to know he was ok and that he still "messes with him" by moving objects at work —like his tape dispenser and other items—just to annoy him since, while the cousin was on the Earth, he liked to perform practical jokes.

Spirits will always provide legitimate proof to the person on the Earth so the person knows it is genuinely their deceased loved one. Typically, you will be provided with ten pieces of evidence. He came through to me on that day because his birthday was the next day. Spirits connect with me on or about their date of birth. The dad of a nurse with whom I have worked for years asked me to call her to let her know he had a message for her. Initially, I had made an appointment (free) for her the following week. But then, he telepathically told me it could not wait, and I rescheduled it for the next day. It turned out the next day was her dad's birthday. I met with the kind-hearted nurse who was in a great deal of pain because her siblings had cut her out of her dad's will. Her dad knew what her siblings had done and, to make up for her pain, he told her he would send her a gift of a granddaughter six to eight months from the time we were meeting. The beautiful nurse is already blessed with grandsons and wanted a granddaughter. Ava was born in June 2020 and we found out it was a girl eight months after we met that day. Spirits come with messages to heal pain from injustices they observe from the other side. I have now learned through my teacher that people/clients must ask me for a reading, but these occurrences happened before I attended his classes. I am truly grateful for these oppor-tunities, and as a G-d-honoring woman, I often thank G-d and those guiding me.

Here is the latest story:

I was upstate looking at art in an art store that was going out of business. I completed a purchase and placed a small piece of art-work into the trunk of my car when I realized I was very hungry. I sat in my car for several minutes (feeling a sense of urgency) debating if I wanted to drive through the quaint town before heading back to the condo. I decided to drive through the town and, while driving, I hap-pened upon the diner. I'd eaten at this diner before and remembered eating a delicious turkey sandwich the last time I was in town. My highly practical side—aware I was only five minutes from my condo with a fully-stocked refrigerator of food--said: "Why don't you just go home?"

But this urgency in my heart made me get out of the car and step into the diner. I enjoyed half of a turkey wrap, enjoyed a brief conversation with the lovely server, and asked for a to-go box for the other half of my wrap. The respectful server brought the box and the check, and I went to the front of the diner to pay the bill. I felt a wave of emotions coupled with a strong inclination to provide a good tip (something that happens frequently) when I meet kind servers. This next part is unusual for me, but I asked the hostess if the servers share their tips and she replied, "no". My tab came to a total of 17 dollars and I gave 'Sophie' 100 dollars as a tip. I normally would not have an issue doubling the total of the bill or even giving a 50 dollar tip. But, this time, I wrote 100 dollars without even blinking an eye. The hostess looked at the amount I had left the server and said, "Oh my goodness …you have no idea what that's going to mean to Sophie… she's going through a really rough time."

I asked what she meant, and she explained that "her brother just died three weeks ago." I asked the server to please call Sophie over to me. Then, I explained to Sophie that I am a medium and that my pattern seems to be that spirits come to me exactly three weeks after they die. So, this was her brother's way of "letting me know that he has crossed over successfully" and "he's letting her know that he's OK on the other side." We then hugged and she thanked me so much for the tip. I told her, "Please, there's no need to thank me. This is from your brother." She then asked if I had a card and I furnished her with one of my business cards.

She told me that her mother is very spiritual, and I explained to her that I was doing free psychic/medium readings over the summer. Two weeks later, her mother called me…in a video chat. We had a beautiful reading together and, at the end of the reading, she said to me:" Jennifer, there's something I need to show you. I was raised Catholic, and in the Catholic religion, you are taught that there is a heaven and an alternate place that you can go. But I believe in spirituality. Because my son died unexpectedly, I needed to know that he had crossed over to the other side successfully. I have a $100 bill of his that I had laminated and a picture of his (she held both of these items up to the camera). The day before you went into the diner to have my daughter wait on you as the server, I held up my son's $100 bill and a picture of my son looking towards heaven and said: 'Please, Sammy—show me that you are ok! Give me a sign that you have crossed over successfully!' The next day, Jennifer, you went into the diner, gave my daughter Sophie the $100 tip, and said "this is from your brother… he is letting you know that he has crossed over successfully." Thank you, Jennifer. That's what I needed to hear and know."

Okay, so I've learned that spiritual law says that if you give *something, it will return to you. The day after the reading with Sammy's mom, I got a call from one of my doctors that, during the pandemic, my insurance company had decided to waive co-payments...and they were going to mail me a check for my $125 overpayment."*

It is a steep hill to climb to ask those who regard the Torah as God's words and its commandments as non-negotiable to make an exception for a modern-day medium who is also a proud Jew. So, I won't do that. But, as you will see in the coming chapters, contact with the dead was not unheard-of in Jewish texts and throughout Jewish history beyond the Biblical period. The power of God can be manifested in ways that we never thought possible and through experiences about which we were never taught. That doesn't mean that they are anti-Jewish, paganistic, idolatrous, or non-Jewish. There are what I call "supernatural" elements that are a vital part of Jewish Tradition that have brought comfort and hope to millions of Jews for many centuries. I can tell you that the experience Jennifer related about "Roger" is 100% true. The spirit that contacted her is the man that I knew as my congregant and friend and student for many years. If you accept the way she described the communication that took place, you should know that it is typical of the sense of humor he had in his all-too-short life. He left behind a love of Judaism and his family, a commitment to his synagogue and his friends, and a devotion to volunteerism and *tikkun olam* (repairing the world). Yet, just because he died, the love of him and from him doesn't have to die, too. As you will see in the next two chapters, Judaism regards the dead as gone but not forgotten, and is full of hope for encounters that are supernatural and miraculous.

CHAPTER 4: THE "WORLD-TO-COME"

"In his classic work on Rabbinic Judaism, J. F. Moore states: 'Any attempt to systemize the Jewish notions of the hereafter imposes upon them an order and consistency which does not exist in them."[31]

"If the soul is immortal, then death cannot be considered a final act. If the life of the soul is to be continued, then death, however bitter, is deprived of its tremendous power of casting mourners into a lifetime of agonizing hopelessness over an irretrievable loss. Terrible though it is, death is a threshold to a new world—the 'World-to-Come.'"[32]

"These are things the fruit of which a person enjoys in this world, while the principal remains for them in the World to Come, and they are: honoring father and mother, acts of loving-kindness, and bringing peace between people. And the study of Torah is equal to them all."[33]

"Every Israelite has a portion in the world to come."[34]

How can we reconcile the first statement with the next three that are all so definitive and emphatic? The first one is from a well-respected historian, the other three from the massive source that is second only to the Bible in its importance. They are also separated by some 1,500 years in terms of when they were written. Moore is not the only historian to offer his view on the subject, and there are other quotations from the Mishnah and Talmud that contradict the one above. Rather than looking for one answer to the question about "Jewish notions of the hereafter," let's consider some important issues and what various sources have had to say about them.

As I indicated in Chapter Two, Jewish history dates back to the 18th century B.C.E. (Before the Common Era), starting with Abraham and Sarah in the Biblical period. That time could be subdivided into before the destruction of the First Temple in 586 B.C.E. by the Babylonians, and then from 586 B.C.E. to 70 C.E. (The Common Era) when the Romans destroyed the Second Temple. The Hebrew Bible was canonized in about the year 90 C.E. The Rabbinic period began around that time and extended to the coming of the 6th Century C.E. The subsequent discussions and writings among the rabbis were considerable, highly organized, and recorded, such as the Mishnah, which was edited around the year 200 C.E. by Rabbi Judah HaNasi and consisted of 500 years of opinions and rulings. There were two versions of the Talmud: the Jerusalem (a.k.a. "Palestinian") Talmud, which was codified about the year 400 C.E., and the Babylonian Talmud, which was codified about the year 500 C.E. The Mishnah was contained in the Talmud, and all of the commentaries and rulings and stories regarding the individual Mishnah verses were collectively called the *Gemara*. If you turn it into an equation, it would be Mishnah + *Gemara* = Talmud.

One of the most famous sections from the Mishnah is the *Pirkei Avot* [also spelled *Pirke Avot*], and the title translates directly as the "Chapters of the Fathers"—although it is also known as the "Ethics of the Fathers" and the "Sayings of the Fathers." In 1993, the UAHC Press published a new edition and translation called *Pirke Avot: A Modern Commentary on Jewish Ethics* by Rabbi Leonard Kravitz and Rabbi Kerry M. Olitzky. Their colleague Rabbi W. Gunther Plaut wrote in the Foreword:

"Next to the Bible and the haggadah, Pirke Avot has been our favorite text. Jews used to read it regularly and knew much of it by heart...It teaches us the essentials of what life might be at its best. It is Jewish ethics in the broadest sense."[35]

In the Introduction to their volume, the authors state:

"Pirke Avot is a Jewish literary classic. It is the most well-known of all writings in rabbinic Judaism.... according to rabbinic Judaism in Pirke Avot, the biblical text, standing alone, cannot provide salvation for the individual; only the interpretations and instructions of the rabbis give us eternal life."[36]

That seems to be a good stepping-off point to share what some of the rabbis said about the afterlife in the post-biblical period. *Sheol* is replaced by the *Olam Haba*, the World-to-Come, and the belief in a soul given by God at birth and put into a body was normative. We will delve into the views of some of the rabbis in *Pirke Avot* next, but here is how it was explained in the Talmud later on:

"As God fills the whole world, so also the soul fills the whole body. As God sees, but cannot be seen, so also the soul sees, but cannot be seen. As God nourishes the whole world, so also the soul nourishes the whole body. As God is pure, so also the soul is pure. As God dwells in the innermost part of the Universe, so also the soul dwells in the innermost part of the body."[37]

This reminds me of how I used to explain the concept of "soul" to my Tenth Grade Confirmation students. I would tell them that, when you stand in front of an x-ray machine, you can see the bones and organs inside of you, but you can't see your soul. That doesn't mean that it's not there. Then I would tell them that your soul is the real you, not your body. Some of them would be relieved to hear that, but my ultimate point was that our souls are given to us by God, that they return to God when we die, and that they are eternal. I believe that, when they "return to God," they do not go to a particular location in a specific direction. Because God cannot be limited to a certain space, our souls become part of a spiritual world that we call "The World-to-Come"—the *Olam Haba* in Hebrew.

The greatest rabbi of them all was Hillel. Rabbis Kravitz and Olitzky tell us: "Hillel was the president of the Sanhedrin…(and) was probably the most eminent of all the sages. He was the very exemplar of the rabbinate. His life reflected the key values of rabbinic Judaism: study, devotion and kindness."[38] He said in Chapter 1, Verse 12 of *Pirke Avot*: "One who has acquired the words of Torah has acquired for oneself a place in the world to come."[39] As you would expect, a rabbi is endorsing the study of Torah in this life as a *guarantee* to a place in the World-to-Come. There is a reward for what he defines as a "good life" and it is given after we die.

Rabbi Tarfon, who lived in the third generation of rabbis from 120 to 140 C.E., affirms Hillel's belief about this world and the World-to-Come:

"He used to say, 'The day is short; there is much work [to be done]; [yet,] the laborers are lazy, [even though] the wages are great, and the Householder is insistent.' Rashi [the 11th Century French commentator] takes the shortness of the day to refer to this life; in the next life, the wages for the service of God will be paid. 'The wages are great'—The study of Torah itself produces joy and happiness. Not only do we acquire wisdom through the study of Torah, but it also secures us a place in the world to come, say the rabbis."[40]

In the next verse, Tarfon declares:

"It is not up to you to finish the work, yet you are not free to avoid it. If you have studied much Torah, then you will receive much in wages, for your Employer is dependable to pay the wage for your work. Know that the giving of the wages for the righteous is in the time to come."[41]

[Moses] Maimonides [the Spanish commentator of the 12th century] notes that the term "the time to come" is also known as "the world to come" ... an unspecified future."[42] In other words, there is a conclusion about what will happen to us in the after-life, but no details are provided about how the righteous will be given wages—and what they will be:

"Rabbi Elazar of Modin [a contemporary of Ben Zoma] used to say, 'One who desecrates holy things, and one who condemns the festivals, and one who publicly shames a fellow human being, and one who breaks the covenant [Berit Milah] of Abra-ham our ancestor, and one who misinterprets the Torah—even if that person were to possess [great knowledge of] Torah and [were a great doer of] good deeds, that person would have no portion in the world to come.'"

[Rabbi Ovadiah ben Abraham] Bartinoro [a 16th century Ital-ian commentator] wrote:

"Such a person acts with presumption and lack of shame... the power of repentance is so great that, should one repent be-fore each one's death, that person will have a portion in the life to come."[43]

This verse intrigues me for two reasons: first, it gives a list of five specific actions that will *guarantee* that an individual will definitely *not* make it to the World-to-Come; and second, the usual qualifications for the afterlife of being knowledgeable and being a good person can't even combine to help that person gain admission.

Did you ever know someone who was very religious or a great scholar, but didn't have a title? Shimon Ben Zoma was a second century Jew who wasn't ordained as a rabbi but who was regarded highly for his scholarship. My father, Joseph Karol, was that kind of man. We read in Chapter 4, Verse 1: "Ben Zoma said, ... 'Who is rich? One who is happy with what one has, as it says, 'When you eat what your hands have provided, you shall be happy and good will be yours.' [Psalm 128:2]. You shall be happy in this world; and good will be yours in the world to come.'"[44] It may have been that Ben Zoma was happy to be a Torah scholar without having been ordained. And this verse provides a sense of perspective that true happiness may be right in front of us and we don't have to think that the grass is greener elsewhere. Apparently, he was happy with the "happy" and looking forward to the "good."

In Chapter 4, Verse 16, we read: "Rabbi Yaakov [a Second Century C.E. scholar who taught the eventual editor of the Mishnah, Judah HaNasi], said: 'This world is like a foyer before the World to Come. Prepare yourself in the foyer so that you will be able to enter the banquet hall.'"[45] His use of the Hebrew forms of the Greek words for "foyer" and "banquet hall" tells us a lot about the influence of Hellenism on Jewish thought and language. Some of the hardest words to read in Hebrew are those that come to it from other languages, including English. This line emphasizes that how we live our lives on earth determines our ability to enter the World-to-Come—referred to euphemistically here as "the banquet hall."

But, in the very next verse, Yaakov uses the term explicitly and compares the two worlds: Chapter 4, Verse 17: "He would often say, 'An hour spent in penitence and good deeds in this world is better than all of life in the world to come. An hour of contentment in the world to come is better than all of life in this world.' Rashi, Maimonides, and Bartinoro all suggest that this world is the place of action and the next world the place of reward. As a result, if something is not achieved in this world, it will be achieved in the next world."[46] There is still an emphasis on the importance of good deeds in this world as establishing the qualifications for entering the next world. To some, this may sound very Christian in regard to what has to be done to get into Heaven. While this may be explained as downgrading the life in this world compared to the afterlife, I see another way of looking at this. In this world, we need to be proactive in admitting when we are wrong and in helping to make the world better. Life in this world is "a sure thing." Our views of the afterlife are speculation and are meant to elicit hope. We have no proof that we will achieve contentment in the next world, but we would like to believe that it is so good that it is worth striving for here and now in our actions.

In the second half of the Second Century C.E., a contemporary of Judah HaNasi alluded to the inevitability of life and death as well as to the possibility of resurrection as indicated in boldface type below:

"He [Rabbi Elazar Ha-Kappar] used to say, 'Those who are born will die. **Those who die will live again.** [Emphasis added] Those who [then] live are to be judged, to know, to make known, and to let it be known who is God, who is the Maker, who is the Creator, who is the One who understands, who is the Judge, who is the Witness, who is the Litigant...Against your will you live. Against your will you will die. Against your will you will make a reckoning before the Ruler of rulers, the Holy One of Blessing.' For Jewish tradition, this life and whatever comes next form a continuum. What we achieve here will be rewarded or punished in the hereafter. Bartinoro comments that the final reckoning, which will take place at the judgment in the world to come, will be 'penny by penny.' Each and every act will be noted."[47]

Elazar portrays life as one big picture with different sections —life on earth and life in the hereafter. While we may not make the choice to live or die or be called to account for our deeds on Earth, we will ultimately be able to speak for ourselves to God—Who is not only the Ruler and all that implies, but is also the Blesser. Bartinoro's comment emphasizes a belief that became so crucial in Jewish mysticism many centuries later— that everything we do in our lives counts. The concept of *tikkun olam*—repair of the world—developed by Isaac Luria in the 16th Century still resonates with Jews today because it empowers the individual to make a positive difference in the world and to join others in doing so.

Three more verses from Chapter Six are not attributed to particular rabbis or scholars, but they reveal theological positions about the World-to-Come. Rabbis Kravitz and Olitzky teach:

"Chapter Six is really a part of neither the Mishnah in general nor of the Tractate Pirke Avot in particular. It is called a *baraita:* a collection of sayings not included in the Mishnah. The word *baraita* means "external," "outside," or "extraneous matter." It is sometimes called *tosefta* (literally an addition to the Mishnah...) it is taught in Mishnaic style and is offered in praise of God, who selected the sages as teachers of the Mishnah."[48]

"This is the way of the [study] of Torah: you will eat bread with salt. You will drink water by measure, you will endure a life of privation. [All] while you labor in the Torah. If you do this, 'Happy shall you be and good will be yours.' [Psalm 128:2]. Happy shall you be in this world and good will be yours in the world to come. Don't seek greatness for yourself and don't covet glory. More than you've learned, do! Don't hanker after the tables of kings for your table is greater than theirs. Your crown is grander than theirs. [Only] your Employer can be depended on to pay you the reward of your labor."[49]

There are probably hundreds of thousands of Torah and Talmud scholars who could identify with the "life of privation" phrase. But the key to their life is that they find joy in their study and that their community is usually there to support them because of the immense respect that exists for scholars. While they may not gain material rewards in this world, they believe that they will reap the benefits of their study in the next world. Furthermore, they are encouraged to put their learning into action, to do so modestly, and to be proud of the crown of knowledge that they have achieved. Their ultimate reward from "The Employer" will be presented to them in the World-to-Come.

A similar unattributed text in Chapter 6 reads: "Great is the Torah because it gives life to those who perform it in this world and in the next, as it says, 'For they are life to them that find them, and healing to all their flesh.' [Prov. 4:22]...The study of Torah promised providence in this life and eternity in the next."[50] It is texts like this one that built the foundation for the inherent value of Jewish study in general, the gaining of knowledge in particular, and the value of Torah most of all. There are no limits on the power of the Torah—it extends beyond this world, beyond death, and into the next world.

The final quotation from *Pirke Avot* is significant because of who said it and what he said. Rabbi Yose ben Kisma lived at the beginning of the Second Century C.E. and, at the end of describing a personal experience while traveling, put forth this detailed account of what happens when we die:

"At the moment of a person's departure [from this world], neither silver nor gold nor precious stones nor pearls accompany the individual, only Torah and good deeds, as it says, 'When you walk, it will guide you; when you lie down, it will watch over you; and when you awake, it will speak to you.' [Prov. 6:22]. 'When you walk, it will guide you'—in this world. 'When you lie down, it will watch over you'—in the grave. 'And when you awake, it will speak to you'—in the World to Come."[51]

There we have, in order, what this rabbi envisions about the end of life on earth and the beginning of the afterlife. Once again, the value of learning and good deeds is emphasized, and the value of material goods is deemphasized. This may be the original "you can't take it with you" statement.

In the transition between the end of the Biblical period and the inception of the Rabbinic period, we see a change from the existence of a dark pit which we can't avoid and from which we can't return to a spiritual existence which has the potential for great rewards. And, for some of the rabbis in these sources, there is a bonus—we can make a positive difference in our actions that can enhance the quality of our lives now and can have an impact on the quality of our lives in the next world.

CHAPTER 5: THE TALMUD, THE "WORLD-TO-COME," AND COMMUNICATION BETWEEN THE LIVING AND THE DEAD

"...The Rabbis...knew that the emphasis of the Torah and of Jewish life is this world. The World-to-Come was described in detail, in part, to reflect an ideal. Everything they envisioned for the next world was a goal, a vision for the world, the world of reality. Thus, they constructed a system of practices and rites that would reflect some of the ideals of the next world in this one.

If in the next world, material possessions would not be a worry, then in this world, they should not be our ultimate concern. What activity would be more worthwhile than study of Torah day and night? Therefore, they strove to combine the concern for worldly possessions and our daily needs with daily study of Torah. Few could exempt themselves from the struggle for sustenance; none could be exempted from daily study.

If the system worked to perfection, this world would become a reflection of the next world. If everyone observed the mitzvot, then strife and warfare would end. If nothing else, this world would be elevated and beautified. That the ideal could never be achieved was not a concern for the rabbis. The ideal itself would become a paradigm for how a person should conduct everyday life. Ironically, if every person lived out all of these ideals—the mitzvot being a crystallization of God's vision of a perfect world —then there would no longer be a need for the mitzvot, for the next world would be achieved."[52]

STEPHEN KAROL

This ideal characterization of the world as we wish it could be is, to me, a Jewish version of "Heaven on Earth." Judaism has long been identified as a religion that emphasizes this life over the next life because it is only about our existence in this world that we can have the chance to be certain. If there is an afterlife in a next world, our beliefs about it are based on hope and faith and speculation rather than fact and logic and proof. Yet, it means that striving for perfection—even if we couldn't attain it—is still worth the effort. If we live with ideals—spelled out for Jews in the commandments, the *mitzvot*—then we can infuse our lives with purpose and meaning. And, for those Jews for whom the details of the commandments are too burdensome, but the principles are valid, there is still a desire to make the world better. In this chapter, we will see how the rabbis had definite opinions about who would make it to the World-to-Come and who wouldn't, whether the dead are aware of us who are still alive, and what difference it could make for us. We will see all of this through sayings and stories, some of which are long, and we need to decide whether they should be taken literally or not. Are they presented by the rabbis as absolute proof of the afterlife? Or are they parables-- stories with a point being made? Regardless of your decision, they reveal insights and interpretations that I believe support the thesis that there is a potential eternal connection between the living and the dead that death cannot defeat.

Having quoted from the Mishnah in the previous chapter, it makes sense to me to begin here with two selections from the Mishnah not only for chronology but also for content. The first selection includes the wording of the third quotation that appears at the beginning of Chapter Four, as well as the list that precedes it. And the translation is a little bit different:

"These are the things that have no definite quantity: The corners [of the field]. First-fruits; [The offerings brought] on ap-

44

pearing [at the Temple on the three pilgrimage festivals]. The performance of righteous deeds; And the study of the Torah. The following are the things for which a man enjoys the fruits in this world while the principal remains for him in the world to come: Honoring one's father and mother; The performance of righteous deeds; And the making of peace between a person and his friend; And the study of the Torah is equal to them all."[53]

These words are so important in the Jewish tradition that they appear in the preliminary section of the Morning Prayers in our prayer books. As you might have noticed, the first group of "things" pertains to commandments to be fulfilled in the context of an agricultural society and with access to the Temple in Jerusalem. Added to them are righteous deeds and Torah study. The second group that can bring enjoyment now and the bonus of rewards in the World-to-Come repeats righteous deeds and Torah study. But it adds parents and peace and places the top priority and emphasis on Torah study because the rabbis believed that being learned meant you would be a good person and be rewarded in the afterlife.

This is the second selection:

"Rabbi Yehoshua ben Levi said: 'In the world to come the Holy One, Blessed be He, will make each righteous person inherit three hundred and ten worlds, for it is written: "That I may cause those that love me to inherit *yesh* (numerical value of 310) and that I may fill their treasuries." (Proverbs 8:21)'"[54]

310 worlds? An explanation will help you understand why Yehoshua said this. Each Hebrew letter has a numerical value. The first ten letters have the value of one through ten. The eleventh letter has the value of twenty, and it continues for the following letters through ninety. The last four letters of the Hebrew alphabet are *Koof* (100), *Reish* (200), *Shin* (300), and *Tav* (400). When Yehoshua ben Levi looked at this verse from Proverbs, he found numerical significance in the Hebrew word

yesh. From there—because the verse expresses God's love for the lovers of God—Yehoshua concluded that there was deep meaning in it. This interpretation of a Biblical verse is an example of proof-texting, which involves having a certain belief or point of view and finding verses to affirm it.

Yehoshua ben Levi was a prominent rabbi and his interpretations were highly respected. Although three hundred and ten worlds for each righteous person is the stuff of science fiction, it was an idealistic expression of how good the World-to-Come would be *if you were a righteous person on Earth.* But what if you weren't so righteous? The Mishnah I quoted in Chapter 4 about all Israelites having a share in the World-to-Come doesn't end with that. Here's a list of those who will not make the cut, so to speak, followed by an explanation:

"These have no share in the World to Come: One who says that [the belief of] resurrection of the dead is not from the Torah, [one who says] that the Torah is not from Heaven, and an *Apikoros* [non-believer]. Rabbi Akiva says: 'also one who reads outside books, and one who whispers [an incantation] over a wound, saying, (Exodus 15:26) 'I will bring none of these diseases upon you that I brought upon the Egyptians for I am the Eternal that heals you.' Abba Shaul says, 'also one who utters the Divine name as it is spelled.'"[55]

This quotation deserves some clarification:
- The Torah "from Heaven" doesn't mean a place up in the clouds. It means that the Torah is of divine, rather than human, origin. This belief contends that God wrote the Torah, and every word is divine, with its contents being passed down to Moses and then through the generations of the Jewish people.
- An *"Apikoros"*—also spelled *"epikoros"*—seems to have been derived from the name of the Greek philosopher Epicurus whose teachings were in direct opposition to those of Judaism. The term came to be understood as referring to a "heretic,"

specifically a Jew who didn't accept the responsibilities as delineated in the Torah.

- "Outside books" may refer to the books of the *Apocrypha*— a collection of mostly Jewish books written in Greek that were not included in the Hebrew Bible when it was canonized, or it may be any books that are not included in the *Tanakh* (the Hebrew Bible).
- The incantation quotation affirms that God is the only Healer of the people, rather than another god or magician.
- And, not uttering the divine name as it is spelled is one of the most influential declarations in Jewish tradition. God's proper name—which consists of the Hebrew letters *Yud, Hei, Vav, Hei*—has become "Jehovah" and "Yahweh" in English, but some Jews consider it to be so holy that they will substitute the words *"Adonai," "Adoshem,"* and *"Hashem"* for it. They won't write it out either, using one of the letters *(Hei)* with what looks like an apostrophe mark next to it.

There is considerable agreement regarding which text in the Torah is being alluded to in this statement from the Mishnah. In his book *The Death of Death: Resurrection and Immortality in Jewish Thought,* Neil Gillman wrote:

"Almost throughout, the Bible views death as absolutely final. Only three biblical passages unambiguously affirm that at least some individuals will live again after their death. ...Genesis 5:21-24 recalls Enoch, one of the ten generations from Adam to Noah. We are told that nine of these men lived a number of years, then they had children, then they lived a certain number of additional years until they died. Of Enoch, however, we are told, 'Enoch walked with God; then he was no more, for God took him' (Genesis 5:24). This enigmatic statement may be a way of telling us that Enoch too died, but here, the text is not explicit."[56]

Mishnah Sanhedrin 10:1 continues with a list of those who

won't be able to have "a portion in the world to come": the generation of the Flood (other than Noah and his family) in Genesis 6, the people scattered because of the Tower of Babel in Genesis 11, the wicked men of Sodom in Genesis 13, the ten spies who gave a negative report about being able to conquer the Land of Canaan in Numbers 14, the entire generation that came out of Egypt except the two spies (Joshua and Caleb) who gave a positive report about Canaan in the same book and chapter, Korach and his rebellious family and followers in Numbers 16, and the residents of any city who have been tricked into worshipping idols.

Now we're going to delve into the Talmud to see what some of the rabbis had to say about the afterlife, how you can get there, what it was like, and if you could communicate with those who arrived there before you. If you're not familiar with the Talmud, this may help to set the scene for you:

"The editors of the Talmud 'cut and pasted' together snippets of teachings from a five-hundred-year period. Sometimes they were conversations that actually took place; other times they created the **appearance** of a conversation by putting together the sayings of two teachers (from two eras) on a single topic. Very often the *Gemara* goes a step further: It puts an argument into the mouth of a particular Rabbi, implying: 'Here's what so-and-so might have said about this had he been there...'

From this approach, we learn that the Talmud is a vibrant, dynamic, organic work. It is not restricted by time or space. It brings us back into the past and enables us to question and address people long since gone about how they dealt with the critical issues in their lives. It also enables us to bring those from the past into the present, so that we can see how they would apply the lessons of the past to the problems of today."[57]

The democratic nature of the Mishnah and *Gemara* in the Talmud was demonstrated in the quote about who would not be able to get into the World-to-Come. Rabbi Akiva and Abba Shaul are reputed to have lived in the same century but may never have had an actual conversation with each other. Their contributions are added to the first list, and all are considered. And there are later opinions given which could be labeled as speculation or faith depending on what one felt was the basis for the rabbinic statement.

The Talmud contains several stories in which the rabbis imagine what happens when we die, what it's like in the World-to-Come, and how we get there. I will have comments about each one of them.

STEPHEN KAROL

What Happens When We Die?

Jewish tradition believes in the existence of angels who are God's assistants and messengers in a variety of situations and for a number of purposes. They enter or are sent to our world by God, but in this quotation, they are introducing the souls of righteous individuals to God:

"Rabbi Yosei ben Shaul said: 'At the time when a righteous individual departs from the world, the ministering angels say before the Holy One, "Blessed be He: Master of the Universe, the righteous individual so-and-so is coming." The Holy One, Blessed be He, then says to them: "The righteous should come forth and they should go out toward him." And the righteous say to the newly deceased individual: 'He enters in peace, and subsequently, the righteous rest in their beds.'"[58]

Rabbi Yehudah HaNasi [Judah HaNasi] was the righteous of the righteous, and it is amazing to me that an account exists of his death. He prays to God for peace in the afterlife, and is answered by a "Divine Voice":

"It is further related: At the time of the death of Rabbi Yehuda HaNasi, he raised his ten fingers toward Heaven and said in prayer: 'Master of the Universe, it is revealed and known before You that I toiled with my ten fingers in the Torah, and I have not derived any benefit from the world even with my small finger. May it be Your will that there be peace in my repose.' A Divine Voice emerged and said: 'He enters in peace; they rest in their beds.'" (Isaiah 57:2)[59]

Next, Rabbi Elazar adds two twists to the flow of the discussion. First, he specifies that there are three contingents of angels that greet the righteous. Second, the wicked are met by the same number of angel contingents but are not met with the same positive message:

"Rabbi Elazar said: 'At the time when a righteous individual departs from the world, three contingents of ministering angels go out toward him. One says to him: "Enter in peace"; and one says to him: "Each one that walks in his uprightness"; and one says to him: "He enters in peace, they rest in their beds." At the time when a wicked person perishes from the world, three contingents of angels of destruction go out toward him. One says to him: "There is no peace, says the Lord concerning the wicked" (Isaiah 48:22); and one says to him: 'You shall lie down in sorrow.'(Isaiah 50:11)"[60]

What Is It Like in the World-to-Come?

According To The Prophets:

The Hebrew prophets are held in high esteem not only by strict Jewish tradition, but also by the more moderate and liberal interpreters and followers of Judaism. As messengers of God, chosen by God, the prophets delivered straightforward and usually unwelcome messages to their fellow citizens in Israel, Judah, and Babylonia. The relevance of their words is considerable regardless of when they are studied or mentioned. But, in these excerpts, even the prophets had their limitations:

"And Rabbi Ḥiyya bar Abba said that Rabbi Yoḥanan said: 'All the prophets only prophesied with regard to the change in world order in the end of days with regard to the days of the Messiah. However, with regard to the World-to-Come, which exists on a higher level, it is stated: "No eye has seen it, God, aside from You."'" [Isaiah 64:3][61]

"What will be in the World-to-Come cannot be depicted even by means of prophecy."[62]

In Blessings:

Blessings are so important in our lives. There are so many prayers from which to choose, and they can be said from the time we wake up in the morning through the time we go to sleep at night. In fact, the Talmud—using a play on words—says:

"Rabbi Meir would say: 'A person is obligated to recite one hundred blessings every day, as it is stated in the verse: "And now, Israel, what [ma] does the Lord your God require of you" (Deuteronomy 10:12). Rabbi Meir interprets the verse as though it said one hundred [me'a], rather than ma."[63]

This citation is also about blessings and recognizes the tradition that blessings should be said in bad times as well as good. But the World-to-Come is different because the only blessing that will be necessary is the blessing for good. What strikes me as unusual and important in this statement is the phrase "In the World-to-Come one will always recite"—meaning that we will somehow, in some way, be reciting blessings in the afterlife. It could be argued that the World-to-Come mentioned by Aha bar Hanina is after the Messiah comes and a new age will begin here on Earth. But it could also be argued that he is referring to an afterlife that is not taking place on Earth. That is because there are different points of view among the rabbis as to the nature and location of the World-to-Come.

"Rabbi Aḥa bar Ḥanina said: 'The World-to-Come is not like this world. In this world, upon good tidings one recites: "Blessed [are You, the Eternal our God, Sovereign of the Universe] Who is good and does good"; and over bad tidings one recites: "Blessed [are You, the Eternal our God, Sovereign of the Universe], the true Judge." In the World-to-Come one will always recite: "Blessed [are You, the Eternal our God, Sovereign of the Universe], Who is good and does good." There will be only one mode of blessing God for tidings.'"[64]

According To Two Other Rabbis:

Rav and Rav Nahman bar Yitzhak start out with the same message that the World-to-Come "is not at all like this world." The difference for Rav is that the physical and emotional aspects of human life on earth will be non-existent, but the souls of the righteous will get to bask in the radiance of God's presence. He bases this contention on a verse from Exodus in which the elders of Israel "saw God" in the Sinai Desert and, instead of being destroyed by God, they were able to have a feast. Nahman focuses on the sanctity of God's proper name, which I wrote about earlier. In order to avoid saying God's actual name, we substitute the Hebrew word that can be translated as "Lord." The end of his comment stands out for me because it states that there will be reading in the World-to-Come. There are no details given about how and why, but it seems to me that reading God's name is an activity that is, by definition, good.

"Rav had a favorite saying: 'The world-to-come is not at all like this world. In the world-to-come there is no eating, no drinking, no procreation, no commerce, no envy, no hatred, no rivalry; the righteous sit with their crowns on their heads and enjoy the radiance of the *Shekhina* (Divine Presence), as it is written (Ex. 24:11) "And they saw God and they ate and drank."[65]

"Rav Nahman bar Yitzhak said: 'The World-to-Come is not like this world. In this world, God's name that is written with the letters *yod* and *heh* is read as *Adonai*, which begins with the letters *alef* and *dalet*. God's name is not pronounced in the same way as it is written. However, in the World-to-Come it will all be one, as God's name will be both read with the letters *yod* and *heh* and written with the letters *yod* and *heh*.'"[66]

How Can You Get There?

You shouldn't be surprised to see a quote that praises the studying of Jewish law as a *guarantee* that one would be destined for the World-to-Come. The verse that is chosen from the book of the rather obscure prophet Habakkuk holds the key to understanding the incredible attraction of entering the World-to-Come. To be "guaranteed" and "destined" for "eternal life in the future world" is well-worth striving for, and the means to the end is to study the *Halacha* [Jewish law]:

"The school of Elijah taught: 'Anyone who studies *halakhot* [the laws of Jewish Tradition] every day is guaranteed that he is destined for the World-to-Come,' as it is stated: 'His ways *[halik-hot]* are eternal' (Habakkuk 3:6). Do not read the verse as *halik-hot*; rather, read it as *halakhot*. The verse indicates that the study of *halakhot* brings one to eternal life in the future world.'"[67]

There are a number of examples in the Talmud in which there is a comparison of the effects and results of doing something or not doing something. In a traditional sense, a *mitzvah* is a commandment, of which there are 613 in the Torah. In a more general sense, a *mitzvah* is variously described as a "good deed" or an "unselfish act." The belief that one deed can make a difference is either tremendously empowering or tremendously terrifying for us:

"And Rabbi Shmuel bar Naḥmani further says that Rabbi Yonatan says: 'With regard to anyone who performs one *mitzva* in this world, the *mitzva* will precede him and walk before him in the World-to-Come, as it is stated: "And your righteousness shall go before you, the glory of the Lord shall be your reward" (Isaiah

58:8). And with regard to anyone who commits one transgression, that transgression will shroud him and lead him on the Day of Judgment, as it is stated: "The paths of their way do wind, they go up into the waste, and are lost.""" (Job 6:18)[68]

I mentioned the prevalence of blessings in Jewish life earlier —the point of which is to express gratitude for what is about to happen or has happened. To be the recipient of hospitality—one of the greatest *mitzvot* that one can fulfill—is worthy of blessing. But the blesser has to get it right because those words can have both a short-term and a long-term impact:

"What is the formula of the blessing with which the guest blesses his host? 'May it be Your will that the master of the house shall not suffer shame in this world, nor humiliation in the World-to-Come.'"[69]

I have a personal wish for the World-to-Come—that it be filled with music, the music I like to hear, and the music I like to sing. If Rabbi Joshua is right, my wish will be fulfilled, and I will be privileged to enjoy it in the World-to-Come:

"Rabbi Joshua ben Levi [said], 'Whoever utters songs of praise to God for this world [olam hazeh] will be privileged to do so in the world to come [olam haba].' "[70]

Rabbi Eliezer's message below is multi-faceted and very much a reflection of the world and the time in which he lived— one in which relationships with colleagues, educating children properly, respecting teachers appropriately, and affirming God positively all added up to being "worthy" of the afterlife:

"Be careful of the honor of your colleagues; restrain your children from [rote] recitation; and seat them between the knees of the disciples of the Sages; and when you pray, know before whom you stand; and on that account you will be worthy of the life of the world to come."[71]

Stories About The Dead

Because of the immense influence of the story of Saul and his fatal decision to consult a witch to bring the prophet Samuel back from the dead, you might think that we would never find any consideration of the next world in the Talmud. If so, you would be surprised to find out that the tractate of *Berakhot* [18b] has an extensive discussion of it that includes a story. Whenever you see the word *"Gemara"* throughout the story, it means that a challenge to a claim is being made or an alternative explanation is being offered. Imagine this story being told, with occasional comments from me—this time appearing after the parts of the story rather than before:

"The sons of Rabbi Ḥiyya went out to the villages to oversee the laborers. They forgot what they had learned and were struggling to recall it. One of them said to the other: 'Does our deceased father know of our anguish?' The other said to him: 'From where would he know? Isn't it written: "His sons are honored yet he shall not know it, they come to sorrow and he shall not understand them' (Job 14:21)? **The dead do not know.**" [Emphasis added][72]

Have you ever wished that you could ask a question of someone who has died? It could be a question about the details that you can't recall from a past experience or a fact that you've forgotten. Wouldn't you like to believe that your deceased family member or friend could help you? Or do you agree with Hiyya's second son that the dead don't even know what's going on with us?

"The other said back to him: 'And do the dead truly not know? Isn't it written: "Only in his flesh does he feel pain, in his soul does he mourn"' (Job 14:22)? Based on this verse Rabbi Yitzḥak said: 'Gnawing maggots are as excruciating to the dead as the stab of a needle to the flesh of the living. **The dead must have the capacity to feel and know.' In order to reconcile this contradiction, they said: 'They know of their own pain but do not know of the pain of others.'"** [Emphasis added][73]

The first brother is still hanging on to the hope that the dead are aware. Rabbi Yitzhak's reply is rather graphic and grants the dead a limited ability to feel pain, even if it's only theirs. But the *Gemara* counters this point of view with an amazing story that goes on for a few paragraphs:

"The Gemara challenges this: 'And is it so that the dead do not know of the pain of others? Wasn't it taught in a *baraita*: "There was an incident involving a pious man who gave a poor man a *dinar* on the eve of Rosh HaShana during drought years, and his wife mocked him for giving so large a sum at so difficult a time? And in order to escape her incessant mockery, he went and slept in the cemetery."[74]

Unfortunately, this story begins with a scene that may resonate not only with men but also with women. When we are mocked—especially for doing something so kind as helping the poor—and that mocking is constant, we may also feel the need to leave. Choosing the cemetery probably wouldn't be what we would do, but it's essential for the plot:

"That night **in his dream, he heard two spirits conversing** with each other. One said to the other:' My friend, let us roam the world and hear from behind the heavenly curtain, which separates the Divine Presence from the world, what calamity will befall the world.' The other spirit said to her: 'I cannot go with you, as I am buried in a mat of reeds, but you go, and tell me what you hear.' She went, and roamed, and came back. The other spirit said: 'My friend, what did you hear from behind the heavenly curtain?' She replied: 'I heard that anyone who sows during the first rainy season of this year, hail will fall and strike his crops.' **Hearing this,** the pious man went and sowed his seeds during the second rainy season. Ultimately, the crops of the entire world were stricken by hail and **his crops were not stricken."** [Emphasis added][75]

Many people that I have met or spoken to in doing the research for this book have told me about their dreams. The first step is to be able to remember what happens, and that is something that I am not able to do, unfortunately. The second step is to interpret what is conveyed during the course of the dream. And the third step is to decide whether to act on it or not. Clearly, this man who is not named but is labeled as "pious" has a precise recall and takes action. This section is also significant because it posits the existence of a "heavenly curtain" between life on earth and the afterlife. If it were not for his recall of the dream and his sowing the seeds, his crops would have been stricken:

"The following year, on the eve of Rosh HaShana, the same pious man went and **slept in the cemetery** at his own initiative, and **again he heard the two spirits conversing with each other.** One said to the other: 'Let us roam the world and hear from behind the heavenly curtain what calamity will befall the world.' She said to her: 'My friend, have I not already told you that I cannot, as I am buried in a mat of reeds? Rather, you go, and tell me what you hear.'
She went, and roamed, and returned. The other spirit said to her: 'My friend, what did you hear from behind the curtain?' She said to her: 'I heard that those who sow during the second rainy season, blight will strike his crops.' That pious man went and sowed during the first rainy season. Since everyone else sowed during the second rainy season, ultimately, the

crops of the entire world were blighted, and **his crops were not blighted.**" [Emphasis added][76]

This is virtually the same narrative as before. In my opinion, the author(s) of this story wanted to convey that what happened the previous year wasn't a fluke, that this pious man can remember his dreams, that two spirits can communicate with each other, that the "heavenly curtain" doesn't prevent the deceased from being aware of what is happening on Earth, that a message from a spirit can be trusted, and that a pious believer can benefit from a message.

"The pious man's wife said to him: 'Why is it that last year, the crops of the entire world were stricken and yours were not stricken, and now this year, the crops of the entire world were blighted and yours were not blighted?' He related to her the entire story. They said: It was not even a few days later that a quarrel fell between the pious man's wife and the mother of the young woman who was buried there. The pious man's wife said to her scornfully: "**Go and I will show you your daughter, and you will see that she is buried in a mat of reeds**." [Emphasis added][77]

Now the mocking wife gets involved, and our opinion of her doesn't get any better. She questions why her [good-for-nothing] husband could be so fortunate and the rest of the world so unfortunate. He lets her in on the secret, and one wonders whether she actually believes him. But she remembers enough of the story that she gets into a quarrel and speaks "scornfully" to the mother of one of the spirits. Why would she reveal what she knows from the dream? And why would she be so impious and cruel?

"The following year, **he again went and slept in the cemetery, and heard the same spirits conversing with each other.** One said to the other: 'My friend, let us roam the world and hear from behind the heavenly curtain what calamity will befall the world.' She said to her: 'My friend, leave me alone, as **words that we have privately exchanged between us have already been heard among the living.' Apparently, the dead know what transpires in this world."** [Emphasis added][78]

For the third year in a row, the pious man—who must have felt that he had all the luck—repeats his ritual of sleeping in the cemetery to get information from which he can benefit. But this time is different because the private words of the two deceased women have been shared by the living. The conclusion of the Talmud is that the dead do indeed know what's going on in the world they left behind.

"The *Gemara* responds: **This is no proof**; perhaps another person, who heard about the conversation of the spirits secondhand, died and **he went and told them that they had been overheard."**[79]

As I mentioned earlier, the *Gemara* challenges everything that has been said up to this point. This is not sufficient evidence that the dead are aware of what is going on here, or that they communicate with each other, or that they communicate with living human beings. So, there has to be a "reasonable and logical" explanation because the alternative is just too farfetched and strange. It is suggested that maybe somebody else's soul (another unnamed spirit) heard about the conversation from another spirit and told the two women in the World-to-Come that their conversation had been overheard. Really? Is that a better instance of proof? Or is it speculation? Some people will go to any extreme to deny the power of spiritual communication.

"With regard to the deceased's knowledge of what transpires, come and hear a proof, as it is told: Ze'iri would deposit his *dinars* with his innkeeper. While he was going and coming to and from the school of Rav, she died, and he did not know where she had put the money. **So he went after her to her grave in the cemetery and said to her: 'Where are the *dinars*?' She replied: 'Go and get them from beneath the hinge of the door in such and such a place',** and tell my mother that she should send me **my comb and a tube of eye shadow** with such and such a woman who will die and come here tomorrow.' **Apparently, the dead know what transpires in this world.**"[Emphasis added][80]

This "proof" may make you laugh, if for no other reason than it mentions a comb and eye shadow. Ze'iri takes the step of going to the cemetery and speaking with the innkeeper. As I mentioned before, sometimes we wish we could ask a question of someone who has died and then actually get an answer. But the dead innkeeper—whose spirit could be dismissed as frivolous because of the cosmetics request—is able to know that someone is going to die and will be in the afterlife the next day. That second comment would seem to bolster the idea that the dead are definitely aware of what is happening and what *will* happen.

"The Gemara rejects this proof: Perhaps the angel Duma [the "Angel of Silence" in rabbinic and Islamic literature] who oversees the dead, comes beforehand and announces to them that a particular individual will arrive the next day, but **they themselves do not know.**" [Emphasis added][81]

Once again, the *Gemara* doesn't find this proof to be believable. It introduces an angel whose job it is to be the "introducer" of newcomers to the afterlife. That tells me that the innkeeper's spirit found out from the angel about this woman for whom it was so important to have a comb and a tube of eye shadow. It must have been important for the sake of the *Gemara* that the power of advance knowledge about new arrivals was concentrated in the angel and not distributed amongst the spirits of the World-to-Come.

"The Gemara cites another proof: 'Come and hear, as it is told: They would deposit the money of orphans with Shmuel's father for safekeeping. When Shmuel's father died, Shmuel was not with him, and did not learn from him the location of the money. Since he did not return it, Shmuel was called: "Son of him who consumes the money of orphans." **Shmuel went after his father to the cemetery and said to the dead: 'I want Abba [Father].' The dead said to him: 'There are many Abbas here'.**

He told them: 'I want Abba bar Abba'. They said to him: 'There are also many people named Abba bar Abba here.' He told them: 'I want Abba bar Abba, the father of Shmuel. Where is he?' They replied: 'Ascend to the yeshiva on high.' Meanwhile, he saw his friend Levi sitting outside the yeshiva, away from the rest of the deceased. He asked him: 'Why do you sit outside? Why did you not ascend to the yeshiva?' He replied: 'Because they tell me that for all those years that you didn't enter the yeshiva of Rabbi Afes, and thereby upset him, **we will not grant you entry to the yeshiva on high.'**" [Emphasis added] [82]

This paragraph features the insulting labeling of Shmuel, who doesn't deserve to be referred to in that way. It's not his fault that his father didn't tell him where to find the orphans' money. His recourse, apparently, is not to try to look for it, but to go to the cemetery to get the answer from the spirit of his deceased father. The story turns somewhat comical over which *"Abba"* he is seeking but ends sadly with the reason for not being granted entry. One wonders what was done that upset Rabbi Afes.

"Meanwhile, **Shmuel's father came,** and Shmuel saw that he was crying and laughing. Shmuel said to his father: 'Why are you crying?' His father replied: 'Because you will come here soon.' Shmuel continued and asked: 'Why are you laughing?' His father replied: 'Because you are extremely important in this world.' Shmuel said to him: 'If I am important, then **let them grant Levi** entry to the yeshiva.' And so, it was that they granted Levi entry to the yeshiva.'" [Emphasis added][83]

There is an extremely crucial point being made again here—that the deceased in the World-to-Come are aware of not only our future (Shmuel's death), but also our present (Shmuel is "extremely important"). How important is he? He is so important that he can appeal for his deceased friend Levi to be allowed to enter the "yeshiva on high" in the World-to-Come, and have that appeal be successful.

"Shmuel said to his father: 'Where is the orphans' money?' He said to him: 'Go and retrieve it from the millhouse, where you will find the uppermost and the lowermost money is ours, and the money in the middle belongs to the orphans.' Shmuel said to him: 'Why did you do that?' He replied: 'If thieves stole, they would steal from our money on top, which the thief would see first. If the earth swallowed up any of it, it would swallow from our money, on the bottom.' **Apparently, the dead, in this case Shmuel's father, know when others will die.** Since Shmuel did not die the next day, clearly the angel Duma could not have informed them. The Gemara responds: '**Perhaps Shmuel is different, and because he is so important, they announce beforehand: 'Clear place for his arrival.'**" [Emphasis added][84]

Shmuel's incredible conversation with his deceased father continues. The text affirms again that the dead know what will happen to the living. The role of Duma is eliminated, and Shmuel's importance is confirmed. Who will announce beforehand? It could be the angels or other spirits or souls. Regardless of the answer to that question, this section of the Talmud is considerably significant in that it discusses communication between the living and the dead.

The story about Shmuel may contradict what some Jews believe, including such great scholars as the late Rabbi Judith Abrams:

"This story is part of a larger section in which the rabbis try to determine how the dead relate to the living. They were anxious to dispel any superstitious notions that the dead can hear us or have any effect on our lives. Why? Because if people believed this, then they might take some, and possibly much, of the intensity they should be putting into their relationship with God and channel it into relating to the deceased, almost praying to **them** rather than to God, to fix things in their lives.

However, this story represents a strong superstitious tradition that the rabbis could not extinguish: the belief that the dead influence our lives and that we could profit from their knowledge if we could but obtain it. The rabbis reject this notion. Even the **spirits** seem to reject the idea."[85]

But what if the possibility still exists? What if contact from the deceased is an extension of a strong belief in the power of God? It seems so illogical and outlandish, so supernatural and wild. What I referred to as "supernatural" in the Introduction to this book is actually quite natural in Judaism. The next chapter provides some examples of that from the Jewish tradition, in ways that some Jews and non-Jews may not even be aware of at all.

CHAPTER 6: THE "SUPERNATURAL" IN JUDAISM: RESURRECTION, ELIJAH, THE DIVINE VOICE, RACHEL THE MATRIARCH, PRAYERS, SONGS, GOOD ANGELS, SATAN, THE ANGEL OF DEATH, AND THE EVIL EYE

Dictionary.com—supernatural:
*of, relating to, or being **above or beyond what is natural**; unexplainable by natural law or phenomena; abnormal.*
*of, pertaining to, characteristic of, or **attributed to God or a deity.** [Emphasis added][86]*

*"Religious **supernaturalism** teaches that religion originates through the initiative of a God Who is beyond the natural order, and Who intervenes in history to reveal a teaching to a specific community...Jewish traditionalism believes that a **supernatural** God revealed the tenets and practices of Jewish religion to our ancestors, most eminently at Sinai." [Emphasis added][87]*

"Many of those that sleep in the dust of the death will awake, some to eternal life, others to reproaches, to everlasting abhorrence."[88]

"He will destroy death forever."[89]

"You are forever mighty, Adonai; You revive the dead."[90]

"and Elijah went up to heaven in a whirlwind."[91]

"He [Elijah] shall reconcile parents with children and children with their parents."[92]

*"Another manifestation of Divine immanence is the Bath Kol, literally 'daughter of a voice.' It refers to the **supernatural** method of communicating God's will to men, especially when the Hebrew prophets had come to an end." [Emphasis added][93]*

"Thus, said the Lord: 'A cry is heard in Ramah—Wailing, bitter weeping—Rachel weeping for her children.'"[94]

"I offer thanks to You, ever-living Sovereign, that You have restored my soul to me in mercy: How great is Your trust."[95] (Modeh/Modah Ani)

"Peace be to you, O ministering angels, messengers of the Most High."[96] (Shalom Aleichem)

"Beloved, come to meet the Bride; beloved come to greet Shabbat."[97] (L'chah Dodi)

"Then came the Holy One, blessed be God, and destroyed the Angel of Death."[98] (Chad Gadya)

"The dread of the Evil Eye was universal in past ages and still persists among the uneducated."[99]

These quotations are about what I—and such respected scholars as Neil Gillman and A. Cohen—refer to as "supernatural" aspects or examples of beliefs within Judaism. You may recall that I mentioned my childhood interest in the supernatural in Chapter One. What I was taught in my temple as an adolescent about Jewish beliefs in the supernatural is that they were illogical or unprovable, impossible or metaphorical, or just pure fantasy. What I have come to accept is that they don't have to be logical in order to be provable, and that what may seem to be impossible is not necessarily just metaphorical or pure fantasy. In particular, the ability for us to receive communication from those who have died is what could be called "supernatural," but it doesn't have to be labeled as "anti-God" or "anti-religious." That is why I provided the dictionary definition as the first quotation—the supernatural may be perceived as "above or beyond what is natural" or "unexplainable by natural law." And what if the same phenomena can be explained as being "attributed to God?" If they are, then the "signs" that some people receive are not "anti-God" and certainly not "anti-religious." On the contrary, they are manifestations of the wonderful quality of the World-to-Come and are examples of God's love for us and of God conquering death. I will address this in a subsequent chapter.

The subjects of the quotations above give a hint about what will be covered in this chapter: Resurrection of the dead, Elijah the Prophet, The *Bat Kol,* Rachel the Matriarch, God's protection of our soul while we are sleeping, good angels, Satan, the Angel of Death, and The Evil Eye. These supernatural events or phenomena—whether they are beliefs or superstition—are incorporated not only in our prayers but also in our culture. They are even integral to holidays, life-cycle events, and our language.

Resurrection of the Dead

Rabbi Neil Gillman—who died in 2017—was affiliated with the Conservative Jewish movement. He taught at the Jewish Theological Seminary and was the author of several books, the most important being *The Death of Death: Resurrection and Immortality in Jewish Thought.* He wrote:

"... the idea of resurrection evolved within Israel as a thoroughly natural development of ideas deeply planted in biblical religion from the outset. If, in fact, God created the world and

STEPHEN KAROL

humanity in the first place, if God is the ultimate force Whose
power extends over all of nature and history, if God can send
Israel into exile and then redeem it once again (from Egyptian
slavery and in the time of Cyrus), if God can renew the natural
cycle each year, if God can, as Isaiah 66 promises, create 'a new
heaven and a new earth,' then why cannot God raise human
beings from the grave?"[100]

In his famous vision of the Valley of Dry Bones, the prophet
Ezekiel declares: "I am going to open your graves and lift you
out of the graves, O my people, and bring you to the land of Israel."[101] Gillman and others refer to this as being a metaphor,
but there are those who see it as an affirmation of the amazing—
and I believe, supernatural—power of God. Gillman stated:

"The prophet's vision was limited to Israel's national regen-
eration, not to the later doctrine of bodily resurrection. This
text remains significant, however, for it marks one of the steps
which, in time, leads the later tradition to go beyond the metaphorical use of this theme and to **understand it in a much more
concrete way, as an even further extension of God's unlimited
power.**" [Emphasis added][102]

In addition, the Book of Daniel (written around the time of
the Maccabees in the second century B.C.E.) contains one of the
few references to resurrection in the Hebrew Bible:

"At that time, the great prince, Michael, who stands beside
the sons of your people will appear. It will be a time of trouble,
the like of which has never been since the nation came into
being. At that time, your people will be rescued, all who are
found inscribed in the book. Many of **those that sleep in the
dust** of the death will awake, **some to eternal life**, others to
reproaches, to everlasting abhorrence. And the knowledgeable
will be radiant like the bright expanse of sky, and those who
lead the many to righteousness will be like the stars forever...But

you, go on to the end; **you shall rest, and arise to your destiny at the end of the days.**" [Emphasis added][103]

The amazing power that God has is enshrined in the *G'vurot* prayer in our daily, Shabbat, and holiday liturgy, and so is Daniel's phrase "those that sleep in the dust"—as a euphemism for those who are dead and buried. The traditional version of the prayer translates as follows:

"Thou, O Lord, art mighty forever. **Thou called the dead to immortal life** for Thou art mighty in deliverance...Thou sustainest the living with lovingkindness, and **in great mercy callest the departed to everlasting life**...and keepest faith with those that sleep in the dust. Who is like unto Thee, Almighty King, who decrees death and life and brings forth salvation? Faithful art Thou to grant eternal life to the departed. Blessed art Thou, O Lord, **who callest the dead to life everlasting.**"[104] [Emphasis added]

As you can see, God's power to revive/restore the dead is referred to four times in this prayer and is motivated by mercy and faith. Although we have seen and experienced scientific methods to prolong the lives of God's creatures, there is no cure for death. We may live longer than before and we may live better than before, but we don't defeat death. Jewish tradition firmly contends and accepts on faith that God—and *only* God—can do that, and it will be done by resurrecting the dead. For more than 150 years, the Reform movement did not accept this power of God and replaced the reference to resurrection in the *G'vurot* with the words "who gives life to all." In *Mishkan T'filah: A Reform Siddur,* which was published in 2007, an option was given to Reform congregations to use those words or the literal words ("revive the dead"):

"You are forever mighty, Adonai; You give life to all (revive the dead...You sustain life through love, **giving life to all (re-**

viving the dead) through great compassion...keeping faith with those who sleep in the dust. Who is like You, Source of mighty acts? Who resembles You, a Sovereign who takes and gives life, causing deliverance to spring up and faithfully **giving life to all (reviving that which is dead)?** Blessed are You, Adonai, who **gives life to all (who revives the dead).**"[105] [Emphasis added]

Whenever I conduct a funeral for a certain funeral home on Long Island, a pouch of Israeli soil is provided for the mourners to put into the grave on top of their loved one's casket. The pouch says: "Holy Earth from Mount Olives, Jerusalem Israel," and also has part of a verse (Deuteronomy 32: 41) on it which reads: "And He will appease His land and His people." The entire quote is: "O nations, acclaim His people! For He'll avenge the blood of His servants, wreak vengeance on His foes, and appease the land of His people." This rather strident line which concludes Moses' final speech to his people has taken on the meaning of resurrection and return to the Land of Israel as the ultimate payback to all the foes of the Jewish people who tried to destroy us.

So, what are the "mechanics" of resurrection? How exactly will it happen?

"Rabbi Ḥiyya ben Joseph said: 'A time will come when the just will **break through** [the soil] **and rise up in Jerusalem**, for it is written', "Let men sprout up in towns like country grass..." (Psalm 72:16). Rabbi Ḥiyya ben Joseph further stated: 'The just in the time to come will rise in their own clothes. [This is deduced] ... from a grain of wheat. If a grain of wheat that is buried naked [i.e., sown] sprouts up with many coverings, how much more so the just who are buried in their shrouds?"[106] [Emphasis added]

I don't remember conducting a funeral and having someone refuse to put the Israel soil into the grave. In a way—and I don't mean this disrespectfully—the custom is like an insurance policy. For someone who doesn't literally believe in resurrection, but might be wrong about it, the soil in the grave can work to the benefit of the deceased. This description of the process of resurrection which appeared on the website *myjewishlearning.com* explains it best:

"Resurrection of the dead — *t'chiyat hameitim* in Hebrew — is a core doctrine of traditional Jewish theology. Traditional Jews believe that during the Messianic Age, the temple will be rebuilt in Jerusalem, the Jewish people ingathered from the far corners of the earth and the bodies of the dead will be brought back to life and reunited with their souls. It is not entirely clear whether only Jews, or all people, are expected to be resurrected at this time...

The resurrection doctrine is fleshed out in a variety of rabbinic sources. Among the ideas associated with it is the belief that during the messianic age the dead will be brought back to life in Israel. According to the Talmud, all bodies not already in Israel will be rolled through underground tunnels to the holy land. Avoiding this process, which is said to be spiritually painful, is one reason some Jews choose to be buried in Israel."[107]

If anything could be referred to as "supernatural," this could be. And it is possible to believe in the supernatural and to also believe in the logical and natural. In the concluding chapter of his book, Gillman wrote:

"I pride myself on being a rational being, on using my critical faculties, and on appreciating the value of scientific methods. ... I cling by my very fingernails to the realization that my rational self is not the whole of me, that there are dimensions of my experience that elude the critical temper, that the world remains for me a realm of enchantment. I do science but I also appreciate poetry; I work but I also play... (I) hope that my life here on earth is not my entire destiny. That kind of hope takes me beyond the conclusions of my rational self. It refuses to surrender to the charges of denial and wishful thinking. It comes from some other dimension of my being, from that intuitive sense that I form a part of a broader order of existence that lends my life coherence."[108]

I will be referring back to this statement later on in this book.

Elijah the Prophet

"When the Lord was about to take Elijah up to heaven in a whirlwind, Elijah and Elisha had set out from Gilgal...Disciples of the prophets at Bethel came out to Elisha and said to him, 'Do you know that the Lord will take your master away from you today?' He replied, 'I know it, too; be silent.'" [Commentary: 'Somehow the groups at Bethel and Jericho knew that the Lord was about to take Elijah. **They do not use words indicating death**'] ...As they kept on walking and talking, a fiery chariot with fiery horses suddenly appeared and separated one from the other; and Elijah went up to heaven in a whirlwind."[109] [Emphasis added]

This is the description of Elijah's "death" from the Book of Second Kings. Because it doesn't mention death per se, it is believed that Elijah's departure from earth was highly unusual and extremely significant. His life spanned the end of the 10th Century B.C.E. through the middle of the 9th Century in the Kingdom of Israel and during the reigns of both Ahab and Ahaziah. Throughout the centuries, he has been accorded a status on a level higher than any other Hebrew prophet. And, because he didn't exactly die, there has been considerable speculation about what happened to him and faith about what he is capable of doing as a spirit. This is especially true in the body of literature known as the "Tales of Elijah" or the "Elijah Legends." Peninnah Schram—a storyteller and author—has written:

"Elijah the Prophet plays three main roles in Jewish life... as the one who will usher in the messianic era—he is the forerunner of the Messiah...A second role is that of arbiter of Jewish law...Whenever a just decision could not be determined, the rabbis agreed to put the entire sum into escrow until the coming of Elijah...

A third role that Elijah plays is that of mediator between parents and children. The Book of Malachi (3:24) describes Elijah as the one who will 'turn the heart of fathers to the children, and the heart of children to their fathers.' As the one who will reconcile families, the one who will settle legal arguments, and especially the one who will announce the imminent arrival of peace and harmony in the world, **we all continue to search and hope for Elijah the Prophet to appear soon in our day.**" [110] [Emphasis added]

Even the way Elijah is referred to in Judaism is special. Having studied and taught about the Hebrew prophets for most of my life, I don't recall any of the other prophets being referred to formally in the way that Elijah is. We have "The Prophet Isaiah," "The Prophet Amos," "The Prophet Jeremiah." *"Eiliyahu Hanavi"* is the Hebrew, "Elijah the Prophet." Most Jews know it because of the song that we sing during the Passover Seder when the door is opened for Elijah. Children are often the ones who have that honor, and he "is present" simultaneously at hundreds of thousands of Seders all over the world and consecutively in different time zones. There is a "Cup of Elijah" on the table representing hope for the future—usually a distinctive and distinguished-looking cup from which no one drinks. The setting for this custom is provided in this way in the *CCAR Haggadah*:

"Elijah, the prophet from the village of Tishbi in Gilead, challenged the injustice of the king and overthrew the worship of Baal. He healed the humble sick and helped the widowed. As to the end of his days on earth, his disciple Elisha had a vision of

Elijah being carried to the skies in a chariot of fire. Legend has it that Elijah returns to earth, from time to time, to befriend the helpless.

This man of mystery became associated with the end of Days, with the Messianic hopes of our people. The prophet Malachi promised that Elijah would come to turn the hearts of parents to children, and the hearts of children to parents, and to announce the coming of the Messiah when all mankind would celebrate freedom."[111]

The text continues: "There are links between heaven and earth which promise an answer to life's perplexities. Elijah opens for us the realm of mystery and wonder."[112] After the door is closed, we sing the song in Hebrew, which translates as: "Elijah the Prophet, Elijah the Tishbite, Elijah, Elijah, Elijah the Gileadite. Soon in our days may he come to us with [the] Messiah [the] son of David, with [the] Messiah [the] son of David." The man who didn't die is the subject of a song expressing the wish that he will return to earth in the company of the Messiah. That same song is part of the Havdalah prayers for the end of Shabbat, and is described so well by my friend, the late Rabbi Mark Dov Shapiro in *Gates of Shabbat: A Guide for Observing Shabbat:*

"Since Shabbat was understood to be a forerunner of the Messianic era, over the centuries Jews have always hoped that Elijah...would arrive with the new week to announce the coming of a time that would be 'all Shabbat.'

Although Reform Jews have not literally subscribed to the notion of an individual Messiah descended from King David, the song 'Eiliyahu Hanavi' (Elijah the Prophet) is still sung here and at the Pesach Seder to express the desire for an era when Elijah's passion for justice becomes a universal human commitment. For us, this would constitute the 'coming of the Messiah.'"[113]

A lesser-known reference to Elijah is on the Sabbath before Passover—known as *Shabbat HaGadol* (the Great Sabbath)

—which receives its name from the previously-mentioned last verse of the *Haftarah* (Prophetic reading) portion from Malachi 3:24: "Lo, I will send the prophet Elijah to you before the coming of the awesome, fearful day of the Lord."[114]

Another "appearance" that Elijah makes is at every *bris* or *b'rit milah* (covenant of circumcision) ceremony:

"A treasured Jewish legend holds that the prophet Elijah is present at every *b'rit milah*. Elijah, most commonly thought of as the forerunner of the messianic age, is also often considered as the 'angel of the covenant' (Malachi 3:1), a protector of little children—in effect, the 'guardian angel.' Jews, therefore, set aside a special chair for Elijah at the *b'rit*, with the baby placed in the chair prior to the circumcision."[115]

Those who sing the *Birkat Hamazon*—the Blessing after Meals —include a line in the longer version of the blessing which is, in essence, a prayer within a prayer, asking God to send Elijah back to earth: "May the Merciful One send us Elijah the prophet— may he be remembered for good—and let him bring us good tidings, deliverance, and consolation." This is clearly not a matter of Elijah being in a particular location on Earth as an ordinary human being would be. The assumption is that God has direct control over Elijah's movement and activity, and this request is also linked to Elijah's coming to announce the Messiah.

What fascinates me the most, though, are the many tales and legends about Elijah. Peninnah Schramm's *Tales of Elijah the Prophet* contains 36 fabulous stories about him, and she provides a wonderful introduction that says, in part:

"In Jewish folklore, Elijah is quite different from the biblical character. He excels in his domain, the domain of miracles…He helps those in need, especially the poor and the pious. He brings hope and reconciliation. He tests and heals. He sees who is unselfish, who offers hospitality, who gives charity, who learns humility, who deserves help.

His chameleon-like disguises are marvelously clever and numerous: an old man, a poor man, a beggar, a student, a traveler, a doctor, an Arab, a robber, a drunkard, a matchmaker, a magician, a dwarf, a farmer, a merchant, a slave, a handsome horseman—always so as to heighten suspense and fantasy, to test people's behavior, to restore faith, and to bring about a happy resolution. Elijah remains as one of the people, in touch with their problems and needs; in other words, a true leader and inspiration. He is indeed a master of miracles."[116]

Among the stories are: "Elijah's Mysterious Ways," "Welcome to Clothes," "Things Could Be Far Worse," "All Because of a Loaf of Bread," "The Man Whose Words Came True," and "The Repentant Rabbi." In most of them, he appears out of nowhere, and disappears in the same way—leaving behind him a person who is changed positively, a community that is better than before, and a world that is improved because this mysterious prophet visited.

The "Bat/Bas/Bath Kol"— The Divine Voice

Elijah was among the first of the great prophets of Judah and Israel over several centuries. Eventually, prophecy came to an end—as our tradition says: "After the death of Haggai, Zechariah, and Malachi, the last of the prophets, the Holy Spirit ceased from Israel; nevertheless they received communications from God through the medium of the *Bath Kol*."[117] Since the words *"Bat," "Bas,"* and *"Bath"* all mean "daughter," and *"Kol"* means "voice" or "sound," it appears that the rabbis believed it important to create and recognize a female connection to God, in addition to the *"Shechinah,"* the "Divine Presence." The prophets experienced direct communication from God and expressed God's messages to the people. With the end of prophecy in the late-400's B.C.E., it would have been unthinkable for God to stop connecting with the people. So, the *Bat Kol* (my preferred spelling) was like a voice from above that was regarded by those who heard it as being authoritative and authentic, "an echo of prophecy."[118] The Rabbis in the Talmud recorded numerous instances of this new source of inspiration and direction:

"Rabbi Abba said that Shmuel said: 'For three years *Beit Shammai* and *Beit Hillel* disagreed. These said: "The *halakha* [Jewish law] is in accordance with our opinion," and these said: "The *halakha* is in accordance with our opinion." Ultimately, a Divine Voice emerged and proclaimed: "Both these and those are the words of the living God." However, the *halakha* is in accordance with the opinion of *Beit Hillel*.'"[119]

Hillel and Shammai were two of the most famous and influential sages during the end of the first century B.C.E. and the early first century C.E. They were scholars and teachers whose schools of thought came to be known as **The House of Hillel** *(Beit Hillel)* and House of Shammai *(Beit Shammai)*. They and their followers and disciples debated matters of theology, customs, and ethics, which became part of the "Oral Law." Their decisions were recorded in the Talmud, and—as the quotation above states—most matters of law became enshrined according to the opinions of the less stringent *Beit Hillel*. These two schools had vigorous debates on matters that were critical for the shaping of the Oral Law and traditional Judaism as it is today. While the final sentence in the above quote is crucial, the most important message is that the words of *both* of them were holy and relevant. The fact that almost all Jewish law followed *Beit Hillel* didn't mean that *Beit Shammai* and its followers were worthless.

The *Bat Kol* had encounters with an amazing array of Jewish scholars, heroes, and even mountains:
- Rabbi Yehudah HaNasi: Which people are destined for life in the World-to-Come—one who earns it in one moment or after

many years of toil?[120]

- Rav: "Forty days before an embryo is formed, a Divine Voice issues forth and says: 'The daughter of so-and-so is destined to marry so-and-so; such-and-such a house is destined to be inhabited by so-and-so; such-and-such a field is destined to be farmed by so-and-so.'"[121]

- Rabbi Yochanan ben Zakkai: Who reported that the *Bat Kol* reprimanded King Nebuchadnezzar of Babylonia for being overly proud of himself.[122]

- The mountains near Mount Sinai that were "jealous" because the Torah was not given on their peaks: "You are all blemished in comparison to Mount Sinai." [123]

- Abraham: Who was crying about the fate of an olive tree— "Just as with regard to this olive tree, its final purpose is fulfilled at its end, when its fruit is picked, so too, with regard to the Jewish people, their final purpose will be fulfilled at their end, i.e., they will ultimately repent and return to Me."[124]

- Rabbi Shimon and his son Rabbi Elazar: They came out from hiding in a cave for twelve years (during which they had studied Torah) and saw the people not being as committed as they should have been. The rabbis' anger then set the people on fire. In reproof of the rabbis' actions, the *Bat Kol* told them to go back inside for twelve more months.[125]

- Rabbi Elazar: He said that when the Jewish people accepted the Torah at Sinai by saying "We will do" before "We will listen," the *Bat Kol* questioned how they had learned the words of the angels.[126]

- Hillel the Elder: About whom the *Bat Kol* had said to his colleagues: "There is one person among you for whom it is fitting that the Divine Presence should rest upon him as a prophet, but his generation is not fit for it."[127]

- Shimon HaTzadik: "Heard a Divine Voice emerging from the House of the Holy of Holies that was saying: 'The decree that the enemy intended to bring against the Temple is annulled, and [the Roman emperor] Caligula has been killed and his decrees have been voided.' And people wrote down that time that the Divine Voice was heard, and later found that it matched exactly the moment that Caligula was killed."[128]

- Rabba bar Naḥmani: "A Divine Voice emerged from above and said: 'Happy are you, Rabba bar Naḥmani, as your body is pure, and your soul left you with the word: Pure.' A note fell from above and landed in the academy: "Rabba bar Naḥmani was summoned to the heavenly academy," [i.e., he has died]. The Rabbis said: 'We can conclude from this that he is there.'"[129]

And the array of subjects is amazing as well! Consider from these quotations what the *Bat Kol* talks about to these people (and a few mountains): the criteria for entering the World-to-Come, predetermining who will marry whom, the wickedness of the King of Babylonia, "blemished" mountains, Abraham's feelings about a tree, the destructive anger of Rabbi Shimon and Rabbi Elazar, the Jewish people's surprising words, the greatness of a rabbi, the death of an evil Roman emperor, and the note announcing the death of another great rabbi. These are not part of the natural order of things, to put it mildly, but neither were some of the experiences and words and actions of the prophets. The *Bat Kol* was a worthy successor to the prophets, and the ways in which it communicated were supernatural, miraculous, and mysterious. For the most part, what the *Bat Kol* said was accepted and respected by those who heard the messages. They were able to recognize it as being divine and regarded its statements as being accurate in its assessments of human beings and its predictions about the fate of certain people.

Rachel the Matriarch

Since I retired in 2014, I have been participating as a student and instructor in the Osher Lifelong Learning Institute (OLLI) program for retirees, which is held at Stony Brook University. It's a nationwide program that meets at 120 universities and colleges across the United States and is funded by a generous grant from the Bernard Osher Foundation. One of the courses I have taught for OLLI is "The Four Foremothers: Sarah, Rebekah, Leah, and Rachel." Although they are usually referred to as "matriarchs"—parallel to Abraham, Isaac, and Jacob being called "patriarchs"—I decided to do a play on words parallel to "forefathers." In the course, we read excerpts from the stories in Genesis about these four women, read from the Midrash literature of Judaism, and talk about how their personalities and their actions had an impact on the beginnings of the Jewish people and Judaism. Rachel is the youngest of the four, but she receives what I feel is a disproportionate amount of attention and, even, power in Jewish tradition, which doesn't even *border* on the supernatural—it *is* supernatural.

Rachel is first mentioned in Genesis 29:6 as being the daughter of Laban, the brother of the matriarch Rebekah. Jacob arrives in his ancestral homeland after fleeing from the wrath of his brother Esau, who is angry because their father Isaac was tricked into giving Jacob the blessing reserved for his older brother. After inquiring about the welfare of his Uncle Laban, he is told that Laban's daughter Rachel is coming toward him with her father's flock. Here is what happens next:

"And when Jacob saw Rachel, the daughter of his uncle Laban, and the flock of his uncle Laban, Jacob went up and rolled the stone off the mouth of the well, and watered the flock of his uncle Laban. Then Jacob kissed Rachel, and broke into tears. Jacob told Rachel that he was her father's kinsman, that he was Rebekah's son; and she ran and told her father...Rachel was shapely and beautiful. Jacob loved Rachel; so, he answered, 'I will serve you seven years for your younger daughter Rachel.'... Jacob served seven years for Rachel and they seemed to him but a few days because of his love for her."[130]

You would think that this seven-year commitment is as clear as can be, but you would think that only if you didn't know Laban. On the evening of the wedding feast—presumably after many hours of eating and drinking—Jacob goes into the tent in which the consummation of the marriage will take place. It isn't until the next morning that he discovers that it was Leah —Rachel's older sister—to whom he has made love. Incensed, he complains to Laban about being deceived. Laban's response basically is: "Too bad. We don't give the younger daughter for marriage before the older daughter. Give me another seven years, and I'll give you Rachel." As the story progresses, Leah becomes pregnant easily and repeatedly, and Rachel does not, arousing a sense of envy in her. After Leah has had four children, Rachel complains to Jacob that she would rather be dead than childless. She resorts to surrogacy through her maid Bilhah, who has two sons, causing Rachel to say that she has won out over her sister. The competition continues, with Leah building her lead with the births of two sons by her maid Zilpah, and then two more sons and a daughter on her own. Finally, Rachel is blessed with a child, and names him "Joseph."

At this point, Jacob is determined to return home to Canaan with his large family and to leave the service of Laban after 20 years. Rachel and Leah agree with their husband that it's time to go, and they are eager to go, feeling that they are not cared about or cared for by Laban. On their way out, Rachel takes her father's household idols, perhaps to get back at her father, or perhaps because she believes in their power. Laban chases after his daughters, son-in-law, and grandchildren, but only because he wants those idols back. Unbeknownst to Jacob, Rachel is hiding them in a camel cushion, sitting on them, and saying that she is experiencing her period. Responding to Laban's charge of theft, Jacob vows that, if Laban finds his gods with anyone, that person should die—unaware that Rachel took them. Later, Jacob signs a pact with Laban, "wrestles" with a "man" who may be an angel, encounters his brother, and reaches the land of Canaan. On their journey south, Rachel experiences a difficult labor and—with her dying breath—names her newborn son "Ben-oni" [son of my suffering]. Jacob immediately changes his son's name to "Benjamin" [son of my right hand]. Finally, the text tells us: "Thus Rachel died. She was buried on the road to Ephrath—now Bethlehem. Over her grave Jacob set up a pillar; it is the pillar at Rachel's grave to this day."[131]

I have shared Rachel's entire story with you as either a reminder or an introduction so that you can understand why she is so revered by Orthodox Jews, in particular. There is a pattern in the Torah of younger children being favored—Isaac over Ishmael, Jacob over Esau, Joseph over his brothers, Ephraim over Manasseh, Moses over Miriam and Aaron—and Rachel and Leah are part of that pattern. Rachel—the favorite wife of the favorite son—has a first-born son (Joseph) who becomes the favorite, and whose sons (Ephraim and Manasseh) become elevated to the level of their uncles when the Hebrew people are organized as tribes. Because the descendants of each of them become a tribe, it's as if Rachel and Jacob's son Joseph is doubly honored by having double the status of the other tribes. And Rachel is the only one of the patriarchs and matriarchs not to be buried in the Tomb of the Patriarchs *(Machpelah)* in Hebron. She lived in the 16th century B.C.E. The prophet Jeremiah lived in the second half of the 8th and the first quarter of the 7th century B.C.E., and it was these words that he declared to the exiles to Babylonia following the siege and capture of Jerusalem:

"Thus, said the Lord: 'A cry is heard in Ramah—Wailing, bitter weeping—Rachel weeping for her children. She refuses to be comforted for her children who are gone.' Thus said the Lord:

'Restrain your voice from weeping, your eyes from shedding tears; For there is a reward for your labor'—declares the Lord: 'They shall return from the enemy's land. And there is hope for your future'—declares the Lord: 'Your children shall return to their country.'"[132]

Jeremiah was right—Rachel's children returned to their country following the Exile, and there has been a Jewish presence in various numbers there throughout the centuries. Rachel's Tomb (*Kever Rachayl* in Hebrew)—with its distinctive dome—has probably been in existence since the Ottoman period (1517-1917). The structure is located on the road to Bethlehem in a Christian and Muslim cemetery. In 1841, the British philanthropist Sir Moses Montefiore had the site renovated, obtained the keys for the Jewish community, and added a large room to accommodate and encourage Muslim prayer. In the 1947 United Nations Partition Plan for Palestine, Rachel's Tomb was supposed to be within the internationally administered Zone of Jerusalem, which meant in reality that the Jordanians controlled it and prohibited Jews from entering. When Israel won the Six-Day War in 1967, the Israeli Ministry of Religious Affairs took over the site, and it became the third holiest Jewish site after the Western Wall and David's Tomb. In a Mosaic Magazine article, Sarah Rindner of Lander College in New York writes about a turning point in its history:

"In 1995, when the Oslo process was in full swing, then-Prime Minister Yitzhak Rabin was planning to hand over several West Bank cities to the Palestinian Authority. Among them was Bethlehem, where the site venerated by Jews as the tomb of the biblical matriarch Rachel is located.

Disturbed at the thought that Israel would relinquish the tomb, Rabbi Hanan ben Porat, an influential settlement activist, met with Rabin to convince him to leave it under Israeli control. On the way to this meeting, Porat was unexpectedly joined by Rabbi Menachem Porush, a Knesset member for the ultra-Orthodox, and formally non-Zionist, United Torah Judaism party.

At the meeting itself, Porat put forth a series of arguments, most of them security-related, to persuade Rabin that handing over Rachel's Tomb would be a mistake. But Porush, to Rabin's surprise, began to weep and grabbed the prime minister's hands: 'Yitzhak, it's Mama Rachel, Mama Rachel!' In Porat's telling, Rabin was so moved that he changed the agreement so that the site would remain under full Israeli control—a decision in which the Palestinians concurred.[133]

My Israeli cousin Esther was a regular visitor to *Kever Rachayl* before the coronavirus pandemic. Having lived her entire life as an Orthodox Jew, she ascribes spiritual significance and power not only to the site but also to Rachel herself. In an email exchange with her, I asked her when she goes and what or whom she prays for when she is there. She replied: "I pray for all relatives, people who need recovery from illness, finding a match, having children ...I go every Friday. *Mama Rachel loves all her children!*" Please notice that my cousin and her Orthodox family and friends assume that Rachel functions as an intercessor for prayer. She speaks about Rachel in the present tense as a matriarch who lives on in spirit approximately 3,700 years after her death. And, like Rabbi Porush, she calls her "Mama Rachel." Lindner concludes her online article with a rationale for why Rachel is so revered:

"Whether it is Jacob's decision or, as with the wedding night, silently orchestrated by Rachel, the fact that Rachel is buried elsewhere allows Leah the role she sought so desperately during her own life, a position next to Jacob as his beloved...In ceding some of Jacob to Leah, both in life and in death, Rachel models the potential to look past one's own sorrow and, where the ego might otherwise dwell, create space for the complex web of relationships among siblings, spouses, parents, and children to flourish and grow into God's chosen nation."[134]

Prayers and Songs

I wrote about the *G'vurot* prayer before in the section on resurrection. While I believe it is the most prominent prayer in our liturgy about the supernatural actions of God, there are other prayers and songs that are also significant.

Many people believe that the only place for prayer is in a synagogue, church, or mosque. But you can pray at home, too. In Judaism, you can start off your day with these words: *"Modeh/ Modah Anee L'fanecha Melech Chai v'Kayam, Shehechezarta Bee Nishmatee B'Chemlah, Rabah Emunatecha."* The translation is: "I give thanks to You, Living and Enduring Sovereign, that You have returned my soul with kindness; your faithfulness is great." Appearing first in the book <u>Seder HaYom</u> by 16th century rabbi and Kabbalist Moshe ben Machir, *Modeh Ani* became so popular that it was eventually designated as the first prayer to say after waking up in the morning. You may ask: My soul has been "returned?" Returned from where? Returned by God? With kindness and faithfulness? What does this mean? Could it be related to the statement in the Talmud that "sleep constitutes one-sixtieth of death"[135], that our souls go into a sort of suspended animation under God's protection while we are sleeping and are recharged all over again when we wake up? Yes.

In the <u>Kitzur Shulchan Aruch</u>, this moment is cause for celebration:

"The first appearance of the exuberance of life brings with it the transcendent joy of holy rejoicing, which finds the fullness of its glorious expression through thanksgiving. Gratitude, recognizing the goodness of the Lord of the world, Master over all works, who in His goodness gives life to the living, is the storehouse of good."[136]

When I attended a Jewish camp for two summers as a teen-ager, and when I was on the faculty at another Jewish camp for seven summers, *Modeh Ani* was sung in the dining hall by all of the campers at the same time. It was our first prayer of the day, preceding even the *Hamotzi*—the blessing for bread (and, symbolically, for all of the food we would eat for breakfast). It is questionable whether the campers actually knew the literal meaning of the prayer, but they totally understood that they were essentially thanking God for waking up that morning and being able to begin their day.

This concept of God guarding our souls while we sleep is reaffirmed in the song *Adon Olam*--"a poetic hymn to God whose author is thought to be Solomon Ibn Gabirol (1021-1058), the poet-philosopher who lived in Spain."[137] Its fifth and final verse is: "Into Your hand I entrust my spirit, when I sleep and when I wake, and with my spirit my body also; Adonai is with me and I shall not fear."[138]

Shalom Aleichem is a song sung on *Erev Shabbat* [Friday even-ing]. Its translation is: "Peace be to you, O ministering angels, messengers of the Most-High, Majesty of Majesties, Holy One of Blessing. Enter in peace, O messengers of peace...Bless me with peace, O messengers of peace...Depart in peace, O messengers of peace."[139] In a footnote in the Reform movement's prayer book *Mishkan T'filah,* we learn:

"A 17th century Shabbat table-song *(z'mirah)*, probably com-posed under the influence of Lurianic Kabbalah, alludes to [the Talmudic page] Shabbat 119b, which states that two angels ac-company each person home from the synagogue as Shabbat begins."[140]

Here is the text that is alluded to in *Shalom Aleichem:*

"Rabbi Yosei bar Yehuda says: 'Two ministering angels accompany a person on Shabbat evening from the synagogue to his home, one good angel and one evil angel. And when he reaches his home and finds a lamp burning and a table set and his bed made, the good angel says: "May it be Your will that it shall be like this for another Shabbat." And the evil angel answers against his will: "Amen." And if the person's home is not prepared for Shabbat in that manner, the evil angel says: "May it be Your will that it shall be so for another Shabbat," and the good angel answers against his will: "Amen."[141]

This fantastic scene described in the Talmud is in keeping with the extensive body of angel literature of Judaism. You will read more about that later.

L'cha Dodi (Come, my beloved) is a song that is at the heart of the *Kabbalat Shabbat* (Welcoming the Sabbath) service as the sun sets on Friday evening. Composed in the 16th century in Safed by the Kabbalist Rabbi Shlomo Alkabetz, its nine verses combine Biblical and Talmudic phrases to emphasize the themes of Shabbat, the city of Jerusalem, God's greatness, and the redemption of the Jewish people. The Midrash depicts God having arranged for the Jewish people and the Shabbat to be a wedding couple. The first letters of the first eight verses are an acrostic of Alkabetz's name, and the last verse is the most significant. In the Talmud, we read:

"Rabbi Ḥanina would wrap himself in his garment and stand at nightfall on Shabbat eve, and say: 'Come and we will go out to greet Shabbat the queen.' Rabbi Yannai put on his garment on Shabbat eve and said: 'Enter, O bride. Enter, O bride.'"[142]

For the final verse, it is customary for worshippers to stand, turn around, and face the door at the back of the sanctuary and sing: *"Bo-i v'shalom ateret ba'lah, gam b'simchah uv'tzoholah, toch emunei am s'gulah, bo-i chalah* (they bow to the left), *bo-i chalah"* (they bow to the right and then face forward and sit down), "Enter in peace, O crown of your husband; enter in gladness, enter in joy. Come to the people that keeps its faith. Enter, O bride! Enter, O bride!"

Protection for our souls while we are asleep, angels on Shabbat, and a Shabbat bride—all are featured in our daily prayers and in the liturgy we use to welcome Shabbat. Whether or not you take them literally or figuratively, the faith they express and the sense of calm and joy they provide are unmistakable.

The Good Angels

I have found over the years that not everyone is aware of the many textual examples of angels in Jewish religious literature. The secular view of angels tends to identify them as having halos on their heads, wearing long, white gowns, and flying around the world as they do good deeds. The Hebrew Bible is actually replete with angels:

In The Torah:

• Genesis 16: an angel finds Sarai's servant Hagar by a spring of water in the wilderness, tells her to go back to her mistress, and informs her that she will have a child that will be named Ishmael.
• Genesis 18: Abraham is visited by three "men" who suddenly appear at his tent following his circumcision. One tells him that Sarah will have a son in the next year. The Midrash identifies the three as "the angels Michael, Gabriel, and Raphael."[143]
• Genesis 21: Hagar and Ishmael are in the wilderness, and the angel encourages her to lift Ishmael because he will eventually be the leader of a great nation.
• Genesis 22: Abraham takes his "favorite son" Isaac to Mount Moriah to offer him as a sacrifice to God. After Abraham picks up a knife, an angel calls out to him to not lift a hand   against

the boy.

• Genesis 28: Jacob is fleeing his brother Esau and is traveling to the ancestral homeland of Haran. He has a dream in which he sees a ladder reaching from the ground to the sky, and there are angels ascending and descending on it. God promises him protection on his journey and Jacob concludes that he is in a holy place.

• Genesis 32: On the way to Canaan, Jacob is encountered by angels. Later, "a man" wrestles with him all night long. The Midrash literature speculates that the man is an angel.

• Exodus 3: Moses flees Egypt after killing an Egyptian taskmaster, ends up in Midian, marries a local woman, and becomes a shepherd for the flock of her father Jethro—a Midianite priest. He comes to "Horeb, the Mountain of God." There, one of God's angels appears to him in the fire of a burning bush.

• Numbers 22: Balaam is a soothsayer who is hired to curse the Israelites on their way to the Promised Land. He is riding a donkey, and an angel of the Lord appears in front of them with a sword in hand. Balaam cannot see the angel and beats the animal, trying to get it to move. Only the donkey can see the angel and goes off the road to avoid it. Balaam beats the donkey two more times, and the animal asks why. Finally, God opens Balaam's eyes, and he sees the angel.

In The Prophets:

• Joshua 5: Joshua is near Jericho, looks up, and suddenly sees a "man" standing in front of him, with a sword in his hand. He identifies himself as the "captain of the Lord's host" [an angel] and tells Joshua to take off his sandals because he is on holy ground.

• Judges 6: An angel comes and sits under a tree belonging to Joash, the father of Gideon. He tells Gideon that God is with him. Gideon is skeptical but is made a messenger of God anyway.

• Judges 13: A man named Manoah has a wife who is barren. An angel of God appears to her and tells her that she will conceive and have a son. He is to become a "nazirite"—a man who is not permitted to drink wine or other intoxicants, eat any unclean food, or have his hair cut. That son will be Samson. Shortly after that, the angel ascends in the flames of the fire on an altar.

• Zechariah 3, 4, 5, and 6: The prophet has a vision in which an angel of God and "The Accuser" appear before Joshua, the high priest. The angel then wakes up Zechariah and   speaks with him. The angel explains the meaning of the prophet's vivid visions.

In The Writings:

• Daniel 3: Three Jews—whose Babylonian names are Shadrach, Meshach, and Abednego—are thrown into the furnace by King Nebuchadnezzar of Babylonia but come out of it   unharmed. The king himself blesses their God who sent an angel to rescue them.

• Daniel 8 and 9: The angel Gabriel comes to Daniel twice to explain the meaning of a vision.

• Daniel 12: The angel Michael is referred to as "the great prince" who will appear in the end times and rescue the Jewish people, including those who have died.

Satan Was an Angel?

Just as most people are not aware of the prevalence of angels in the Hebrew Bible, they are also not aware that Satan started out as an angel rather than as "The Devil." In his book *A Gathering of Angels: Angels in Jewish Life and Literature*, Rabbi Morris B. Margolies writes:

"Satan has a bad reputation as the incarnation of evil, sin, temptation—hell itself. Satan is the antagonist of God, pitting his hateful nature against the loving Deity—even plotting to unseat the Lord and to occupy His throne.

That's a heavy load to carry, especially given that Satan is a law-abiding citizen of the Angelic Host, an agent of God who goes about doing his job as faithfully as he knows how. What is his job? It is to look into the behavior of human beings and to report back to his divine employer any wayward deeds and aberrations he can discover. He is the celestial prosecuting attorney who gathers his evidence carefully and sets it before the Supreme Judge."[144]

The Hebrew word *sahtahn* generally means "accuser" or "adversary," and is sometimes preceded by the prefix *"ha,"* which means "The." It even is in one of our prayers in the traditional evening service—the *Hashkiveinu* [Cause us to lie down]: *"v-ha-seir sahtahn milfaneninu u'meiachareinu,"* "remove The Adversary from before us and from behind us."[145] In *The Jewish Book of Why,* Alfred Kolatch provides this information in a question-and-answer format:

"Why do some Jews arise very early on the morning after Yom Kippur to attend a morning service? In Jewish folklore the belief was prevalent that Satan will make one final effort to entrap Jews and cause them to sin. Convinced that now that Yom Kippur is over Jews will become lax and will not carry out all their religious resolutions, Satan believes he may yet succeed. To prove Satan wrong, many Jews attend the earliest morning service on the day after Yom Kippur."[146]

These prayer customs developed after the mention of Satan in the *Tanakh.* Here are some examples of the Adversary/Satan:

In The Torah:

- Numbers 22: The angel of God is referred to as "an adversary."

In The Prophets:

• First Samuel 29: Philistine officers suspect that David will become "an adversary" rather than an ally against Saul, their common enemy.
• First Kings 11: The Edomite Hadad is listed as "an adversary" of Solomon raised up by God.• Zechariah 3: The word *hasahtahn* "The Accuser" occurs three times in the prophet's vision.

In The Writings:

• Psalm 109: The Psalmist feels surrounded by haters as if he is the accused in a courtroom charged by "an accuser."
• First Chronicles 21: Satan convinces David to do a census.
• Job 1 and 2: "The Adversary" comes along with the divine beings to present themselves to God, Who begins a conversation with him about Job. God refers to Job as "a blameless and upright man who fears God and shuns evil!"[147] Satan says that Job is so upright because he is so blessed. He suggests that if Job were to be deprived of all that he has—including family   and possessions—he wouldn't be so faithful. God gives Satan the power to take away all that Job cherishes as blessings. The story then proceeds with interaction and theological disagreement between Job, his friends, and God.

In addition to these Biblical references, *sefaria.org* lists 728 texts mentioning Satan in Torah commentaries, the Midrash, and the Talmud. Among them are his convincing Sarah that Isaac is dead [*Midrash Tanchuma, Vayera* 23:5], showing the Israelites at the foot of Mount Sinai that Moses is dead (leading them to compel Aaron to make the Golden Calf) [Rashi commentary to Exodus 32:1], tricking David into looking at Bathsheba (Sanhedrin 107a), making men get foolish with drink (Bamidbar Rabbah 20:23), and the double blowing of the shofar to confuse Satan (Rosh Hashanah 16b). This evil involvement in the lives of famous and ordinary people reveals a wide range of powers. It's no wonder that the blowing of the shofar was employed as a means to rid the community of Satan's influence.

The Angel of Death (Malach HaMavet)

As you would expect, the Angel of Death's title tells what his function is. This quotation from the Talmud contends that Satan and the Angel of Death are one and the same:

"Reish Lakish says: 'Satan, the evil inclination, and the Angel of Death are one, that is, they are three aspects of the same essence...He is the Satan who seduces people and then accuses them, as it is written: 'So the Satan went forth from the presence of the Lord, and smote Job with vile sores.' [This] teaches that the evil inclination is to be identified with the Satan...He is also the Angel of Death, as it is written: 'Only spare his life'; apparently Job's life depends upon him, the Satan, and accordingly the Satan must also be the Angel of Death.'"[148]

Much superstition arose regarding the presence and powers of the Angel of Death both at the time of a birth and the time of a death:

"Throughout Jewish history, names were viewed as having special power. Accordingly, many superstitions grew up around names, especially during the Middle Ages. Some Jews had secret names, which they would not reveal to anyone. Other Jews refused to marry a person who had the same name as their mother or father and would even hesitate to live in the same town as an individual bearing their name. All of these customs derived in large measure from a fear that the Angel of Death might confuse two people of the same name, leading to the premature demise of one or the other.

To further 'confuse' the Angel of Death, Jewish families often took unusual steps in selecting names. In Poland, in a household where several young people had died, babies would sometimes receive names indicative of advanced years, such as *Alter* (old) or *Zaida* (grandfather). A custom followed by some Jews, even in modern times, is that of changing the name of a person who is near death. In accordance with talmudic, rabbinic, and mystical traditions, the individual is given a name such as *Chaim* (life) or its female equivalent, *Chayah*."[149]

"Sometime after the thirteenth century it became customary to place a towel and a glass of water near the memorial candle. According to popular belief this would appease the Angel of Death, who might want to wash his sword in the water and dry it with a towel. There also existed the belief that man's soul returned to cleanse itself in the water. Nineteenth-century scholars condemned this practice and forbade it."[150]

Covering mirrors is a custom that is observed by some Jews for the period of *shiva*—literally, seven days beginning with the day of the funeral. There are many reasons given for doing this, but these are the most common:

"Why are all mirrors covered? We recall two superstitious fears: a. The soul of a person in the home might be 'caught' in the mirror and snatched away by the ghost of the deceased. b. Due to the supposed presence of the Angel of Death, those seeing their reflection might place their own lives in jeopardy."[151]

But not all customs are universal. Sephardic Jews who come originally from Spanish-speaking or Middle Eastern countries and Yemenite Jews have unique traditions. I was not aware of the following custom until recently:

"In recent centuries, the practice among the Jews of Yemen has been to remove the *mezuza* and sacred books from the room of a dying man who is in great pain. The Yemenites believe that the presence of holy objects lessens the power of the Angel of Death, and when they are removed the power of the angel increases. Thus, the Angel of Death is able to take the life of the patient sooner."[152]

The Evil Eye (Ayin Hara)

Although the "Evil Eye" has its origins in rabbinic sources, it is more well-known in Jewish folklore and belongs in the category of superstition among Jews. Saying the Yiddish word *"kinnehora"* (which means "against The," or, "no Evil Eye" from *"kein ayin hara"*) is used by some Jews hopefully to ward off harm from the powerful Evil Eye. In a 2014 article for Moment Magazine online, George E. Johnson wrote:

"The evil eye is one of the world's oldest and most widely held superstitions. Its place in Jewish lore is rooted in classical Judaism and Jewish folk religion dating to the Bible, the Talmud and rabbinic Midrash. There's a rich history, particularly from the Middle Ages onward, of often bizarre and elaborate folk practices—invocations such as *'kinehora'* being a rather tame example—aimed at thwarting the malicious intent or effect of the evil eye. The evil eye stems from the Greek theory that the eye can shoot rays that strike with harmful or deadly force...

The evil eye may have been introduced into Jewish thought by Talmudic authorities exposed to Babylonian culture, according to Joshua Trachtenberg, the late author of *Jewish Magic and Superstition: A Study in Folk Religion.*"[153]

I will have more to say about *kinnehora* and compliments below. Long before it became a part of folklore and superstition, the Evil Eye was mentioned in a great philosophical discussion in the *Pirkei Avot* in the *Mishnah*. Rabbi Yochanan ben Zakkai, "who lived in the first century C.E.—was the leading rabbinic sage toward the end of the Second Temple period and during the years following the destruction of the Temple."[154] He asked his colleagues to consider this: "Go and see which way one should follow." The different answers he received were: "a good eye... a good friend...a good neighbor...anticipate the future...a good heart ..." [Then he said] Go out and see from what should one flee... an evil eye *(ayin raah)*...a bad neighbor...one who borrows and does not repay...an evil heart... "[155] For the 12th century commentator Moses Maimonides and the 15th century commentator Ovadiah Bartinoro, "the evil eye is the pursuit of excess."[156] Shortly after that verse comes another reference, which is more direct and precise: "Rabbi Yehoshua said: 'The evil eye, the evil urge, and hatred of [one's fellow creatures] takes one out of the world."[157] Rabbis Leonard Kravitz and Kerry Olitzky say:

"Although the commentators do not make a distinction between an evil eye and the evil eye, it is necessary to do so. *An* evil eye is simply the dissatisfaction with what one has, envious of the possession of others. *The* evil eye carries a much more sinister meaning. It connotes envy tinged with malevolence, an envy that not only begrudges the other the possessions but also wishes evil upon that individual for having them."[158]

Sefaria.org indicates that there are 317 texts in Jewish traditional writings that mention the Evil Eye. Here is a sampling from different sources:

The Torah (Commentaries):

• Rashi on Genesis 21:14: "...the child [Ishmael], too, he [God] placed on her [Hagar's] shoulder, for Sarah had cast an evil eye upon him, so that a fever seized him, and he could not walk." [159]
• Rashi on Exodus 34:3: "Because the first tablets were given

amidst shouting, sound, and throng, the evil eye prevailed against them. There is nothing more desirable than modesty."[160]

• Rashi on Numbers 24:2: "And Balaam lifted up his eyes — he wished to cast the evil eye upon them."[161]

• *Or HaChaim* on Deuteronomy 28: "The evil eye does not exercise any influence on hidden places; this is why the Torah emphasized that this blessing will occur in places which are out of reach of the evil eye."[162]

The Talmud:

• "One who enters a city and fears the evil eye should hold the thumb *[zekafa]* of his right hand in his left hand and the thumb of his left hand in his right hand and recite the   following...: 'I, so-and-so son of so-and-so, come from the descendants of Joseph, over whom the evil eye has no dominion ...'"[163]

• "One day, the Sages gave him the evil eye, i.e., they were envious of him, and his legs became singed in the fire. And from then on they referred to him as: The short one with   singed legs."[164]

• "Rav went to a graveyard, and did what he did, i.e., he used an incantation to find out how those buried there died, and he said: 'Ninety-nine of these died by the evil eye, and only one   died by entirely natural means.'"[165]

The Midrash:

• "By universal custom when one goes to a banquet house, he does not take his children with him for fear of the evil eye."[166]

What would such a negative force as the Evil Eye have to do with compliments? It's the same as when someone says "Don't jinx it" when someone else talks about how well things are going. Or it's like when someone says that something positive will happen, "knock on wood." You could use *kinneahora* when speaking positively of someone's appearance or age or mile-stone. For example, "she is a beautiful girl, *kinneahora.*" Or "he's going to be 90 years old next month, *kinnehora.*" Or "they're going to celebrate their 50th anniversary next month, *kinnea-hora.*"

"From the 17th century onward, according to Trachtenberg, 'no evil eye' expressions had 'become automatic accompani-ments on Jewish lips of the slightest compliment.'"[167]

"… one can either prevent or counteract the evil eye by the avoidance of any expression of praise or by 'qualifying' any praise with an expression like the Yiddish *kein ayen hore,* 'may there be no evil eye,' sometimes shortened to *keinahora.*"[168]

"Rashi…considers that Tzipporah [the wife of Moses] was in-deed beautiful but that the term Cushite—which implies the op-posite—was meant to ward off the evil eye, to make sure people would not be jealous of her."[169]

I know many Jews who are not superstitious in regard to most aspects of their lives, and I know many people who are not Jewish and not really superstitious for the most part. Yet, *"kinne-hora"* and "knock on wood" come out of their mouths at certain times, and they are not thinking then about the origins of these phrases and why they were originated.

You should be able to recognize by now that there are many manifestations of the supernatural in Jewish texts, beliefs, and practices. Some of them are religious, but you don't have to be Orthodox to follow them. Some of them are common know-ledge, and some are unheard-of among some Jews. Not all of our beliefs are rational and logical. Superstition is often regarded as a lower level of human functioning. Yet, what we do on a daily basis or just on a holiday or just when a life-cycle event occurs can be based on emotion as much as on ideology. We are, after all, complex creatures and we are often fascinated by the supernatural.

Resurrection...Elijah...the *Bat Kol*...Rachel Our Mother...
Prayers and Songs...Good Angels...Satan...The Angel of Death...
The Evil Eye. That is quite a number of supernatural influences
in religion and folklore, and they combine to form a strong foundation of belief and practice.

CHAPTER 7: THE "MAGICAL MYSTERY TOUR" OF MYSTICAL BELIEFS AND HASIDIC STORIES ABOUT THE "SUPERNATURAL"

"Jewish mysticism in its various forms represents an attempt to interpret the religious values of Judaism in terms of mystical values. It concentrates upon the idea of the living God who manifests himself in the acts of Creation, Revelation and Redemption."[170]

"Kabbalah has a long history that began in the mystical elements that are already found in the Bible and which began to flower in the early rabbinic period around the time of the destruction of the Second Temple in Jerusalem in 70 C.E. and the following centuries. What can properly be called Kabbalah emerged in the twelfth century and drew from all the previous forms of Jewish mysticism, centering on a specific language of divine emanations and powers called Sefirot, and a transcendent, infinite, ultimately Unknowable Divinity called Ein Sof."[171]

"One of the most vital aspects of the Hasidic movement is that the hasidim tell one another stories about their leaders, their 'zadikkim.' Great things had happened, the hasidim had been present, they had seen them, and so they felt called upon to relate and bear witness to them. The words used to describe these experiences were more than mere words: they transmitted what had happened to coming generations, and with such actuality that the words in themselves became events. And since they serve to perpetuate holy events, they bear the consecration of holy deeds."[172]

"The men who are the subject of these tales, the men who quicken, are the zaddikim, a term which is usually translated by

'the righteous,' but which actually means 'those who stood the test' or 'the proven.' They are the leaders of the Hasidic communities. And the men who do the telling, whose tales constitute the body of transmitted legends, the men who were quickened, are the hasidim, 'the devout,' or, more accurately, those who keep faith with the covenant. They are the members of such communities."[173]

I have to admit that I didn't grow up with much exposure to mysticism and Hasidism (also spelled "Chasidism"). But I learned about mysticism in rabbinical school and throughout my 45 years as a rabbi, and I have had experiences with Hasidic Jews (especially *Chabad*) during my career. While I may not agree with most of the mystical and Hasidic beliefs and practices, I am open to learning other interpretations about our relationship with God and one another and the resulting approaches to life and death. Out of all of the mystical concepts that exist, *tikkun olam* (repair of the world) resonates the most with me spiritually. Like the Reform priority of social action, it empowers the individual to seek to make a positive difference in our world. The *Chabad* Hasidic efforts to engage in proactive outreach to Jews—as conceived of and developed by The Lubavitcher Rebbe, Menachem Mendel Schneerson—emphasize a personal touch that can be meaningful, although I don't agree with the tactics that are used sometimes.

It is what mysticism and Hasidism have to say about life and death, and life after death, that are of interest to me for this book. Scholem's description above of a living God manifested through creation, revelation, and redemption is extremely relevant for considering whether or not God has created an afterlife which includes the ability of souls to communicate with their loved ones who are still alive. That communication could be regarded as a sort of revelation, and the positive feelings generated could comprise a sense of redemption for both the living and the dead. God as *"Ein Sof"* (without end), as transcendent, infinite, and unknowable fits in with what I called "supernatural." I believe that the potential ties between the living and the dead are inherently transcendent, that the possibilities for contact are infinite in the form of "signs," and that we may not know how it happens but be glad that it does happen. In terms of Hasidism, you will see in this chapter some examples from the Hasidic tales that deal with the eternal nature of our souls. And I should mention that there are those adherents of The Rebbe who believed during his lifetime that he was the Messiah and who visit his gravesite weekly at the Montefiore Cemetery in Queens, New York. To them, he was a true *"zaddik"* (also spelled *"tzaddik"*).

Mysticism

I have taught courses about mysticism that have lasted for several weeks, but I am condensing that information here. Some basics, though, are in order:

- *Kabbalah:* pronounced either with the emphasis on the second or third syllable—means "Receiving," a term which refers to the teachings of mysticism being received by one generation from the previous generation(s). Mark Elber relates that the word became connected to mysticism in the early 1200's in southern France.[174]

- *Zohar:* meaning "Enlightenment"—is the name of the most well-known source of mystical belief. Some say that it was written in the second century C.E. by Rabbi Shimon Bar Yokhai, who was a disciple of the great Rabbi Akiva. A vocal opponent of the Roman occupation, he escaped and lived in a cave for twelve years, supposedly writing what became the *Zohar.*

- Rabbi Moshe de Leon: a Spanish Kabbalist in the 13th century who claimed that a manuscript of the *Zohar* came into his possession, and he was responsible for its promulgation.

Rabbi Simcha Paull Raphael has written a wonderful book,

entitled *The Grief Journey and the Afterlife: Jewish Pastoral Care for Bereavement.* He states:

"In the Zohar, the post-mortem journey is conceived as a four-fold process of: separation from the physical realm; emotional cleansing: transcendent awareness; and, ultimately, divine union. Terms used to describe these processes are: *Hibbut ha-Kever* (pangs of the grave as one departs the physical realm); *Gehenna* (a state of emotional purification and purgation); *Gan Eden* (the heavenly Garden of Eden, a realm of transcendent divine recompense); and *Tzror ha-Hayyim* (a return to the Source of Life, wherein the highest level of soul qualities merge with the divine)."[175]

Hibbut ha-Kever takes three to seven days in which the soul separates itself from the body. The *Zohar* says:

"At the hour of one's departure from the world, one's father and relatives gather 'round, and one sees them and recognizes them, and likewise all with whom one associated in this world, they accompany one's soul to the place where it is to abide...for seven days, the soul goes to and fro from the house to the grave, from the grave to the house, mourning for the body."[176]

The second step of the process is not new to me, but it may be for you. *Gehenna* or *Gehinnom* has roots that extend all the way back to the Hebrew Bible. The valley of *Hinnom* is where, according to the book of the prophet Jeremiah, "the children of Judah have done that which is evil in My sight...And they have built the high places of *Topheth*, which is in the valley of the son of *Hinnom*, to burn their sons and their daughters in the fire."[177] Rather than worshipping God, they were paying tribute to the pagan god Molech. Later on, Jeremiah decries the allegiance to the pagan god Baal, whose followers "have filled this place with the blood of innocents, and have built the high places of Baal, to burn their sons in the fire for burnt-offerings unto Baal."[178]

I have always thought that *Gehenna/Gehinnom* was the Jewish version of "hell on earth"—literally sacrificing your future by killing your children. Like *Gehenna* on Earth, *Gehenna* in the afterlife is full of fire, which serves to purify rather than to destroy. The *Zohar* affirms: "The body is punished in the grave and the soul in the fire of *Gehinnom* for the appointed period. When this is completed it rises from *Gehinnom* purified of its guilt like iron purified in the fire and is carried up to *Gan Eden. (Zohar III*, 53a)."[179]

The third step is probably more familiar to anyone who knows the story of Adam and Eve and the serpent in the Garden of Eden *(Gan Eden* in Hebrew). The *Kabbalah* portrays it as "a period of intellectual contemplation of supernal bliss, experienced by the transcendent dimensions of the soul. Eternal in nature, the cleansed soul in the heavenly *Gan Eden* experiences a state of consciousness reflecting the level of spiritual development attained during life."[180] Rabbi Raphael connects the ascent of the soul through *Gan Eden* with the recitation of the *Kaddish*—a point that you will read about in a later chapter.

The fourth step, *Tzror Ha-Hayyim,* is "a cosmic storehouse of souls, the point of origin and termination for all souls in the universe...achieved by the most supernal elements of soul capable of direct perception of God...an experience of spiritual union with the divine."[181] The *El Malei Rachamim* prayer recited at funerals and *Yizkor* memorial services specifically refers to souls being bound up in the bond of eternal life. You don't have to be a Jewish mystic to believe that the soul of your loved one will be united with God and reunited with other souls.

Another important Kabbalistic concept is *gilgul hanefesh*—which is generally translated as "transmigration of souls" or "reincarnation." It should surprise a lot of people to read that any Jewish movement would promote a belief in having at least a second chance at life. After all, many Jews were taught in Religious School and in rabbis' sermons that we should emphasize the value of life as our only opportunity, and that we should make the best of it. Reincarnation sounds so Eastern, so non-Jewish. But it is also so mystical, so Kabbalistic. Raphael writes: "The doctrine of *gilgul* first appeared in *Sefer ha-Bahir* (ca. 1150-1200), as an esoteric doctrine explicated indirectly through metaphor and parable...Ultimately, the aim of *gilgul* was to further purify the soul and provide further opportunity for self-improvement, and the fulfilling of *mitzvot*." [182] Elber remarks that Kabbalists have interpreted certain verses in the Hebrew Bible as references to reincarnation.[183]

The primary citation is from Chapter 34 of Exodus in which God tells Moses to carve a second set of tablets because he smashed the first set in anger when the Israelites worshipped the Golden Calf. God comes down on Mount Sinai in a cloud, "stands" there, and proclaims a list of qualities to Moses—among which is "extending kindness to the thousandth generation."[184] The interpretation of that phrase is that those living in the present generation will get to experience God's kindness in a future generation.[185] I am particularly mystified by this concept because a few people who believe in reincarnation have suggested that my memories of the first house in which I lived are so vivid because my grandfather Wolf's soul is reincarnated in my body. Those memories are affirmed by two of my cousins whose descriptions of that house appear at the end of this chapter. Reincarnation is another example of the supernatural, and in this case, it is made possible by God.

Hasidism

"Hasidism was the last religious movement to be born within the older world of Jewish piety, that is, before the Jews entered the world of modernity. Its founder, Israel ben Eliezer, was born c. 1700 in the village of Okup on the eastern border of the Polish province of Podolya. Few facts about his life are known... It is said that at the age of thirty-six he revealed his miraculous powers of healing and prophetic foresight, and became known as the Baal Shem Tov (Master of the Good Name). He taught his disciples that God is present everywhere and that all Jews can connect with the Holy One through joyful prayer and unbound enthusiasm. The Baal Shem Tov and his disciples infused all the inherited pieties with spontaneity and cheerfulness.

After the Baal Shem's death in 1760, the mantle of leadership passed to his disciple Dov Ber, known as the Maggid (preacher) of Mezritch. Dov Ber surrounded himself with dozens of charismatic figures who brought the teachings of Hasidism to all the Jewish communities of eastern Europe. These Hasidic masters came to be known as tzaddikim, or rebbes, and they were thought by their disciples to be the mediators between heaven and earth—not themselves divine, but something of divinity graced their presence."[186]

The Baal Shem Tov instigated a spiritual revolution within traditional Judaism and, subsequently, through all of Judaism. Joyful prayers sung or chanted with incredible enthusiasm presented a worthy and viable alternative for Jews who wanted to find another way to connect with God. *Niggunim*, or "chants without words," became a new and different way to reach out and up to God, with *"Bim-Bim-Bam"*, *"Lai-Lai-Lai"*, *"Yai-Yai-Yai"* or *"Ai-Ai-Ai"* being the most popular. This approach opened the door for those who didn't know how to *daven*—to pray the set liturgy with chanting and swaying back and forth being done simultaneously. Often, the Hasidic chanting would lead to dancing, and that is when the "unbound enthusiasm" would kick in. The sense of discipleship was crucial as well, and many *tzadikkim* had many disciples. With more and more adherents to Hasidism being groomed, and with the charisma of *tzadik-kim* or *rebbes* leading to utmost respect and incredible reverence, it makes sense that stories would be passed down through the generations. They were told with a sense of wonder and gratitude, and nothing was considered to be impossible for God and the heroes of the stories to do or make happen.

The great Martin Buber (1878-1965) was a theologian, philosopher, author, and teacher. One of his most significant works was <u>Tales of the Hasidim</u>, which was originally published in 1947 and then re-published in 1991, with a foreword by well-known author Chaim Potok. There are approximately 1,250 stories or statements arranged in two groups—The Early Masters and The Late Masters. I have selected several of them to share with you that emphasize the link between the living and the dead. They are arranged by subject and titles:

About The Baal Shem Tov:

"The River and the Light"
Several years after his (The Baal Shem's) death, his son lost his way, as he was walking by night, and suddenly found himself close to the river which he did not recognize because of its tiding waters. He tried to cross but was soon seized and swept away by the current. Then, above the shore, he saw a burning light which illumined the banks and the river. He mustered all his strength, fought free of the current, and reached the shore. The burning light was the Baal Shem himself.[187]

"The Fiery Mountain"
Rabbi Zevi, the Baal Shem's son, too, told this: "Sometime after my father's death, I saw him in the shape of a fiery mountain, which burst into countless sparks. I asked him: "Why do you appear in a shape such as this?" He answered: "In this shape I served God."[188]

Communication From The Dead:

"The Vision of the Vegetable Vendor"
Rabbi Yitzhak of Neskhizh, the son of Rabbi Mordecai of Neskhizh, told this story:
"On the day before the Rabbi of Apt suddenly fell ill and died,

an old woman who sold vegetables in the marketplace said to her neighbor: 'This morning at dawn—I don't know whether I was awake or dreaming—I saw my husband, may he rest in peace, who has been dead these many years. I saw him rush past without looking at me. Then I burst into tears and cried to him: "First you go and leave me to a miserable life with my orphaned children and now you don't even look at me!" But he kept on running and didn't turn to give me a glance. As I sat there crying, I saw him coming back. He stopped and said: "I couldn't take any time off before. We had to fumigate the road and cleanse the air because the *Zaddikim* from the land of Israel cannot stand the air here, and they will soon be coming to receive the Rabbi of Apt and escort him to the other side."'"[189]

Reincarnation?

"The Grave in Tiberias"

"Once the Rabbi of Apt sat deep in thought. He looked bewildered and a little sad. When his Hasidim asked whether anything was troubling him, he said, 'Up to now, during my soul's every sojourn on earth I occupied some post of honor in Israel, but this time I have none.' At that very moment a messenger from the land of Israel arrived and handed the rabbi an official letter. In it was stated that the Palestinian community made up of emigrants from Volhynia whose seat was in Tiberias, nominated him their head. The Rabbi of Apt had a feast prepared to celebrate his happiness. Then he gave the messenger a sum of money for the purpose of acquiring a plot of ground for him beside the grave of the prophet Hosea, and of the same size.

The night Rabbi Abraham Yehoshua [the Rabbi of Apt] died, a knocking was heard at the window of the Volhynia meeting house in Tiberias: 'Go out and escort the Rabbi of Apt to his eternal rest,' it said. When the caretaker opened the door, he saw a bier being borne through the air. Thousands of souls were swarming around it. He followed it to the cemetery and watched them lower the body into the grave."[190]

Two-Way Communication:

"From the Look-Out of Heaven"

"At a time for great anguish for Israel, Rabbi Elimelekh brooded more and more on his griefs. Then his dead master, the maggid of Mezritch, appeared to him. Rabbi Elimelekh cried out: 'Why are you silent in such dreadful need?' He answered: 'In Heaven we see that all that seems evil to you is a work of mercy.'"[191]

Appearances In Dreams:

"Inheritance"

"It is told:
After his death, the maggid appeared to his son and—invoking the commandment to honor one's parents—ordered him to give up his life of perfect seclusion, for whoever walks a way such as this, is in danger. Abraham replied: 'I do not recognize a father in the flesh. I recognize only one merciful Father of all that lives.'

'You accepted your inheritance,' said the maggid. 'With that you recognized me as your father even after my death.'

'I renounce my father's inheritance,' cried Rabbi Abraham, the Angel. At that very moment, fire broke out in the house and consumed the few small things the maggid had left his son—but nothing besides."[192]

"The Other Dream"

"In the night after the seven days of mourning for Rabbi Abraham, his wife had a dream. She saw a vast hall, and in it thrones, set in a semi-circle. On each throne sat one of the great. A door opened, and one who looked like those others, entered. It was Abraham, her husband. He said: 'Friends, my wife bears me a grudge because in my earthly life I lived apart from her. She is right, and therefore I must obtain her forgiveness.' His wife cried out: 'With all my heart I forgive you,' and awoke comforted."[193]

"Sanctified"

"Rabbi Israel of Rizhyn told:
A few years after the death of Rabbi Abraham, the Angel, his widow, my blessed grandmother, received an offer of marriage from the great *zaddik* Rabbi Nahum of Tchernobil. But the Angel appeared to him in a dream and looked at him threateningly. So, he let her be.

My blessed grandmother lived in want. When the Rabbi of Tchernobil had taken her son, my father, into his house, she went to the Land of Israel. She told no one there who she was. She took in washing and supported herself with the money she got for this. She died in the Land of Israel."[194]

"From World to World"

"Many years after Rabbi Mikhal's death, young Rabbi Zevi Hirsh of Zhydatchov saw him in a dream. The dead man said to him: 'Know, that from the moment I died, I have been wandering from world to world. And the world which yesterday was spread over my head as Heaven, is today the earth under my feet, and the Heaven of today is the earth of tomorrow.'"[195]

"The Offer"

"The story is also told that when his master had died and Rabbi Mendel was greatly troubled as to who would now be his teacher, the Yehudi appeared to him in a dream and tried to comfort him, saying that he was willing to continue to teach him. 'I do not want a teacher from the other world,' answered Mendel."[196]

Pride And Humility:

"In the Last Hour"
"On a certain New Year's night, the maggid of Zlotchov saw a man who had been a reader in his city, and who had died a short time ago. 'What are you doing here?' he asked.

'The rabbi knows,' said the dead man, 'that in this night, souls are incarnated anew. I am such a soul.'

'And why were you sent out again?' asked the maggid.

'I led an impeccable life here on earth,' the dead man told him.

'And yet you are forced to live once more?' the maggid went on to ask.

'Before my death,' said the man, 'I thought over everything I had done and found that I had always acted in just the right way. Because of this, my heart swelled with satisfaction and in the midst of this feeling I died. So now they have sent me back into the world to atone for my pride.'

At that time a son was born to the maggid. His name was

Rabbi Wolf. He was very humble."[197]

Just A Voice:

"The Soul of the Cymbalist"
　　"It is told:
　　Once, on a midnight, a voice drifted into the room of the maggid of Koznitz and moaned: 'Holy man of Israel, have pity on a poor soul which, for ten years, has been wandering from eddy to eddy.'
　　'Who are you?' asked the maggid. 'And what did you do while you were on earth?'
　　'I was a musician,' said the voice. 'I played the cymbal and I sinned like all wandering musicians.'
　　'And who sent you to me?'
　　Then the voice groaned: 'Why, I played at your wedding, rabbi, and you gave me praise and wanted to hear more, and so I played one piece after another and you were well pleased.'
　　'Do you still remember the tune you played when they conducted me under the wedding-*baldachin* [canopy]?'
　　The voice hummed the tune.
　　'Well then, you shall be redeemed on the coming Sabbath,' said the maggid.
　　On the Friday evening after that, when the maggid stood in front of the reader's desk, he sang the song: 'Come, my friend, to meet the bride,' in a tune no one knew, and not even the choir could join in."[198]

A Visit From A Dead Man:

"In the World of Confusion"

"They tell this story:

To Rabbi Yisakhar of Wolborz there came a dead man whom he had once known when he was alive and prominent in his community, and begged the rabbi's help, saying that his wife had died some time ago and now he needed money to arrange for his marriage with another.

'Don't you know,' the *zaddik* asked him, '"that you are no longer among the living, that you are in the world of confusion?'

When the dead man refused to believe him, he lifted the tails of the dead man's coat and showed him that he was dressed in his shroud.

Later Rabbi Yisakhar's son asked: 'Well, if that is so—perhaps I too am in the world of confusion?'

'Once you know that there is such a thing as that world,' answered his father, 'you are not in it.'"[199]

A Feeling About A Death:

"Do Not Stop!"

"On the Day of Rejoicing in the Law, the rabbi of Ulanov, who was a dear friend of the rabbi of Roptchitz, lay dying. In Roptchitz the *hasidim* had just begun the great round dance in the court of the *zaddik's* house. He was standing at the window and looking down at them with a smile, when suddenly he raised his hand. Instantly they stopped and gazed up at him with faltering breath. For a while he kept silent and seemed as someone who has been overcome by bad news. Then he signed to the *hasidim* with his hand and cried: 'When one of the generals falls in battle, do the companies scatter and take to flight? The fight goes on! Rejoice and dance!' Later it became known that the rabbi of Ulanov had died that very hour."[200]

In *The Essential Kabbalah: The Heart of Jewish Mysticism*, Daniel C. Matt wrote: "On the one hand, Kabbalah refers to tradition, ancient wisdom received and treasured from the past. On the other hand, if one is truly receptive, wisdom appears spontaneously, unprecedented, taking you by surprise."[201] Rooted firmly in Jewish tradition, mysticism as conveyed in the *Kabbalah* on the subject of death and the afterlife will indeed take many people by surprise. For Jews who are absolutely certain that our religion has nothing to say about the afterlife, and certainly not even a thought about reincarnation, what I have cited in this chapter will be unexpected, to say the least, and I hope that it is enlightening. I come back to the word "supernatural" to describe what the *Zohar* presents in vivid detail, and with those details can come hope and faith in signs for the living from the dead—if you choose to accept it as I do.

Martin Buber has written an extremely relevant insight about the *zadikkim/tzadikkim,* which reflects on the stories that I've included here:

"... the *zaddik* has the greatest possible influence not only on the faith and mind of the *hasid,* but on his active everyday life, and even on his sleep, which he renders deep and pure. Through the *zaddik,* all the senses of the *hasid* are perfected, not through conscious directing, but through bodily nearness. The fact that the *hasid* looks at the *zaddik* perfects his sense of sight, his listening to him, his sense of hearing."[202]

Like the stories from our multi-century tradition that have been told over and over again, these *Hasidic* tales have been passed on repeatedly over a much shorter period of time. These tales have an underlying, inherent sense of power and influence because of the position of the *zaddik.* To those for whom the *zadikkim* were unknown or irrelevant, the tales would probably be viewed as being outlandish or crazy. But, for the *hasidim,* anything was possible—even, and sometimes especially, the supernatural. Nothing was beyond their power. Everything was in God's power. Although I didn't start out believing that the dead could communicate with the living, I have come to believe it because I am convinced now that God can make anything happen. Our deceased loved ones and friends are in their eternal home, and our connection to them can be eternal if we are receptive to it. And I believe that God makes it all possible—through "signs."

Rabbi Stephen Karol—The House I Lived in Until I Was 15 Months Old:

"As Rod Serling used to say occasionally on The Twilight Zone *in his introduction to an episode, 'For your consideration.' What you are about to read is true. I mention it in this chapter because the subject of reincarnation appeared earlier. Whether reincarnation is the reason behind the story or not, I don't know. But it's an interest-*

ing possibility:

I have a vivid memory of the house where I lived with my parents and grandmother from the day I was born until I was about 15 months old. Over the years, I used to ask my parents why I could take someone on a virtual walking tour and point out pieces of furniture and the general floor plan of the house, even though I was so young. Psychologists and therapists who know more about memory than I do have not been able to explain it. Occasionally, it was suggested that I saw and remembered photos of the house, but that doesn't sound right. My parents were sort of freaked-out by what I recalled, but they affirmed whatever I told them. Two of my older cousins have done the same, as you will see below. Although it sounds far-fetched in terms of logic and reason, some of my Orthodox relatives who believe in reincarnation, and colleagues who are well-versed in mystical interpretations, have suggested that I have within me the soul of my deceased grandfather, for whom I am named.

Before you dismiss this suggestion, consider that I have been open to more rational explanations. Despite that, none of them have made sense to me. My maternal grandfather died in 1930, and I was born in 1950. My Hebrew name is Yisrael, as was his. My cousins are Audrey and Eileen. We didn't consult with each other before I asked them to tell me what they recalled about the house. What they each describe is exactly the way I remember the house:"

Audrey: "*I do remember the layout fairly well. There was a large front porch with a glider, like a swing that two or three people can use at once. Then there was an entrance hall. Directly ahead was the living room, and beyond the living room was another room.*"

Eileen:" *I lived in the house from the time I was four to seventeen. It was gray stucco with a large front porch, half of which was roofed. There was both a swing and a glider. There was a small entry hall with another door into the living room, which acted like an airlock. The living room was quite large, and, on either side of the entry, there were wide built-in mahogany benches. I used to curl up on the western one and read. It was by a window. There was a gray stone*

fireplace on the west wall with either a gas or electric grate, and be-
yond that, a bay window. Through an archway at the back was the
den, containing a daybed and Ruth's large upright piano." [Ruth was
my mother and Eileen and Audrey's cousin]

Audrey: *"Upstairs were four bedrooms and, I think, two bathrooms.*
There was an attic above the bedroom level. I think that there were a
couple of bedrooms there as well."

My main question for this memory has always been "why?"
Why do I remember this house in such vivid detail? Who decides what is the best explanation for it? If you think that the
reincarnation explanation is outlandish, is there a better one? In
the next chapter, I explore how we decide why things happen.
We have plenty of choices, and—although we may not always
agree—just being exposed to the various possibilities can be fascinating.

CHAPTER 8: WHY DO WE NEED TO KNOW WHY?

A superstition is "a belief or practice resulting from ignorance, fear of the unknown, trust in magic or chance, or a false conception of causation."[203]

"People tend to see cause and effect relationships, even where there is none!"[204]

"A coincidence itself is in the eye of the beholder."[205]

GODWINK: 1. Not a coincidence but an event or experience so astonishing it must be of divine origin. 2. Another term for answered prayer.[206]

A sign is a message sent to you by the universe ...the term I use when I refer to God energy—the all-encompassing force of love that connects to us all and that we are all a part of.[207]

"Praised are You, the Eternal our God, Sovereign of the Universe, Who has kept us alive, sustained us, and brought us to this time."

Shehehcheyanu blessing

"Praised are You, the Eternal our God, Sovereign of the Universe, Who brings forth bread from the earth."

Motzi blessing

"Praised are You, the Eternal our God, Sovereign of the Universe, Who rewards the undeserving with goodness, and Who has rewarded me with goodness."

Gomeil blessing

Why do things happen the way they do? Why do some people see certain experiences as "signs" and others see them as "coincidence?"

Why do we need a reason for why things happen the way they do? When Supreme Court Justice Ruth Bader Ginsburg died in September of 2020, I heard someone say in a television interview that God wanted her in Heaven because she was so good. Really? How about: "God wanted her on Earth and healthy so that she could continue her great work for our country?" Why not say that she died because she couldn't fight off cancer anymore? That is a sad reality, but it is reality.

Why do people die at all? What happens to them after they die? Does God *make* them die? Does God cause cancer, heart attacks, car accidents, plane crashes, Lou Gehrig's Disease, high blood pressure, obesity, wars, violent crime, climate change, racial tensions, the Coronavirus, deadly fires, tornadoes, hurricanes, tsunamis, etc., etc., etc.? Do some of these happen because human beings are not perfect or take risks, or because we don't eat right or inherit certain conditions and tendencies? Do they happen because we haven't found the cure yet or don't take care of the environment as we should? Or is it because "Mother Nature" is beyond our control and all we can do is plan ahead for an occurrence and react when it happens?

And what about the good in our lives? You fall in love. Did God arrange it, is it Fate, was it "meant to be," or did you do everything right? You make a lot of money all of a sudden. Did God cause that to happen, or was it just "dumb luck," or are you a financial wizard? You achieve success in your job—whatever "success" may mean. Is God taking care of you, or does your boss like you, or are your clients or customers, patients or readers, congregants or members responsible, or do you get all the credit? Your favorite team wins the championship. Is it because God answered their prayers and your prayers, or did they just perform better, or did your wearing of their cap and jersey during the game make it happen, or is it simply because your team scored more runs or points or goals than the other team?

You have experienced a death, but you also have experienced what you believe is a "sign" from the spirit of the person who died. Why is it happening? Why do you feel that it is a "sign?" Is this God's way of bridging the gap between this world and the next world, or is it evidence of your wishful and, perhaps, delusional thinking? Is it a coincidence, or is it the result of your religious faith, or is it the product of supernatural forces that we can't explain but can truly enjoy?

When I would counsel congregants whose loved one had died, the question "why" would come up frequently. I would usually ask what kind of answer they wanted to that question. Did they want an answer that would make sense out of a tragic or premature death? Did they want an answer that would comfort them emotionally or provide an explanation intellectually? And, once they had the answer they were seeking, then what? Did that make mourning easier? Did that answer enhance their relationship with God or family or friends or life itself? Or did that answer make them feel regretful or sadder or hopeless? And, if they felt worse than when they asked the question, what was good about that? Sometimes, we seek answers about death because we think that having them will bring us consolation through explanation and comfort through theorizing.

When I would counsel couples about getting married, many of them told me that they believed, as my wife and I do, that they were "meant to be." So, was God the matchmaker, or was it Fate (which I do not associate with God)? Was it a computer program, or was it their own human actions? I believe less in Fate, and more in God and computers and humans. Regardless of the rationale claimed for them being together, the end result is that there are two people who are extremely happy that they love each other. And that's what really counts the most.

There are religious people who believe that good things happen to them because they prayed for good health or love, success or happiness. They believe that good things happen to them because they live a life according to the laws of the Torah, or in keeping with the Gospels, or in devotion to the Koran, or with a sense of always doing what is right and ethical. For them, there is a cause-and-effect relationship between their thoughts and actions, and their rewards and benefits. There are religious people who believe that prayers are not answered and bad things happen because whoever prayed didn't deserve a good result. It can be contended that the pray-er was not religious enough or good enough or kind enough. Or it could be—in an example I have heard far too often (and with which I disagree)—that the parchment in their *mezuzah* on their doorpost wasn't *kosher* enough. We are told that bad things happen because someone has not accepted a particular religious belief or practice, or because they are heretics or infidels. We are told that, if you think that things are bad now, wait until your life after death in Hell or some other equally scary place. For some who hear such an intimidating message, that is motivation enough to change their ways.

Yet, whether the messages we receive are scary or encouraging, here's what they have in common: they ascribe to us a certain degree of responsibility and a certain amount of control. They inform us that what we believe and think and do all make a difference. It doesn't mean that we have total responsibility and total control, but it does mean that we are not just the victims of Fate and the guinea pigs of God's whims and the recipients of dumb luck. In Judaism, the mystical belief in *tikkun olam* (repair of the world) empowers the individual to engage in positive acts to make the world a better place. For some Jews, praying for the coming of *Mashiach* (the Messiah) involves following what God wants us to do. For other Jews, knowing that every contribution we can make to social equality and social justice will help bring about the Messianic Age is incentive to join others in seeking to create an ideal society, country, and world.

Sometimes, people decide that their actions will have desired outcomes, and superstition is their means to achieve those outcomes. It can be defined as "a belief in the supernatural, which is to say, a belief in the existence of forces or entities that do not conform to the laws of nature or a scientific understanding of the universe."[208] Writing about the science of superstition, Neil Dagnall and Ken Drinkwater from Manchester Metropolitan University have said: "For many people, engaging with superstitious behaviours provides a sense of control and reduces anxiety ..."[209]

I have been a sports fan longer than I've been a rabbi, and I used to be convinced that my team would win if I followed the required (in my mind) superstitious rituals. Some of them were and, unfortunately, still aremy sitting in the same place on the couch, wearing a hat or jersey or sweatshirt of my team, saying "hit it" before a basketball player from my team took a shot, saying "let's get the first (down)" for my football team, saying "do something good" before a batter from my team swung, and texting my daughter throughout the game—among others. But it isn't just fans who are superstitious. I discovered some player superstitions online, a few of which I already knew. They all share the "belief" that a particular action leads to a desired result:

- Professional baseball player Wade Boggs would eat chicken before every game.
- Professional basketball player Michael Jordan would wear his University of North Carolina shorts under his Chicago Bulls shorts.
- Professional tennis player Serena Williams would not change her socks during a tournament.
- Professional football player Brian Urlacher would eat two chocolate chip cookies before every game.
- Professional hockey player Ed Belfour would tell his teammates every season: "If you touch my stuff, I'll kill you."[210]

There are so many Jewish superstitions (called 'bubbe misehs", "old wives' tales" in Yiddish) that they can be the subject of entire books. Here are several of them, provided in an online article from the Jewish Federation of Baltimore[211]:

- Don't sit at the corner of the table if you are an unmarried woman. You won't get married for the next seven years.
- Don't step over someone. You will cause them to stop growing.
- Never leave your purse on the floor if you want to keep your money.
- Spit three times after seeing, hearing, or learning something horrible to ward off the Evil Eye. Say "pu pu pu" after receiving good news.
- Don't take a direct path home from the cemetery. You wouldn't want the demons of the cemetery to follow you home.
- Bring jam to a housewarming party as a tasty gift, which is a distraction to evil spirits that nosh on it instead of wreaking havoc in the new home.
- Only bring an odd number of flowers for a special occasion since an even number is reserved for funerals only [although flowers are not encouraged at Jewish funerals].
- Wear a metal pin on your clothes when embarking on a trip because the metal is thought to be a powerful protective substance and can successfully ward off the evil spirits.
- Never hand a knife directly to another person—to avoid getting into a fight.
- Close open books—or else demons will steal the "holy knowledge" and use it for evil plans!

The field of psychology has a lot to say about cause-and-effect in what is called "attribution theory." In the article I cited in the first quote of this chapter, Saul McLeod states:

"Attribution theory is concerned with how ordinary people explain the causes of behavior and events... [Fritz] Heider (1958) [in his book *The Psychology of Interpersonal Relations*], didn't so much develop a theory himself as emphasize certain themes that others took up. There were two main ideas that he put forward that became influential: dispositional (internal cause) vs. situational (external cause) attributions...

Dispositional attribution assigns the cause of behavior to some internal characteristic of a person, rather than to outside forces... [Situational attribution is] the process of assigning the cause of behavior to some situation or event outside a person's control rather than to some internal characteristic."[212]

Both psychology and religion deal with "why" questions and providing answers for them. In terms of explaining the phenomenon of "signs," you could attribute them to the personalities of the people who receive them—their needs, their character traits, their imaginations. And you could attribute them to situations or events outside their personalities—so-called "random occurrences," supposedly "unexplainable" events, and "strange" happenings. Or, if you believe as I do, you can attribute them to God providing a bridge between the living and the dead. Why do people receive "signs?" Because they believe that it's all part of God's plan.

As long as we're talking about psychology, let's talk about the psychology of coincidence. In an article for The Atlantic, Julie Beck cited Dr. Bernard Beitman, who was well-known for his research into coincidence:

"Beitman in his research has found that certain personality traits are linked to experiencing more coincidences—people who describe themselves as religious or spiritual, people who are self-referential (or likely to relate information from the external world back to themselves), and people who are high in meaning-seeking are all coincidence-prone. People are also likely to see coincidences when they are extremely sad, angry, or anxious.

For Beitman, probability is not enough when it comes to studying coincidences. Because statistics can describe what happens but can't explain it any further than chance'" I know there's something more going on than we pay attention to,' he says.

'Random is not enough of an explanation for me.'"[213]

The argument for coincidence as the reason for "signs" is frequently offered as an explanation of why people feel a sense of the presence of a deceased loved one, why certain animals appear, why significant numbers repeat, why coins mysteriously show up, why photos have images in them that weren't there when taken, why important music plays suddenly, why electric fixtures go off and on, why certain shapes are seen over and over again, and why long-lost objects are found. And, when it is offered, it frequently means that the one who hears the story or experience just can't believe it is possible and downgrades it to "just a coincidence." Yitta Halberstam and Judith Leventhal have written a series of books from a Jewish perspective on this topic, with titles like *Small Miracles, Small Miracles from Beyond: Dreams, Visions and Signs That Link Us to the Other Side*, and *Small Miracles for the Jewish Heart: Extraordinary Coincidences from Yesterday and Today*. In the second book, they write:

"...When a loved one dies, the soul-connection that he or she has forged with friends and relatives is not obliterated but remains eternal. **This everlasting bond is expressed by the continuous involvement of the deceased in the lives of those the person leaves behind.** [Emphasis added] Parents continue to watch over the lives of their children, deriving pride in their accomplishments and interceding on their behalf before the heavenly throne...Not only is God carrying us, but our deceased relatives and loved ones are supporting us as well. Their presence continues to bless us in the small, personal, and ordinary events we experience every day, events that may very well provide important clues or small hints that they are with us still. Sadly, some of us are not attuned to the messages of the coincidences, even when we encounter them repeatedly."[214]

I find this perspective to be interesting for several reasons: 1) It's Jewish; 2) It affirms the belief in everlasting life; 3) It indicates that the souls of our deceased family members are aware of what's going on here; 4) It theorizes that they take an active role in shaping our lives; and 5) It contends that there are clues that are provided to those who are receptive. Halberstam and Leventhal also mention the belief in *melitzas yosher*—someone who prays for mercy on your behalf...and is your direct intermediary with God, interceding whenever necessary."[215] This injects into the discussion a new element of not just mysterious contact, but of an active existence of a spirit in the World-to-Come that continues a strong connection between the living and the dead. It means that we have advocates on our behalf in the afterlife.

Coming at coincidences from a different place is SQuire Rushnell, who created the term "Godwinks." Rushnell is a former television network executive and is the author of about a dozen books, such as *When God Winks: How the Power of Coincidence Guides Your Life, The God Wink Effect: 7 Secrets to God's Signs, Wonders, and Answered Prayers* (with Louise Duart), *Godwinks & Divine Alignment: How Godwink Moments Guide Your Journey,* and *When God Winks at You: How God Speaks Directly to You Through the Power of Coincidence.* Before becoming an author, Rushnell was a network executive responsible for the success of *ABC's Good Morning America, Schoolhouse Rock,* and *ABC Afterschool Specials.* In the first book I mentioned above, he wrote:

Godwinks are signs of hope; God's way of providing you with encouragement, comfort, and certainty...what you thought were coincidences, were actually Godwinks, little messages to encourage you on your journey through life, nudging you along the grand path that has been designed especially for you... Learning to identify Godwinks—hopeful communications directly to you out of seven billion people on the planet—will help you to develop a confident sense of direction. It will be an affirmation that, no matter how often you may think it, you are never alone. Somewhere up above, there is a universal guidance system, and you are on the radar screen.[216]

Rushnell's most relevant insight for this book is this:

At times when you are deeply grieving, you may not understand *why* a loved one was called to the other side. But Godwinks are loving messages of hope meant to reassure you that life is not a continuum but a circle, and that **connections to loved ones are never lost** [Emphasis added]...When someone you admire or someone close to you dies, hold tightly to this truth: Everything *will* be OK. You are seeing but one small piece of the overall puzzle. From God's perspective, it all makes perfect sense.[217]

While Rushnell has a definite Christian orientation and quotes from both the Hebrew Bible and the New Testament in each chapter, he and I are in agreement that God can connect with us, that those connections are positive, that they can provide us direction, that we are not alone, that we don't lose touch with our loved ones who have died, and that we must have hope that everything will be OK. These are all important messages that I express in my book *Finding Hope and Faith in the Face of Death: Insights of a Rabbi and Mourner.* And they are messages with which I think most of my clergy colleagues would agree.

In my research for this book, I have ventured into areas of thought and belief with which I was not familiar previously. I certainly never expected to get into the subjects of mediums, coincidence, superstition, and attribution theory. In regard to "signs," I have a wife and stepdaughter, congregants, friends, and strangers who have related to me amazingly similar experiences and touching stories. Before I move on to stories about "signs," I want to repeat and expand on a definition from Laura Lynne Jackson, author of *Signs: The Secret Language of the Universe:*

"A sign is a message sent to you by the universe...the term I use when I refer to God energy—the all-encompassing force of love that connects to us all and that we are all a part of. The universe also includes the angelic realm, spirit guides, and our loved ones who have crossed to the Other Side...Signs are a method of communication from the Other Side. Signs can come from different sources—our departed loved ones, our spirit guides, and God energy. These are all part of the universal Team of Light that each of us has working for us every single day."[218]

She uses somewhat different terminology than I would. But Jackson speaks of the universe, God, angels, spirits, and light —all of which I am very comfortable with as a Jew and as a rabbi. There are many reasons that can be cited for why things happen. If there is such a phenomenon as "signs", why do they happen? I have become convinced through repeated instances in my life and the lives of others that coincidence and randomness and luck are not sufficient explanations for "signs." I believe that when I or anyone else feels the sense of a deceased loved one's presence, it is an example of God facilitating communication from the World-to-Come (also known as "The Other Side"). I further believe that those who have such experiences are not delusional or wishful thinkers. Actually, I believe that they are blessed.

In Jewish tradition, we have quite a number of blessings that express our gratitude. The *Motzi*—which is said over bread—is: "Praised are You, the Eternal our God, Sovereign of the Universe, Who brings forth bread from the earth." Does God *literally* bring forth bread from the earth? If not, why does the prayer say so? This sounds supernatural to me. The *Shehehcheyanu*—which is recited to express joy for a first-time experience or special occasion—is: "Praised are You, the Eternal our God, Sovereign of the Universe, Who has kept us alive, sustained us, and brought us to this time." Does God *literally* keep us alive? If not, why does the prayer say so? This also sounds supernatural to me. The *Birkat Hagomeil*—which is said after someone has recovered from serious illness or has arrived home safely after a trip—is: "Praised are You, the Eternal our God, Sovereign of the Universe, Who rewards the undeserving with goodness, and Who has rewarded me with goodness." If the *Gomeil* is recited in the presence of a congregation, their response is: "May the One Who rewarded you with all goodness reward you with all goodness forever." Is God *literally* responsible for our recovery or our safe arrival? If not, why does the prayer say so? And this, too, sounds supernatural to me. Could it be that the blessings are simply an acknowledgment of God's role for the good in our lives?

Literally, these blessings are examples of attribution theory that do not rely on superstition or coincidence as explanations for why things happen. It's no surprise that a blessing is inherently linked with God. And I would contend that, when Rushnell talks about Godwinks, it's pretty much the same as when I talk about blessings—the active and conscious recognition of what has happened, attributing it to God, and not taking something good for granted. It is within our control to decide how we relate to and understand and explain having food to eat, having a reason to express joy, and having survived a difficult experience. In a way—as I said about the result being the most important for the wedding couples—it is the "*what*" that has happened that matters most. But thinking about the "why" can give us a sense of structure and purpose. To be able to relate to and understand and explain "signs" as a gift from God, as a blessing, can enhance our lives and help us to realize that love never dies.

CHAPTER 9: THE POWER OF THE KADDISH FOR THE LIVING AND THE DEAD

"Death ends a life, not a relationship.
Lost love is still love.
It takes a different form, that's all. You can't see their smile or bring them food or tousle their hair or move them around a dance floor.
But when those senses weaken, another heightens.
Memory. Memory becomes your partner. You nurture it. You hold it. You dance with it."[219]

"It is hard to overstate the importance of Kaddish within the liturgy; it is part of virtually all communal Jewish worship. Indeed, because the sanctification of God's name is considered one of the primary functions of Jewish worship, Kaddish has been called a 'self-contained miniature service.'"[220]

"By ruling that Kaddish for a parent should not be recited for more than eleven months, Rabbi Isserles was eliminating the possibility of ascribing wickedness to the parent."[221]

"The firstborn son of a family in Yiddish-speaking Eastern Europe was referred to as its 'Kaddish,' the guarantor that there would be someone to say the prayer for his parents when they died, even if no more male children were born after him. Mourners unable or unwilling to attend synagogue regularly often hired stand-ins to say the Kaddish in their place."[222]

"I have a Kaddish."

Daniel Handelman to his daughter Donna before he died

When I was growing up in a Reform congregation in Kansas City, I was well-acquainted with the *Kaddish*. I was not aware that, in other synagogues, only the mourners stood to recite this prayer in memory of family members who had died. When I attended Friday night services with my parents, I knew that I was supposed to stand up with the rest of the congregation. When I sat with my buddies at Saturday morning services, I knew that this was not a time to converse or, God forbid, to joke around. We were taught that the *Kaddish* was a prayer that is said to honor the memory of people who died—not just people we knew —but also people who had been members of the congregation and were complete strangers to us. Occasionally, when a famous Jew or a world leader died, their name would be mentioned before the rabbi said, "Please rise." I remember that it was the custom to stand up with people in the sanctuary who were actual mourners because our standing symbolized our support for them. The names that were recited by the rabbi included members who had died at that time of year since the founding of the congregation in 1870, as well as those members or relatives of members who had died during the last year or the last week. The *Kaddish* was "the prayer for the dead," and they deserved mention and attention and respect.

As I became older and more knowledgeable, I found out that the prayer doesn't mention death, that it is a praise of God, that the Mourner's *Kaddish* is only one version of the prayer, and that another version of it could be chanted. Having experienced deaths of family and friends in my teens, I decided when I became a teacher and a tutor to make sure that my Religious School and B'nai Mitzvah students learned this important prayer before they needed to know it. I would like to believe that it wasn't just my projection of my own neediness, but that it was practical preparation for an inevitable situation. For me, it was: "At some point, you're going to have to say *Kaddish*. Better to know it now so that you can feel comfortable and ready when the time comes." When I became a rabbi, I would feel empathy for congregants who didn't know how to read the prayer in Aramaic [the ancient spoken language of our ancestors written with Hebrew letters]. I would guide them through the English transliteration so that they could participate in reciting the prayer. At funerals and unveilings, at festival *Yizkor* services and *Shabbat* services, and—especially at High Holy Day services with hundreds of people present—I could feel the warmth and the power and the strength of a community coalescing around those who were mourning. At all three of the temples I served, my office staff and I were proactive in encouraging mourners to actually be there to say *Kaddish* on the *yahrzeit* [death anniversary] or during the year following the death. I did not want to be their intermediary, their surrogate, or their substitute. I always used to say that reciting the *Kaddish* doesn't just honor your deceased family members and friends—it honors you.

In my book *Finding Hope and Faith in the Face of Death: Insights of a Rabbi and Mourner*, my last chapter is entitled "The Mystery of the *Kaddish*." I begin with this quotation from the *Authorised Daily Prayer Book* edited by Rabbi Joseph H. Hertz, and it is very appropriate here as we consider the importance of the *Kaddish*:

"Its origin is mysterious. We find foreshadowings of it in the Biblical books; prayers for the dead are mentioned in the Books of Maccabees; snatches of the Kaddish reach us in the legends of Talmudic teachers; and echoes of it in the writings of the early Mystics; but the Prayer in its entirety we find neither in the Bible, nor in the *Mishna*, nor in the vast Talmudic and Midrashic literatures. It seems to be a gradual growth, continued from generation to generation, from age to age, until in the period of the *Gaonim*, some twelve centuries ago, it attained the form which we have before us in our prayer books."[223]

Whether you are familiar with the words of the prayer or not, it is crucial to know what the prayer says, and I will provide that translation below. Then, I want to elaborate on what Rabbi Hertz suggested about its origins and follow that with what I consider to be the supernatural aspects of the *Kaddish*—what it is supposed to do for the deceased and what the deceased can do for us.

The *Kaddish* is, by definition, a doxology—a liturgical praise to God. The word *"Kaddish"* in Aramaic corresponds to the word *"Kadosh"* in Hebrew—which means "holy." I am focusing here on the Mourner's *Kaddish* (sometimes called the "Orphan's *Kaddish*"), but we also have the *Chatzi Kaddish* (the "Half" or "Reader's" *Kaddish*), which separates one section of the service from another: the *"Kaddish "D'Rabanan"* (the Rabbis' *Kaddish*), which follows the studying of an excerpt from the Mishnah or Talmud; the *Kaddish "Titkabbal"* near the end of a prayer service; and the *Kaddish "Achar Hak'vura"* (the *Kaddish* after Burial) as the primary versions of it. Here is the English of the Mourner's *Kaddish*:

"May God's great name come to be magnified and sanctified in the world God brought into being. May God's majestic reign prevail soon in your lives, in your days, and in the life of the whole House of Israel; and let us say: Amen.

May God's great name be blessed to the end of time.

May God's holy name come to be blessed, acclaimed, and glorified; revered, raised, and beautified; honored and praised. Blessed is the One who is entirely beyond all the blessings and hymns, all the praises and words of comfort that we speak in the world; and let us say: Amen.

Let perfect peace abound; let there be abundant life for us and for all Israel.

May the One who makes peace in the high heavens make peace for us, all Israel, and all who dwell on earth; and let us say: Amen."[224]

In *The Jewish Mourner's Book of Why*, Rabbi Alfred J. Kolatch writes about the origins of the *Kaddish*:

"The idea of reciting the Kaddish for the dead was encouraged by the thirteenth-century Kabbalists (mystics), who contended that **this prayer has the power to redeem the souls of the deceased.** [Emphasis added] This belief may have stemmed from a widespread legend that Rabbi Akiba had helped redeem the soul of a deceased man from the tortures of hell *(gehinnom)* by teaching the man's son to recite the Kaddish at a synagogue service."[225]

I am positive that most Jews I know are not aware of the belief about the redemptive power of the *Kaddish.* Nor would they be aware of the term *gehinnom,* and they would most likely think that saving a soul from the "tortures of hell" is what Christians would want to do. Maurice Lamm provides a little more background to the story:

"Rabbi Akiva had a vision of a well-known sinner who had died and was condemned to intolerable punishment. The sinner informed the rabbi in the vision that only if his surviving son would recite the *Barchu* and Kaddish would he be redeemed. The rabbi proceeded to teach the youngster those prayers. When the youngster recited the Kaddish, he saved his father from perdition. The child endows the parent!"[226]

Hillel Halkin adds to this concept of the redeeming power of children who pray for their deceased parents. For me, this is proof of the belief in a supernatural connection that transcends death:

"By the end of Talmudic times, therefore, Judaism had arrived at the notion that prayer—and specifically, **the Rabbis' Kaddish—could redeem the souls of the damned** [Emphasis added] ... here is historical irony in this when one considers how opposed Biblical Judaism was to the pagan practice of sacrifice and prayer for the dead, and to the belief that human intervention could improve their lot. Yet paganism, for all its deficiencies, addressed human needs that monotheistic faiths like Judaism, try as they might to ignore them, repeatedly discovered could not be repressed forever—and such was the need to feel there must be something one can do for those in the next world whom one has loved in this one.[227]

I doubt whether most non-Orthodox Jews who recite the *Kaddish* are consciously aware that there are traditional beliefs like these that stress the great power of the prayer. In particular, most of those Jews would tell you that they say *Kaddish* either because it's "tradition" or because they want to honor the memories of their parents or anyone else for whom they say the *Kaddish*. Rabbi Simcha Paull Raphael finds another benefit for the mourner:

"The act of saying Kaddish can be a powerful way of keeping one's own internal conversation with the soul of a deceased loved one. On a psychological level, saying Kaddish is a way to remember the deceased with respect and reverence, and it facilitates a gradual acceptance of death and loss. On a spiritual level, saying Kaddish mediates the ongoing relationship between the bereaved and the soul of the person who has died. It is a way of continuing the healing and 'finishing old business' between the living and the dead."[228]

But what if you can't or don't want to say *Kaddish*? You may have noticed the end of the quotation from Halkin at the beginning of the chapter in which he said that "mourners unable or unwilling to attend synagogue regularly often hired stand-ins to say the Kaddish in their place." A modern version of that practice is indicated in an ad that frequently appears in *Hadassah Magazine*. It's entitled: "Who Will Say Kaddish?":

"Hadassah's Perpetual Yahrzeit Program ensures that Kaddish will be recited in Jerusalem for your loved ones every year. Forever.

Perpetual Yahrzeit: Kaddish will be recited annually for your loved one in perpetuity in the Fannie and Maxwell Abbell Synagogue at Hadassah Medical Center beneath Marc Chagall's iconic stained-glass windows.

Enhanced Perpetual Yahrzeit: Kaddish will be recited for your loved one daily for 11 months after burial, after which Kaddish will be recited annually.

Advance Yahrzeit: A reservation to ensure Kaddish will be recited for you and your loved one upon their death. Available in standard and Enhanced Perpetual Yahrzeit."[229]

There are times, too, when you can't say *Kaddish* even if you want to do so. Our tradition stipulates that it can't be recited unless there are enough people present, as Rabbi Elie Kaunfer explains:

"The Mourner's Kaddish is the quintessential prayer associated with a *minyan* (a prayer quorum of ten). One needs a *minyan* to recite it, and its entire structure is call and response. It is one of the few prayers in our liturgy that has the leader address other people in the room, as opposed to God, directly ("in *your* lives and in *your* days…*You* say: Amen!"). For this reason alone, it feels disorienting to consider reciting it without others…There are recent rabbinic rulings that have permitted saying Kaddish with an online *minyan*."[230]

While this is a common practice in Orthodox synagogues and in most—if not all—Conservative synagogues, most Reform congregations do not require a *minyan* for Kaddish to be said. Whenever I led a service where there were less than ten people in attendance, we would nevertheless say it because I didn't want someone who came to the service to be "penalized" and unable to recite the *Kaddish*. The same approach would apply to a *"shiva minyan"*—a prayer service held in a house of mourning during the memorial period.

Having said that, there are many Jews—especially men—

who have had the experience of being asked to be in a *min-yan*. It could have occurred in a neighborhood or on a city street, outside of a synagogue or on a cruise ship, in a hospital or on a plane, for *shiva* or for a weekday service. Women can be included in a Conservative *minyan* of ten and in Reform and Reconstructionist and other *minyans* as well. There are syna-gogues and prayer groups all over the world that will call people or text them in order to have a *minyan,* and I have found that some who respond are those who will show up for a *shiva* ser-vice because they know the person who is mourning. Although a non-traditional mourner could theoretically say the *Kaddish* alone, it is just not the same as reciting it as part of a community —especially a community that cares about you.

What benefit does someone gain from the recitation of the *Kaddish*? It is an affirmation of faith, it offers the opportunity to gain or give communal support, and it directs one's attention to remembering and honoring the person who has died. Alfred Ko-latch cites an additional benefit, which happens to be mutual:

"The concept of "merit of ancestors" *(zechut Avot)* as a contributing factor to our salvation is underscored throughout Jewish literature. The Midrash (Exodus Rabba 44:1) emphasizes this point in its comment on the verse in the Book of Psalms (80:9), 'Thou didst pluck up a vine out of Egypt.' The Rabbis comment: 'Just as a vine leans upon dead pieces of wood, so does living Israel lean upon the [dead] Patriarchs [Abraham, Isaac, and Jacob].'"[231]

This concept is applied not only to the customs of death and mourning, but also to our lives in general. To me, it is the op-posite of "guilt by association." It involves inheriting a sense of goodness and righteousness from our ancestors and having that lead to positive outcomes for us just because of their exemplary lives. In Judaism, it goes all the way back to Abraham. After circumcising himself and his son Ishmael and every male in his

household, Abraham is visited by three "men," and enthusias-
tically plays the role of host. The beginning of Chapter 18 of
Genesis tells us that he *runs* to greet the men, *hastens* to the tent
to tell Sarah to make some cakes, *runs* to the herd to get a first-
rate calf, gives it to a servant boy who prepares it *quickly*, and
then on his own, takes curds and milk and the calf, and serves
them to his visitors. Abraham is praised in Jewish tradition as
performing the mitzvah of *hachnasat orchim*—hospitality. The
concept of *zechut Avot* says that Abraham's descendants benefit
from his praiseworthy actions, as the Talmud relates in regard to
the Exodus:

"In reward for providing them with curd and milk, the Jewish people merited the manna; in reward for: "And he stood
[*omed*] by them," the Jews merited the pillar [*amud*] of cloud; in
reward for Abraham saying: 'Let now a little water be fetched,'
they merited the well of Miriam."[232]

Another citation from the Talmud attributes the manna, the
pillar, and the well to Moses, Aaron and Miriam:

"Rabbi Yosei, son of Rabbi Yehuda, says: 'Three good sus-
tainers rose up for the Jewish people during the exodus from
Egypt, and they are: Moses, Aaron and Miriam. And three good
gifts were given from Heaven through their agency, and these
are they: The well of water, the pillar of cloud, and the manna.'
He elaborates: 'The well was given to the Jewish people in the
merit of Miriam; the pillar of cloud was in the merit of Aaron;
and the manna in the merit of Moses. When Miriam died the
well disappeared, as it is stated: "And Miriam died there" (Numbers 20:1), and it says thereafter in the next verse: "And there
was no water for the congregation" (Numbers 20:2). But the well
returned in the merit of both Moses and Aaron.'"[233]

Thus, *zechut Avot* transcends history and the wall between
life and death. In terms of time, it extends far beyond the Exo-

dus more than 3,000 years ago and can be applied to our lives. That is the relevance and the staying power of our link to our ancestors through *zechut Avot*. And it is implicit in the custom of visiting the cemetery, an ancient practice that is still followed by many Jews. Rather than viewing a cemetery as a spooky place, Jews have regarded it as sacred. In Hebrew, it can be called *"bet kevarot"*—"the house of graves," *"bet olam,"*—"the eternal home," or *"bet hayyim"*—"the house of the living." Kolatch continues:

"Visiting the cemetery on fast days in order to pray at the graves of loved ones and saintly persons is an old Jewish tradition. (*Taanit* 16a). It was believed that prayers recited at graveside would be more efficacious than prayers recited elsewhere, and that **the dead would be more inclined to 'intercede' for the living** [Emphasis added...

The Rabbis of the Talmud [*Taanit* 16a] discouraged frequent visits to the graves of relatives because the living were in the habit of praying to their dead to intercede in their behalf. This was considered a sacrilegious act. In Judaism, unlike other religions, prayers are to be addressed to God alone, not to an intermediary.

To curb excessive cemetery visits, the Rabbis specified when it is proper to visit the grave of a deceased relative. The approved times include the month of *Elul* [which precedes the High Holidays], the days between *Rosh Hashana* and *Yom Kippur, Tisha B'Av,* and the anniversary of the loved one's date of death *(Yahrzeit)*. Visits are also sanctioned at the conclusion of the *Shiva* and *Sheloshim* [thirty days] periods and at the end of the twelve-month mourning period. Cemetery visits on the Sabbath and holidays (including the Intermediate Days of festivals, *Rosh Chodesh* [the first day of the month], and *Purim*) are not permitted.[234]

There are many congregations that provide a special memorial service at cemeteries, usually on the Sunday between *Rosh Hashanah* and *Yom Kippur*. The idea that the dead might "intercede" on behalf of the living is indicative of an eternal connec-

139

tion, but there is a difference between praying to the dead and praying to God that Kolatch emphasizes. His list of approved times to visit the cemetery is pretty much adhered to by the Jews that I know. The unveiling ceremony for a tombstone is not mentioned because it is a relatively recent custom, and usually takes place between six months and a year after the death.

It should come as no surprise to anyone that there is a blessing to be said upon entering a cemetery. But it may be surprising that the blessing is addressed to the deceased:

"Blessed art Thou, O Lord, King of the Universe, Who created you justly, who knows justly how many you are, and who will justly return and restore you to life. Blessed are Thou, O Lord our God, Who quickens the dead.'...It addresses the dead, as if to provide them with an analysis of what has befallen them. **The intercession of the dead for the living is replaced by the intercession of the living for themselves.** [Emphasis added] Mournful reflection passes into moral reflection, and it is the role of the dead to stimulate such a passage."[235]

This blessing is tremendously unusual because—in most of our blessings—God is the One being addressed or is the One to Whom reference is being made. What Halkin says is illustrative of four key points: 1) a belief that we can address the dead at all; 2) an acknowledgment of the traditional belief that the dead can intercede on behalf of the living; 3) a sense that we can be motivated by the dead to engage in moral reflections; and 4) the dead have a role through which they can "stimulate" our reflections.

The *Kitzur Shulchan Aruch*—written and published by Rabbi Shlomo Ganzfried in 1864—summarizes the *Shulchan Aruch*, which was written in 1563 by Joseph Karo, and represents a codification of Jewish laws, which emphasizes how to apply them to daily life and special occasions. The *Kitzur* deals with the subject of going to the cemetery and adds an element with which most Jews today are very familiar:

"It is customary to go to the cemetery *erev Rosh Hashanah* after the *Shacharis* [morning] prayers and bow prayerfully at the graves of *tzaddikim* [righteous men]. Charity should be given to the poor, and many fervent applications offered to arouse the saintly *tzaddikim,* in their eternal resting place to intercede for us on the Day of Judgment.

An additional reason for going to the cemetery is that the place where *tzaddikim* are buried is sacred and pure, and prayers are more readily accepted when they are offered on sacred ground, and the Holy One, blessed is He, will show us kindness for the sake of the *tzaddikim.*

But it should not be your intention to appeal to the dead who rest there, for that would be tantamount to "Inquiring of the dead," (Deuteronomy 18: 11), which is forbidden, but you should ask of Hashem, blessed is His name, to have mercy on you for the sake of the *tzaddikim* who rest in the dust...

When you approach the grave, you should say, 'May it be Your will, that the repose of [so-and-so] who is buried here, be in peace, and may his merit aid me...May you lie in peace, and may you sleep in peace until *Menachem* [the Comforter,] *Moshiach* [Messiah] comes, announcing peace.'"[236]

The element I am referring to is the giving of charity, otherwise known as *tzedakah.* Occasionally, when I go to certain cemeteries, I will see "a poor person" there, asking for *tzedakah.* Some cemeteries have a *tzedakah* box, or more than one, located at certain locations. More important is the fact that the custom of giving *tzedakah* in memory of the deceased is prevalent in Judaism and also in Jewish culture. I know Jews who say that they are not "religious," but who are very generous with their *tzedakah,* and do this *mitzvah* primarily when someone dies. Synagogues, Jewish organizations, hospitals, and other institutions benefit from *tzedakah* given in memory of the departed. Obituaries will usually say that the family would prefer donations to an organization "in lieu of flowers." Many people know that synagogues have *yahrzeit* boards with memorial plaques on them that are paid for by donations from the family of the deceased. This *tzedakah* also includes scholarship funds, wings of buildings, sections of libraries, units in hospitals, rooms in museums, and programs at colleges that are named in memory of someone and that are funded by initial and subsequent donations. My temple in Stony Brook has a youth scholarship fund named in my father's memory. The temple in which I grew up has a Sisterhood leadership training fund named in memory of my mother. So, *tzedakah* is not limited to the poor in a cemetery.

The clear emphasis on *tzaddikim* is fascinating as well. The translation of the word above says, "righteous men," but both women and men, of course, can be righteous—as I mentioned in Chapter Seven. "Arousing" them to "intercede" for us on The Day of Judgment is an example of the reciprocal relationship between the dead and the living that is mentioned in a number of traditional sources. The inherently holy nature of a cemetery makes it an ideal place for prayer, but those who pray there have to understand that they are praying to God and not to their deceased relatives. The prayer shown in the last paragraph from the *Kitzur* is definitely one which benefits both the living and the dead, especially with its message of peace occurring four times, and with its request "may his merit aid me" being spoken by the person who is praying. It concludes with a reference to the resurrection of the dead—a firm belief in Jewish tradition. I will use the word "supernatural" again to describe what is going on here. **The assumption of the prayer is that the living and the dead are linked by their ability to do something of benefit for each other.**

While I believe that men and women can be righteous and can be recognized during their lives and honored because of their character and their deeds, there is a special class of *tzaddikim* whose graves are visited by more people than their family members. Halkin writes:

"A belief in the dead's ongoing presence in the grave even as they dwell in other worlds or haunt this one exists in many cultures. No doubt this is why some visitors to cemeteries feel they can commune with the dead and even talk to them...

Pilgrimages to the graves of revered rabbis have also been a feature of Jewish folk religion... The main such event in today's Jewish world is the annual *Lag B'omer hilulah* at the tomb of Shim'on Bar Yohai on Mount Meron in the Galilee, which attracts hundreds of thousands of participants. Well attended, too, is the *Rosh Hashanah* pilgrimage to the burial site of Rabbi Nachman of Bratslav in the Ukrainian city of Uman. Gatherings of this sort do not commemorate a death. **They pay homage to a life that exerts its power even from the grave."**[237] [Emphasis added]

I would add to this short list the grave of the Lubavitcher Rebbe Menachem Mendel Schneerson at the Old Montefiore Cemetery in Queens, New York; the Tomb of Rachel near Bethlehem in the West Bank; the Tomb of King David in Jerusalem; and the grave of Moses Maimonides in Tiberias, Israel.

The Jewish tradition essentially has created a two-way street between the living and the dead. It is, potentially, an opportunity for mutual communication and mutual influence. In spite of —or because of—the belief that the soul of a deceased relative might experience punishment, the rabbis came up with a solution. Rav makes what I consider to be an amazingly negative statement about the dead being forgotten, but at least there was an attempt to institute a practice that would eliminate that possibility. A number of centuries later, it was modified and improved:

"The dead are not forgotten until after twelve months [from the time of death], says Rav in the Talmud [*Berachot* 58b], and therefore the Kaddish for a deceased parent was originally recited for a twelve-month period. In talmudic times there was also a belief that the wicked are consigned to hell (*gehinnom* or *Gehenna*) and are subject to punishment for a maximum of twelve months.

To avoid the possibility of people erroneously concluding that the parent for whom Kaddish is being recited (for a twelve-month period) was wicked, scholars of the caliber of Rabbi Moses ben Israel Isserles (c. 1525-1572) of Cracow reduced the requirement for the recitation of Kaddish for parents to eleven months."[238]

Leon Wieseltier elaborates on the important relationship between parent and child when he refers to a particular Kabbalistic source—*Ma'avar Yabbok,* or "Crossing the Jabbok," by Aaron Berachah ben Moses of Modena, an Italian Kabbalist of the late sixteenth and early seventeenth centuries:

"'Just as the son must honor his father in life,' Aaron maintains, 'so in his death he must take the judgment of his father upon himself.' The duty of the son survives the death of the father. 'And the son must do so because he is capable of unburdening his father of it, with the power of the commandments that he performs and the good deeds that he does for the purpose of blocking that judgment.'

The Kaddish has the power to extinguish the fire of Gehenna and to subdue the strange and hostile forces. **With the power of the Kaddish, the son rescues his father** [Emphasis added] and gets him into Eden...With every Kaddish, he freezes hell for an hour and a half.[239]

This Kaddish...is based on the son's righteousness, which is so great that the name of heaven may be sanctified by him, and in this manner the son acquits the father by demonstrating the merit of him who begat someone who sanctifies the name of heaven.

When the mourner appeals for God's mercy for the deceased's soul, the appeal is not made in the name of blood; it is made in the name of character. The mourner does not say: have pity on the soul of my father because he was my father. The mourner says: have pity on the soul of this man because he raised a man who stands before you and submits to your authority.

In rising to say the Kaddish, you have given an answer: he was the kind of father who taught his son to do this. And a man who directs his son toward truth deserves mercy. It is based on the son's righteousness, which is so great that the name of heaven may be sanctified by him, and in this manner the son acquits the father by demonstrating the merit of him who begat someone who sanctifies the name of heaven."[240]

I started this chapter with the quotation from Mitch Albom because I love his writing style, his content, and his perceptiveness. The statements that "death ends a life, not a relationship" and "memory becomes your partner" describe the *Kaddish* without mentioning it. Anita Diamant's characterization of it as a "self-contained miniature service" because it is about the sanctification of God's name highlights the importance of the *Kaddish* throughout the centuries. The quotations from Kolatch and Halkin are all about who keeps the memory of a loved one— especially a parent—alive, and how it is done in a positive way.

I conclude this chapter with my wife's story of talking with her father the night before he died and her being the only child left to say *Kaddish*. It illustrates the absolute emotional and spiritual power of the prayer, but it needs some background and perspective first:

"When I would go to the synagogue with my dad before I became a Bat Mitzvah, he insisted that I leave when the Kaddish was recited during a memorial service. It was considered to be inappropriate for a child to say that prayer when his or her parents were alive—and, especially, for a girl. As an adult, I began to read it at services in my Reform synagogue—Temple Isaiah in Stony Brook, New York— when we all stood up in support of the mourners.

My twin brothers were born on 1/11/55. I was born three years later. Throughout his life, Michael had severe learning disabilities, took multiple prescribed medications, and underwent various treatments in mental hospitals, and Joseph eventually became very successful but was an alcoholic. Like a lot of twins, my brothers were close from the time of their birth, communicated in their own language (including when they were sleeping), and could feel each other's feelings. For example, when they were 16, Joseph woke up in the middle of the night complaining of extreme pain in his arm and stomach—but there were no signs of any injury. The next day, we found out that Michael (who was 3,000 miles away) had been robbed and stabbed in his arm and stomach at the exact time that Joseph felt the pains.

They were in a tragic car crash in California in February of 1990. Michael was driving and wasn't injured as seriously as Joseph, who would never again be able to talk or walk, feed himself or express emotion, and was in various rehab centers for the rest of his life. At the beginning of May of 1992, Joseph requested to have his feeding tubes removed—meaning that he would die within days. We weren't able to reach Michael because of the chaos caused by the Rodney King riots in Los Angeles at that time. We learned subsequently from the police that Michael had died of an accidental drug overdose at exactly the same time that Joseph had the feeding tubes removed. The following day, Joseph communicated with the nurses with a "thumbs-up" gesture to have the tubes reinserted. It was almost a week later that the police found Michael's body in his apartment.

My parents and I believed that the boys had communicated with each other somehow, even though Joseph had suffered severe brain damage. It was the same sort of communication between the twins that had occurred throughout their lives and that no one else could explain or understand. We believed that Joseph gave the thumbs-up to be reconnected because—despite his condition—he must have been aware somehow that his brother had died. We also believed that Joseph didn't want my dad to have to say Kaddish for two sons at the same time. After Michael's funeral and shiva, my parents flew to California. My dad wanted to tell Joseph in person that his brother had died—even though he wasn't visibly aware of what he was being told. Despite that, my dad was determined to say Kaddish for Michael with Joseph, and that's exactly what he did. He ultimately died on July 27th, and we buried him next to his brother.

My parents belonged to an Orthodox synagogue when we were growing up and, although they weren't Orthodox in their practice, my dad believed in certain traditions. One of them was that his sons would be his "Kaddish"—in other words, they would have the obligation to say Kaddish for their father who (it was assumed) would die before them. The tradition didn't provide for daughters to be designated with this title, this obligation, this honor. So, when Joseph died, my dad had no "Kaddish" according to Jewish tradition.

At the time, I was married to a non-Jewish man who had two children from a previous marriage. We had two children of our own —a daughter and a son—and divorced when they were 5 and 3. During the last eleven years of my dad's life, and after his death, I was a congregant at Temple Isaiah. When he saw my strong commitment to raising my children as Reform Jews and sending them to Religious School and to camp, and when he saw me being so involved at my synagogue, he was really happy.

In 2003, my dad received a diagnosis of pancreatic cancer, and died six weeks later. The night before he died, we were talking on the phone about his funeral plans. During that conversation, he said to me, approvingly: "Although your brothers are gone, I know that, in you, I have a Kaddish." My mother died in 2018. I am their "Kaddish," and so is my husband, as I am for his parents. For us, saying the Kaddish when their yahrzeits occur and when we observe Yizkor is powerful and meaningful, and helps us maintain a loving connection with our parents that will endure for the rest of our lives."

CHAPTER 10: THE APPEARANCE OF ANIMALS AND THE SENSE OF A LOVED ONE'S PRESENCE

"When I was 4 years old, my brother, who was 7, told me I could be president of his bee club if I stuck my hand in a jar with a bee in it. I did it and was stung. He made fun of me for being so gullible for the rest of his life. On the day of his shiva [mourning period], my best friend found a bee in our house. We caught the bee and let it go. We laughed and said it was my brother, because—knowing my brother— he would return as a bee.

For four years after his death, a bee would appear in my house during the middle of winter, and then it would disappear. The last time the bee appeared, I forgot the bee could be my brother and tried to kill it. I cried and felt I was trying to kill him all over again. The following spring, I walked into a gift store, and there was a display of stuffed animals, which were bees. I bought a bee and have it in my house. A bee has not appeared in my house since that last winter."

Mindy—a friend and former congregant at Temple Isaiah in Stony Brook

"A cardinal landed in my tree, beautiful colors so nice to see.
The thought of a loved one brings a smile to my
face, away it flies with such grace.
Visitors from Heaven, they are said to be.
I feel blessed that you came to see me."

Etsy.com

"[My twins] were so little, sleeping in the same crib, before they could roll around, very shortly after their birth. We had a baby animal jungle-themed mobile hanging above their crib that we hadn't

turned on for them yet. It was a manual, wind-up one. In the middle of the night, I heard music. I got the strong sense that [my husband] Craig's mom (who passed away when Craig was a teenager) was with the babies. I went to the nursery and found the mobile playing its lullaby with the rotating little animals gently spinning. Craig hadn't turned it on, and neither had I. My only answer was that it was his mom Cheryl giving us a sign that she was watching over Cayla and Iris."

Raina—a friend

"My daughter was almost two years old when she died during open-heart surgery. On the evening of the day she was buried, my husband and I allowed our seven-year- old son to sleep with us in our bed. About 2 a.m., I awoke out of a sound sleep for no apparent reason. My husband and son also woke up at the same time, as did our dog, who was sleeping on the floor near us. The dog began to whimper, and my son said, 'I think Paula is here.' Both my husband and I had the same impression. A wonderful sense of calm came over me."

Nancy—a friend from Temple Isaiah

Animals

Most of the time, we don't pay attention to the animals around us—unless they are our or someone else's pets. But there are those who believe that certain animals are the carriers of messages or the symbols of spirits from our loved ones and friends who have died. Here are some examples that I have collected:

Amy and her husband Monte have written fifty books and sold three million copies in eighteen languages. Their website —*www.The EnchantedWorld.com*—states: "The Enchanted World is all about personal growth through self-discovery." For over thirty years, they have been involved in "the work of inner-exploration and self-discovery...[and] have helped millions answer questions, find deeper meaning, and follow their own spiritual paths." Amy—an author, jewelry maker, and clothing designer—identifies herself as a "luxury artist" on *www.Amyzerner.com*. I came into contact with her through a friend, and this is what she shared with me:

"A young deer practically walked into our front door yesterday! The strange thing is that I had been going through tons of family photos, and many of my mother Jessie, and so I was feeling her beautiful presence so deeply. She drew animals all the time in her artwork, and connected strongly to them, and especially deer—and we used to tease her that she actually was a deer! So, the close encounter with the deer yesterday was no accident."

Diane, a pre-school teacher and the mother of three, was married to Sam, and they were members of my synagogue in Hingham, Massachusetts. One of his hobbies was flying his private plane, and his last flight resulted in a crash that killed him. The suddenness of Sam's death shocked his family and friends.

When I officiated at the funeral at our temple, hundreds of people attended, and we had to open the sliding wall between our sanctuary and social hall so that we could accommodate 500 people. Diane later wrote a beautiful tribute to Sam, called "When Hawks Fly":

"There are two ways to think about the red-tailed hawk. The first is with your mind, absorbing the fact that describe this majestic bird that is the most common hawk in North America. Whether soaring over open fields or sitting on a telephone pole, the hawk searches for its prey, its sharp vision and high intelligence making him an able hunter, ready to swoop down and catch his next meal in his sharp, powerful claws. A closer inspection reveals a rich brown color on top of his body, broad rounded wings, a short tail streaked with a cinnamon-red on top, a hooked beak, and talon feet.

The other way to consider the hawk, however, is through a spiritual lens, a lens that asks the question, "What does it mean when a hawk comes to you?" The Internet is filled with accounts of people sharing their personal experiences. The common thread that links these reports is the belief that the hawk brings messages from the spirit world. Its presence, some believe, is a symbol of courage, intelligence, protection, healing, and, perhaps most important, the need to use the hawk's guidance to discover the purpose of one's own soul or to overcome problems in one's life.

So how do I look at the hawk? With my mind or with my heart? If you had asked me this question before March 30th, 1996, my answer would be logical—with my mind. Life changed for me and for my children on that day, the day of the accident, the day the crash of a small plane brought my husband Sam's life to an end. How could it be a coincidence that the following day a hawk appeared over my house—soaring, circling, and gliding—and he continued to fly over my home for the next two weeks? That's when I began to see the hawk with my heart, not my head, wanting to believe that Sam had found a way to let us know that his spirit was soaring.

Some months after Sam's death, in observance of the Jewish custom of visiting the graves of loved ones around the time of the High

Holidays, I drove to the cemetery. I waited by my car for my brother and mother to arrive and join me in this difficult first visit. My brother pulled his car beside mine, walked over to me, and said, 'Look up at that pole.' There, perched on a tall pole, sat a red-tailed hawk, his own gaze meeting ours, as if he was trying to connect with us, or at least that's what I wanted to believe.

My next encounter, several years later, occurred as I was taking a walk with a friend. We were in the process of planning a bike trip in Vermont, an adventure way out of my comfort zone. We were approaching my house when, directly in front of us, so close as to be within my reach, flew a hawk. 'It's an omen,' I said. 'I think that hawk is telling us to follow our dreams.' If I had any doubt, a re-peat visit from the hawk the next morning was all the confirmation I needed to take that trip.

Knowing that the hawk continues to hold a special place in my heart, I guess the next, very recent incident, should come as no sur-prise. I'm sitting in a classroom with fifteen other students, our ages ranging from teens to seniors, and we are listening to a lecture from the local animal control officer. After sharing a description of her job, and adding some personal anecdotes, the officer tells us that she has brought a special guest for us to meet. The guest remains hidden in a covered cage, one that would hold a cat or small dog. The officer pulls on a pair of long, heavy gloves, uncovers the cage, and gently coaxes our guest—a red-tailed hawk—out of the cage and onto her arm.

We learn that this hawk has been injured in an encounter with some electrical lines and can no longer live in the wild. The bird seems as fascinated by us as we are with her, and all is going along fine when, suddenly, the bird—frightened by the glare from a stu-dent's eyeglasses—pulls away and attempts to fly. That beak and those talons are looking very sharp. Within seconds, her handler has her back, under control, whispering softly to her agitated charge. When I walk out of the class at the end of the evening, I overhear two women admitting to being a little unsettled. At least I wasn't the only one ready to dive under the table!

A few days later I tell this story to Mark, a personal trainer at my gym. I've been working with Mark for several years, ever since an orthopedist described my right knee as 'bad, really bad—no cartilage, full of arthritis, bone spurs. You'll need a knee replacement in a year, maybe two. Call me when it hurts 24/7.' Since I dread the surgery, I'm working hard to delay it as long as possible, building up the muscle to compensate. Anyhow, between sets, I tell Mark about my most recent encounter with a hawk, and then, between more lifting and lowering, I share some more of my hawk stories.

Mark listens attentively, while still managing to count and to check my form and, somewhere between bicep curls and chest presses, Mark decides to share something with me: 'You've never seen what's tattooed on my right arm, under my sleeve,' he says. I know the answer before he tells me. "'t's a red-tailed hawk.' We're both quiet for a moment. I contemplate his disclosure, wondering if it means something. I'm open to the possibility of something deeper. At the very least, it's a comforting image, that of the hawk protecting and watching over, as he soars with his wings outstretched."

Lisa is what I would call a "young" widow—being in her 50's—who has developed her own podcast called *Widow Walking Forward*, and is a veritable fountain of energy, spirituality, and joy. In fact, her middle name is "Joy," and her podcast listeners are referred to as "Joysters." She is a former member of my synagogue in Stony Brook, and I officiated at her sons' Bar Mitzvah services. I knew her husband Doug better than I knew her for a while through his involvement in our Temple's Brotherhood and got acquainted with Lisa as well with her participation in our Religious School Parents Association and then as a teacher in our school. When Doug got sick and eventually was in hospice, I spent some quality time with him and Lisa. During the last few years, she has branched out and become a medium, prompted by her ongoing spiritual connection with her late husband. In one of her podcast episodes, "Do You Believe in Signs?", she talks about seeing a blue butterfly:

"'Is that you, Doug?'

I took a picture through the door. When someone died in hospice, the staff would put a plastic butterfly on the door to indicate that they had died. I started to cry after taking the picture.

'Doug—why are you visiting me today?'

'Because I'm always flying around you.'

'Are these figments of what we want to happen? Or are they signs from the Other Side? We're okay, and we want you to know that you're okay.'

There are other signs that I receive—a cardinal, significant numbers appearing, a certain distinctive and familiar smell. We need to continue to move forward."

Kendra is my stepdaughter. Her mother Donna and I were married in 2016. We had met at our temple in Stony Brook when I became the rabbi in 2002 and she was the music teacher in our Religious School. Kendra and her brother Alec were both my students through their senior year in high school. Here she writes about a love in the family for butterflies:

"Butterflies are the signs I see the most. My grandmother loved her sister, my Tanta [Yiddish for "Aunt"]. They shared a love for butterflies and especially the Monarch because of its beauty and color. They loved the field butterflies, the white and yellow ones that suck the nectar from the flowers on a warm day. There hasn't been one day that goes by that I don't see a butterfly. Living down south, I've been blessed with warm weather. I know it's going to be a good day when it's 12:34 p.m. and I see a butterfly."

Etsy.com is a website that features jewelry, clothing, gift ideas, wedding accessories, and a variety of other products usually made by individual crafters and artists. Among the art you can find an incredibly large number of cardinals that are on handmade greeting cards, the subject of a painting or drawing, and

part of a design that is meant to be inspirational. The messages that are conveyed are practically identical:

"A cardinal can be a special sign from your loved one in heaven.

If a cardinal should appear, a loved one came to bring you cheer.
A memory. A smile. A tear. A visitor from heaven's near.

Those we love don't go away, they walk beside us every day.
Unseen, unheard, but always near, so loved, so missed, so very dear.

When you believe beyond what your eyes can see ...
Signs from heaven show up to remind you love never dies.

A gentle reminder that we're never far apart.
My spirit will live on forever within your heart."

One of my friends made me aware of the website *soul-proof.com*, which is about Dr. Mark Pitstick, who has worked for almost 50 years in private practice, hospitals, mental health centers, and pastoral counseling settings. He has been involved in suicide prevention counseling and education professionally and has had "revelatory and spiritually transformative experiences" personally since the age of ten. Here is a story told to him by a patient, in which an animal appeared:

"Ted, a long-time patient of mine, passed on after suffering with lung cancer. His wife Elizabeth is a salt-of-the-earth Christian woman whom I have known for many years and trust completely. She told me about a unique shared ADC [After Death Communication] that happened after she prayed for a sign that Ted was at peace. In the first spring after Ted's burial, the family planted flowers by his grave and videotaped the scenery. As soon as they arrived at the grave site, a sparrow flew to Ted's monument and perched there, cocking its head and looking intently at the family.
Elizabeth remarked that it seemed as though the sparrow were

*trying to tell them something or that perhaps Ted's soul was commu-
nicating through the bird. Throughout their visit, the same sparrow
continued to chirp and hop on the gravestone. The family excitedly
videotaped the bird with the idea of showing it to other family members. When they played the tape at home, however, there was the
grave site, grass, trees, family members, and flowers—but no sparrow! They considered this anomaly to be a sign from Ted. This story
also corroborates reports that spirit beings are difficult to capture on
film."*[241]

Sense of Presence

When people speak of sensing the presence of a deceased
loved one or friend, it isn't done with a feeling of foreboding,
spookiness, or terror. Instead, it is expressed with love and a
feeling of comfort. Sometimes, it can be the experience of a
chill running up and down your spine when it isn't cold outside,
and you wouldn't normally feel a chill. Sometimes, it can be
described as an intuition or awareness that there is a spirit near
you—invisible but tangible. Or, it can be more literal, as Janis
Heaphy Durham wrote in her book *The Hand on the Mirror: A
True Story of Life Beyond Death:*

*"On Sunday, May 8, 2005, my reality changed. That was the day
I discovered a large handprint on the mirror of a bathroom in my
home in Sacramento, California. It was not an ordinary handprint.
Seemingly made of a soft, white, powdery substance, it showed all
the facets of the bone structure, as if it were an X-ray. Looking closer,
I could see it was the hand of a man because of the masculine shape
of the fingers and the wide base of the palm. The handprint stood
alone, the image affixed to the mirror and perfectly formed. It had
appeared out of nowhere. Literally, nowhere. The day the hand appeared was the first anniversary of the death of my husband, Max
Besler."*[242]

This is not described in a ghoulish way and, like most other similar experiences, Janis does not refer to this as a "ghost" or a "haunting." Typically, when people have unsolicited experiences such as this, they are taken by surprise, curious, amazed, intrigued, and thankful.

Cantor Jerry wrote about a comforting sense of presence:

"My father attended the first time I officiated as a student cantor at high holiday worship. Six months later, he passed away. During the next high holiday worship while I was singing Max Hellman's setting of Sh'ma Kolenu, rays of energy like lightning flowed up and down my spine. Afterwards, [I was] sitting next to [the] Rabbi [who] turned to me offering a handshake, [and] saying how beautiful it was. The handshake I recognized immediately was that of my father!"

When my cousin Esther visited Auschwitz—where her father's grandparents had been killed—she felt their presence and was inspired to write a poem on behalf of her father and aunt, the 13 great-grandchildren (including her), and the 35 great-great grandchildren:

"Rutke, your town, lies 200 km from Auschwitz.
I do not know where you returned your holy souls.

When standing in the killing room of Auschwitz,
I felt your presence, overpowering.
Tehillim [Psalms] was my only recourse.

Your greatness is so precious to us.
Please accept our packages, express to Heaven.

We will learn Torah in your memory,
` *Work on Avodas Hashem [Godly work]*
Be nicer and help another Jew.

Continue to shine your special light on us.
We will beam back Torah [learning] and Mitzvos [unselfish deeds]."

My friend Rabbi Jonathan shared this experience with me:

"My fiancée and I bought a house together in 2015 and, soon after, she bought a large and sonorous wind chime for the porch. Six months later, she was killed when a dump truck lost control and rolled over onto her car. Since then, every time I hear that wind chime, I experience Lisa speaking to me."

Kendra writes about the impact of death on her and her family, and about an extraordinary experience. While this experience does not fit into the category of the others that appear in this book because it is an example of seeking contact with the dead, I find it to be fascinating:

"My experiences began around 5 years old after the tragic death of my twin uncles. Signs showing me God, miracles and treasured moments that only few can understand. My Nanny, Poppy and my mother always had a look on their face. From as early as I can re-member, they were sad.

When I was 14, I lost my grandfather. It was one of the hardest days I've ever had. I hated seeing my mother cry, and I hated that Nanny was in denial and kept trying to wake him up. It was scary. I didn't want to see my family go through another loss. I didn't want to go through another loss. It was my Poppy—the glue that held our family together.

When I was 16, we flew to Florida. My best friend Gina came with us and brought her Ouija board. She and my brother Alec and I turned off the lights. We lit a candle at the foot of Poppy's bed. Nanny and my mother were in the kitchen and talking about the garage door. Here is the "conversation" we had with my grandfather:

Us: "Poppy… Are you here?"
P: "Yes" "ADCHAI"
Us: "GOD?"
Us: "ADONAI?"
P: "YES"
P: "Kendra, Believe in yourself."
P: "Alec Be nice to Mommy."
P: "R U Ready to go?"
Us: "Yes."
P: "Goodbye."

Mindy:

"When I was 13, my grandmother Esther told me that, if I married a non-Jew, she would haunt me from her grave. Eleven years after her death, I met Thomas Lee. We fell in love and were married.

The day before my wedding, I was getting my nails done. A very cute 6-year-old girl, who was Asian, was playing with me. After we were done playing, she asked me if I wanted to know her name. She told me her name was Esther Lee, combining my grandmother's first name with Tom's last name. The girl was so cute, smart and fun that I figured this was my grandmother's way of giving me her blessing."

Lynn is the wife of a colleague, and sent a story about a mysterious white Zinfandel:

"When my almost 102-year-old father died in 2016, our family

gathered in Marinette, Wisconsin, to bury him in our family ceme-
tery. Arriving from California, New York, Colorado and Texas, we
gathered the night before for dinner at a hotel in Green Bay, Wiscon-
sin, where none of us had previously been. Dad normally would be
seated at the head, so we left it empty, and we all filled up the 10
chairs on either side.

Dinner was spent sharing "Dad/Grandpa" stories that were fun,
funny, and poignant. After we had all finished our desserts and
coffee, I asked for the bill. Just before the server returned with the
bill, she suddenly reappeared with a glass of wine and said to all of
us, 'Who ordered the white Zinfandel?' We were startled, and I asked
everyone who was over 21, if they had, indeed, ordered the white
Zinfandel. Not one of the adults had done so, and suddenly my niece
said, 'Grandma, take the white Zinfandel.' We all gasped.

For decades, my parents had shared one glass of white Zinfandel
at restaurants, and now, here. In an unfamiliar hotel dining room,
the bartender had sent over a glass of white Zinfandel! We then real-
ized that Dad seemed to be making his presence known and felt from
the Great Beyond."

Rabbi Ken was the Dean when I was a rabbinical student at
the Hebrew Union College in Cincinnati in the mid-70's. He left
before my classmates and I were ordained, but he always had a
special place in our hearts because he was such a caring and kind
man. I received permission from him to reprint an excerpt from
an article he wrote that was published about a month before
he died from the coronavirus. He is retelling an experience that
someone had:

"Twelve years ago, I had gotten into my car after leaving Publix
(a grocery store). It was Hanukkah time, and I was depressed. My
husband, Joseph, had died the month before. An elderly man carry-
ing a large bouquet knocked on my car window. As I rolled down the
window, he thrust the bouquet into my car and said: 'To Flo from Joe-

B' (my husband's and my pet names for each other). When I looked around, the man was gone. I drove all over the parking lot looking for him, but he had vanished. Ironically, the flowers were the same as the ones in my bridal bouquet many years before. I thought it was G-d's way of saying Joseph was okay and I would be also. My three children, Benjamin, Rebecca, and Sarah, agreed."[243]

Pamela was a congregant at Temple Isaiah, and I knew both of her parents, as well as the doctor who surprised her and her friends. I officiated at her father Shelly's funeral:

"Seven years ago, for my 50th birthday, my parents wanted to give me money to go on a trip to celebrate. A year prior to that, my parents had asked me: 'Where would you like to go for your 50th?' I said: 'I don't care' because, at the time, both of them were in separate nursing homes and my father wasn't doing well. I was more concerned with their health than I was with planning a trip. My father continued to pursue and ask me: 'Where do you want to go?' Finally, I gave in and asked: 'Where is your favorite place you have traveled?' He replied with no hesitation: 'Paris, the city of love!'

Throughout my father's last 20 years, I would take him regularly to his neurologist, Dr. Mark, who my son Alex also has been seeing for over 15 years now. Eight months later, after my Dad passed away, my mother insisted that I take a trip to Paris to celebrate my 50th birthday. So, my husband, our closest friends, and I all started to plan this wonderful trip to Paris for ten days in October.

Before I knew it, we were in Paris—enjoying and celebrating our (my friend's and my) 50th birthday right in the Eiffel Tower! Having the time of our lives! In the days following, as we were touring the Arc de Triomphe, I was entering the building and Dr. Mark was coming out of the building! I couldn't believe my eyes! Instantly he said: 'Pam! What are you doing here?' And to that, I said: 'Mark! What are you doing here?' He was in Paris for a conference seminar regarding Parkinson's Disease—the same ailment that affected my father. The five of us looked at each other and, at that moment, I felt my father's presence and spirit with us as well. He was able to make my wish come true, and Fate had us all placed there at the same time.

If that isn't a sign that a loved one who has passed away stays with you or was present in that moment of time, I don't know what is. And we all felt it and experienced it together. His memory will forever be a blessing, and I will never forget the things that he did as a man and as my father. To this day, I still get reminders and signs of his presence and love. Thank you, Shelly, for always being there for me. "

Jim is a friend and was a congregant at Congregation Sha'aray Shalom in Hingham, Massachusetts. His wife Donna and their children Diana and David were friends of ours, and I conducted Donna's funeral, Jim's wedding to his second wife Linda, and Diana's wedding to Ben:

"Donna was my beloved wife of 24 years who lost her eight-year battle with cancer on July 28, 1995 (a day after my birthday because she was too much of a lady to spoil my birthday). Those who really knew her can attest to her sense of humor. At the party when our son David became a Bar Mitzvah, on the name cards she put table numbers that did not exist for some friends.

Months after she died, we were having an unveiling one Sunday morning. Our daughter Diana, David, and I went to the supermarket to get food so we could feed people after the unveiling. Our shopping cart was piled high. When we got to the register, I handed my credit card to the cashier. She ran it and said, "I'm sorry, sir, but your card has been declined." I knew I had plenty of credit left and that the bill had been paid in full. I had her run it three more times.

Finally, I asked her if I could call the credit card company, which I did. They could not understand why it had been declined. There was no problem with the card or the account. At that point, as if on cue, both kids looked at me and, as though it had been rehearsed, we looked at each other and said, 'MOM!' They then accepted the card and we had a story to tell people back at the house."

Rabbi Ron is a rabbinical school classmate and one of my best friends for almost 50 years. Here is a remembrance of his father:

"Growing up, there were times when I would follow my father around. One of the activities I found fascinating was watching him shave. I would stand at the bathroom sink and observe him take a mug of shaving cream, place a brush in it, and apply the brush of lather to his face.

He was the only one I knew who shaved that way. My older brothers used a can of shaving cream. When it was time for me to shave, they taught me to use a can of shaving cream also.

After my father died, for a reason I cannot explain, I was drawn to purchase a shaving mug and brush. I have been shaving that way for many years, and rarely shave using shaving cream from a can. I feel a closeness to my father and often think of him when I am shaving."

Rabbi Adam is my predecessor at Temple Isaiah in Stony Brook and Rabbi Emeritus. The first experience is more common than you might imagine, and the second may sound familiar:

"After my mother died, I saw a woman from the back who looked like my mother. She was driving and, while I knew that she could not be my mother, I followed her all the way to Smithtown to be sure.

Eileen and I sometimes see people who look very much like my dear friend Bob, although I know it could not be him. When I make coffee, I often think about Bob because he used to tease me about not being able to fold a filter properly. There are other times when similar things happen.

I also think that we all carry around our parents with us because they make such an impression on our lives from what we think, to how we feel, to how we react to situations, to how we do things."

Carol is a friend, therapist, and the wife of a colleague. She writes about how the ability to sense the presence of a deceased family member can be multi-generational:

"My parents remodeled the house to add on a dining room in the back of the house. It was very cool—round, with planters outside the ceiling-high windows, and a window seat inside with velvet cushions. It even had an indoor barbecue! We had an open house. The party went on for a while, and at some point, the adults were having coffee and I went to stand next to my mom, who was sitting on one side of the maple dining room table. Her cousin Marilyn was sitting opposite her.

All of a sudden, my mom looked at Marilyn, who was looking over my mom's head, and her mouth dropped open. She became quite pale. My mom turned around to look, and what they both told me they saw was my grandmother standing behind my mom, with her hands on my mom's shoulders, smiling at everyone! I was about 12 at this time and was a bit freaked out, but not surprised, having grown up with all these other stories. They said she was there for about five minutes before they couldn't see her anymore. I didn't see or sense her there. I was happy for mom, though. She felt so happy her mom was there! So was Marilyn.

One of my daughters had felt my grandfather's presence more than once. In all the years since he died, that only happened for me once at Kol Nidre—which is really funny—as he hated formal Judaism! I sensed him standing next to me. My mom died at 95. I sense my mom often, particularly when I look at my kids, or sometimes when I catch on my own face an expression that I know is hers.

I was talking with my middle daughter yesterday about this stuff, and she mentioned that she thinks her daughter may have some of it as well. Even as an infant, she would be feeding her in the middle of the night, and she would be staring at something 'over my shoulder that I couldn't see.' She seemed to be looking, not just staring, at something, according to my daughter. My granddaughter has always been extremely sensitive to other's feelings and emotions in movies, books, etc. At times, my daughter has reported being sensitive to specific places, which brings her comfort or dismay that she cannot explain. So, we call it 'gypsy' in our family—that something unexplainable that we seem to have that others don't understand, that makes us more aware of our surroundings, people, etc. We just kind of go with it when it happens!"

Winnie attended one of my Zoom presentations:

"I had a pleasant feeling when my first daughter was born. We were naming her after my Grandmother Goldie. A slightly older nurse came in my room and smelled like my grandmother who always wore "Evening in Paris" cologne. She said she grew up on a farm and took care of me. In those days (1962), we stayed in the hospital at least 5 to 7 days, but this nurse only came in that one time. I felt she came to check on the baby my grandmother was named after."

Jill Sandra is a former congregant at my synagogue in Stony Brook who has had a few experiences:

"My late mother-in-law's name was Sasha. When my father-in-law went to make funeral arrangements, he was told to provide an outfit for her body in the casket. He was standing outside and, out of nowhere, a balloon floated over to him and landed on him. It was the exact color that he was thinking about, and so she was dressed in that color. He also would have the scent of her perfume around him often following her death.

At some time after her death, I went shopping with a friend at a mall that I had never been to before and haven't been to since. We walked into one of the entrances, and the first store I saw was called 'Sasha.'

I had surgery after her death and couldn't sleep that night. While I was up all night, I received messages that I should call my father-in-law. The messages were from his wife, and she screamed them three times.

The owner of my cleaning service died. A number of months later, my husband and I went to a bagel store. We were standing in line and I heard a voice that sounded exactly like the owner of the cleaners. I turned around—and the man I saw looked like his twin! I asked him if he was related to my cleaner, and he said 'no.' My husband Jeff asked if we could take a picture of him, and he allowed us to do it. The next day, the cleaning crew came to my house and the deceased owner's daughter came with them, took a look at the picture, and said that it was her father. This occurred a year to the day that his death had been posted on Facebook.

I had a friend named Mary in kindergarten and first grade. We used to make fun of the boys who liked to eat paste. I switched to a different school in second grade, and Mary eventually died from cancer before her seventh-grade year. When I became a professional, I was working with a teacher's aide by the name of Kathy, who was a number of years older than me. I knew her for years, and we had one particular conversation and found out that we had been in the same school district as children. She told me that her sister Mary had died before she could start seventh grade.

When I shared with her that her sister was my friend for a couple of years, she said: 'Mary sent you to me.' She also said that her mother was still having a hard time dealing with Mary's death and that her other sister was not helping. I told her that the seventh-grade yearbook had been dedicated to Mary's memory, and she said that the family wasn't aware of it. I took the yearbook to her mother, and she loved it! The name on the cover was my homeroom teacher's name—and it was the same as Kathy and Mary's mother's maiden name."

Maureen W. is the sister of one of my friends and shared this multi-generational story:

"In October 2016, my daughter Tracey, her husband Marc and their then-four-year-old daughter Marissa were in a horrible car accident two blocks from their home in L.A. A woman was texting while driving and plowed into their SUV, spinning them around and flipping their car over. Miraculously, they all survived without severe injuries. The story lies in the circumstances surrounding the accident. The accident occurred on Overland Avenue, right in front of Congregation Adat Shalom, which my Grandfather Benjamin had founded 70 years ago in his living room. He helped to build the shul [synagogue] and, years later, my aunt and uncle became leaders of the congregation. A mile west of the synagogue is the house where my grandparents lived. A mile south of that location is the building where my Grandmother Annie resided before she passed away. And that day was Grandma's yahrzeit. I know she was watching over my dear children."

You may have questions after reading this chapter, such as:

- Are these people reliable? Yes. Are their accounts true? Yes.
- Are they examples of wishful thinking? No.
- Are they just trying to get attention? Not at all.
- Could the reason for these experiences just be coincidence? Possibly, but I strongly doubt it.

And here's my question for you:

Is it conceivable that the "signs" people receive from their deceased loved ones are neither fake nor coincidence, but are experiences made possible by God?

And here's my answer to you:
I believe they are.

CHAPTER 11: "HERE COMES THAT DREAMER!"

"Sometime in the early 1960's, your mother and I had a falling-out and did not speak for several months. I cannot remember the exact reason, but I think it might have been when Temple Beth El did not renew the rabbi's contract, and your parents left Beth El and joined B'nai Jehudah. We stayed at Beth El.

After a while, I had a very vivid dream in which our grandmother came to me and said that this ill will was very disturbing to her. The next day, I called your mother, and we resumed our close connection."

Eileen—my cousin

"The more my mother aged, the more she measured life by mortality. During her final years in Pittsburgh, she and my wife Alice sometimes talked about death drawing near and the question of whether there is such a thing as life after death. My mother often ended these conversations with, 'If there is, Alice, I'll come back and let you know.' When she died, we then traveled to the New Jersey cemetery to bury my mother next to my father, and near her parents. On the drive back to Pittsburgh, Alice fell asleep. She then suddenly awakened, crying. Through the tears, Alice said, 'Your mother just spoke to me. She said, "We did a good job together in Pittsburgh."'"

Rabbi Mark—a colleague

"Rav Ḥisda said: A dream not interpreted is like a letter not read."[244]

"All dreams follow the mouth of the interpreter."[245]

"Sleep is one-sixtieth of death; and a dream is one-sixtieth of

prophecy."[246]

If you are familiar with the Bible, it's likely that your first word-association answer with someone in the Bible as a dreamer would be Joseph. After all, it is his dreams about his parents and brothers bowing down to him—and his adolescent behavior of telling the dreams in great detail to all of them—that get him into trouble with his brothers in Chapter 37 of Genesis. In fact, when they see him coming to check up on them, they say: "Here comes that dreamer!"[247] Yet, it is his interpretation of the dreams of the baker and cupbearer while in prison in Egypt, described in Genesis 40, that eventually leads to his being summoned to interpret the dreams of the Pharaoh. In Genesis 41, it takes two years for the cupbearer to remember him, but Joseph is brought out of jail, has his hair cut, changes his clothes, and listens to the recounting of the dreams. Giving credit to God for his ability to ascertain their meaning, the formerly obnoxious teenager predicts that Egypt will have seven years of plenty followed by seven years of famine. He proposes that a reserve of grain be collected and stored during the first seven years so that the people of Egypt can survive during the second seven years. He also recommends that the Pharaoh "find a man of discernment and wisdom and set him over the land of Egypt."[248]

What does Joseph get out of this? A job as second only to Pharaoh, the king's signet ring, fine linen robes, a gold chain, a chariot at his disposal, a tremendous amount of power, an Egyptian name, a wife who is the daughter of an Egyptian priest, and the ability to travel all over the land of Egypt. Clearly, the importance of dreams is emphasized in this story. Although Joseph is not the one dreaming, and although it doesn't involve communication from a deceased person's spirit, the content of the dreams is predictive of what will become reality.

But Joseph is neither the first nor the last to have experiences with dreams in the Hebrew Bible—as evidenced in the following excerpts. Please note that God initiates the dream in the first three instances below. Then, God makes it clear that dreams are not the most direct means of contact in the hierarchy of communication. Following that, a dream is overheard, and its content comes true, and God initiates again and rewards Solomon. The Book of Daniel (from which the three quotations are taken) is similar to the story of Joseph, in that a Jew's ability to interpret dreams enables him to become second only to the king in a story that takes place in the Diaspora. And then, I cite examples from the Torah, the Prophets, and the Writings that are not so favorable about dreams. Mainly, that is because those dreams are not from God, or approved by God. It seems to me, then, that our judgments about the validity of a dream depend on what or who we believe is the "instigator" or source of the dream, as well as who is doing the interpretation.

Torah:

- Genesis 20: God comes to King Abimelech of Gerar in a dream and warns him not to touch Sarah or else he will die.
- Genesis 31: Jacob has a dream in which he is told by God to leave his uncle Laban and return home with his wives and children.
- Genesis 31: God appears to Laban in a dream and tells him not to harm Jacob.
- Numbers 12: After Miriam and Aaron criticize Moses, God emphasizes that divine communication with Moses is face-to-face and not in a dream.
- Deuteronomy 13: A warning is given against listening to a "dream-diviner" instead of God.

Prophets:

- Judges 7: Gideon hears a man describing a dream he had, and another man responds that it means that Gideon and the Israelites will defeat the Midianites.
- First Kings 3: God appears to Solomon in a dream and asks what he wants from God. He requests the ability to judge his

subjects in a positive way, and God grants him that <u>and</u> what he didn't ask for—riches, glory, and a long life (if Solomon will observe God's laws and commandments).

- Jeremiah 27: Pay no heed to [pagan] prophets, augurs, dreamers, diviners, and sorcerers because they are false prophets.
- Zechariah 10: Augurs give false predictions; dreamers are liars and provide consolation with illusions.

Writings:

- Daniel 2: King Nebuchadnezzar of Babylon has a dream that makes him anxious, and no one feels capable of offering an interpretation—which causes the king to get angry and order his wise men to be executed.
- Daniel 2: Daniel not only relates to the king what occurred in his dream but also interprets it for him.
- Daniel 7: Daniel has a dream and a vision in which he sees four beasts representing four kingdoms in an apocalyptic future, which will end with God's people becoming "an everlasting kingdom."[249]
- Ecclesiastes 5: "Just as dreams come with much brooding, so does foolish utterance come with much speech."[250]
- Ecclesiastes 5: "For much dreaming leads to futility and superfluous talk." ("The reference to 'dreams' may stand as a negative image for anything ephemeral and unstable…Alternately, the reference may be to the widespread Near Eastern, including biblical, appeal to dreams as a form of divine communication, here warning against undue reliance on them because they could be vague and misleading.")[251]

With this biblical analysis in mind, and with a sense that dreams can be important in Jewish tradition, I want to share with you some examples of dreams that I received. These descriptions of dreams were sent to me by two rabbinic colleagues, the wife of a colleague, a congregant/friend, and my wife's friend. They are, in my opinion, incredible!

Rabbi Irwin—a friend:

"My mother Cecilia lay on her death bed. Gathered around were numerous family members and friends. She carefully (as was her way) apportioned this and that, assembled commitments for the future, and bravely faced her end.

She looked at us all: 'Everything is in order. I know all will be OK. My sister (an elderly childless woman, whom Mom cared for) will be OK, Sam (my father who required aid) is planned for. Just one thing is left—who will take care of Tzimmie, my dog?' I volunteered, but she knew my own beast of a dog would tolerate no intrusion into our house. She responded with an unsatisfied 'Hmph!'

Three weeks later, she passed around 3 a.m., my wife Marta at her side. Marta informed me, and that morning I stopped at my study to prepare for the short trip from Buffalo to Erie. Our cousin Ilene stopped by and, before I could share our sad news, she excitedly regaled me concerning a strange dream she had the night before:
'I dreamed of your Mom last night—real as real could be. She asked me to take care of her dog! It was so startling to me that I woke up.'
'And what did you tell her in your dream?' I asked.
'I said "of course"!'
'Did you happen to notice the time?'
'Yes, it was 3:15!'
My careful mother took care of the last loose end herself, seeing no one capable.
And Ilene indeed took care of Tzimmie the rest of her doggie life."

Rabbi Mark—Cemetery Meditation:

"Over the years, I've always considered this cemetery service meditation the first of my High Holy Day sermons. After the Holy Days, when I compile and publish the anthology of my sermons, this meditation is always the prelude. This, then, is the first of my last

High Holy Day sermons. As such, it would be special enough, but the night before I sat down to write this meditation, I dreamed about my sister Gail.

In my dream, I was standing with a handful of other people in a parking garage with enough room for only a few more cars. One car entered carefully between a parked car and a steel post. Another car then did the same. Both cars were compact cars; still they navigated the tight spaces carefully. My sister Gail then pulled in, driving a bronze-colored Cadillac, vintage 1975 and big as a boat. We called out to Gail, "Don't pull in, the car won't fit," but Gail ignored our warning. Between the post on the left and the car to the right, she dented both sides of her Cadillac, and the other car to boot.

The scene then changed. I was now in the car with Gail, and we were driving along a verdant country road. Gail gave me a warm "hello." I wanted to respond with a kiss on her cheek, but I was afraid that it might distract her from driving, on top of which she had just banged up the car, so I took her hand and kissed it.

Clearly, the dream's first scene in the parking garage expressed some of life's basic experiences: finding your comfortable place, navigating narrow straits, giving good advice, ignoring good advice, and then dealing with the damage. But the dream's second scene with my sister driving us down a country road is best understood in light of the fact that my sister died in 2004.

Surely you, too, have dreamed about loved ones who died. And surely, you'll agree with me that, in the totality of life's experiences, there is nothing like a dream about a loved one who has died. At that indescribable place between heartache and comfort, that unique place between emotional hollowness and emotional fulfillment, and always, always mysterious, there is nothing like a dream about a loved one who has died.

Thus, this dream, especially the second scene, proves so appropriate for this morning, this service, this time, and this place.

My sister was taking me on life's ultimate journey. The car may have been dented and damaged, but it was still drivable. The journey also is ultimately inevitable. Life's bumps and bruises, the dents and damage all quicken the journey; my sister died at sixty-one.

The best advice, indeed, the only advice, is to accept this because it cannot be ignored. Yes, my sister and I were happy to be with one another, but it was also important to me that she focus on the road ahead and keep us both safe. My kiss on her hand affirmed my love. Finally, we traveled gently downhill on a road bordered by green grass and trees.

This morning, I will liken it to the hill that rolls gently down behind me and in front of you, the hill where one, or some, or many of our loved ones are buried, the hill where one day some, or many, of you will be buried, and where one day I, too, will be buried. As for the distinctive color of the Cadillac, bronze coffins are a popular choice for many people today, although my sister was buried in a traditional wood coffin. So, too, will I.

What should we think of all this? How should we feel?

In the second century Midrashic collection of Pirkei D'Rebbe Eliezer, Rabbi Zechariah taught, "Sleep at night is like this world, and the awakening in the morning is like the World to Come." The World to Come is God's reign of peace on earth, heaven on earth. This cemetery and every cemetery might be called heaven <u>in</u> earth. And what of our dreams about our loved ones who have died? They are heaven in us."

Carol:

"In 1959 my Nana died from a brain tumor. She was only 59 years old, and the family was distraught. She had come through the surgery but died of a heart attack when still in the hospital. My mom never really got over her death, nor did my grandfather.

In 1960 my family moved into a new home in the Westchester area of L.A., and it was very hard on my mom. My mom's older sister and her family lived across the street. Often, my grandfather would just go over to my aunt's home. I think my mom began to suffer from anxiety about this time. She had developed a condition she called 'lockjaw' and could only open her mouth a little bit. I was 9 years old and would come home from school and sit with her, while she curled up on the couch with our little dachshund, Mitzi.

I think that is the beginning of my learning to become a therapist, as mom would tell me stories about her family and childhood, and I would listen. She was a wonderful storyteller! One day, she was lying on the couch and told me she dreamed of her mom cupping her cheek —the side that hurt her—and said that her mom told her it wouldn't hurt her anymore. She could feel her mom's hand on her cheek. The pain stopped and never returned.

When I was 18, my mom and I were talking one morning in December, and she was telling me she had been having dreams of her parents walking towards each other for several nights. My grandfather had remarried several years earlier, and no one really liked Rose very much, but she kept Grandpa company, so that was okay. But she did talk about her kids <u>all</u> the time, which really bothered my mom and her siblings! Anyway, that morning Mom told me that the dream had changed, and that her parents were walking and holding hands. A minute later the phone rang, and it was Rose, my grandpa's wife, telling us that he had died. He had no health issues, and so there was no reason that they could point to other than that he was 78 years old. It is the way we all want to go—peacefully, in our sleep. I have never forgotten my mom's dreams that week, though. She told me about them every morning!

Mom would tell me that she dreamed that dad was coming to pick her up, that he was downstairs in the car. She saw my cousin and her mom, my aunt, both of whom had died, and related whole conversations she had had with them. Sometimes I was there, and she would ask me if I saw them. She was disturbed that I didn't. She did not have dementia. It is not uncommon for people who are in the midst of a UTI to hallucinate—and that did happen—but those visions go away when the infection passes. Some of these did not. She would tell me of conversations with my dad, which became more common as she came closer to dying. "

Ilene—a friend and congregant in Stony Brook:

"My father and I were very close, he loved me unconditionally, and his loss was a tremendous sorrow for me. I often dreamt that he and my mom would be coming through our front door in Setauket, and each dream portrayed my same feeling of 'oh Daddy, you're here!', apparently wishful thinking and lack of acceptance of his no longer being with us. One night, however, I dreamt that he and my mother were arriving, and I asked, 'Daddy, what are you doing here?' It was so clear to me when I awoke and remembered the dream that I had finally accepted that he was gone!"

Christine—a friend of my wife:

Months before I met Gary, I had a very vivid dream that someone kissed me on my cheek. The feeling was so real that it woke me up. I remember sitting up in bed and looking toward the bedroom door. The early morning light was pouring into the doorway, and standing there were two people. One looked like a very old man, and he was standing with a young woman with long dark hair, and they were both bathed in white light. The man had his arm around the young woman's shoulder, and he was pointing towards me. She was looking straight at me and nodded.

I had the strangest feeling, because I was confused by this, but not frightened at all. I just put my head back on my pillow and went back to sleep. On my way to my teaching job that morning, I kept thinking about the feeling of that kiss on my cheek, because I could still feel it. And it occurred to me that a woman kissed me, and it was that woman in my dream.

Months later, I met Gary on a blind date. I was a teacher in his son's school and actually taught his art, music, and PE classes. I knew that Gary had lost his wife to cancer and found himself a single dad with two small boys. I think by the second date we both knew this relationship was going to work. One day, he invited me to his house for dinner. As I walked around the living room, I noticed photos of the boys on the bookcase. I took a closer look and, there in the photo, was the young woman with the long dark hair I had seen in my dream months ago. I knew right then and there that she was the one who kissed me on the cheek.

We were married in 1981, and I never told Gary about my dream. Then one day, years later, we were talking about all the heartbreaking confrontations we were getting from his former mother-in-law, and Gary didn't understand why we were getting this reaction, and then he said, "I think if Karen could have hand-picked someone for me and the boys, I know she would have picked you out." And my response was, "I think she did."

We were married for 37 years.

We aren't the only ones who are interested in dreams and their meaning. It is a major subject in the Talmud, specifically in *Masekhet Berakhot* 55a, 55b, 56a, 56b, and 57b. Various rabbis are cited, and the *Gemara* quoted is the discussion of the points made by the rabbis.

Prayers and Dreams

Dreams can be the subject of prayers and, in the first case, should be. And, of course, we would pray for good dreams and that they would be fulfilled—unless you are Rav Ḥisda. In the second case, it is apparent that dreams were important enough to be inserted in a crucial part of the service when those of priestly descent bless the congregation:

"Rav Yehuda said in the name of Rav: 'Three matters require a plea for mercy to bring them about: A good king, a good year, and a good dream. These three, kings, years, and dreams, are all bestowed by God and one must pray that they should be positive and constructive.'"

Related to what was stated above, that one should pray for a good dream, the Gemara cites additional maxims concerning dreams and their interpretation. Rav Ḥisda said: 'One should see any dream, and not a fast.' In other words, any dream is preferable to a dream during a fast. And Rav Ḥisda said: 'A dream not interpreted is like a letter not read.' As long as it is not interpreted it cannot be fulfilled; the interpretation of a dream creates its meaning. And Rav Ḥisda said: 'A good dream is not entirely fulfilled, and a bad dream is not entirely fulfilled.' And Rav Ḥisda said: 'A bad dream is preferable to a good dream, as a bad dream causes one to feel remorse and to repent.' And Rav Ḥisda said: 'A bad dream, his sadness is enough for him; a good dream, his joy is enough for him.' This means that the sadness or joy engendered by the dream renders the actual fulfillment of the dream superfluous."[252]

"The Gemara relates: 'Ameimar and Mar Zutra and Rav Ashi were sitting together. They said: "Let each and every one of us say something that the other has not heard." One of them began and said: "One who saw a dream and does not know what he saw should stand before the priests when they lift their hands during the Priestly Blessing and say the following:

'Master of the Universe, I am Yours and my dreams are Yours, I dreamed a dream and I do not know what it is. Whether I have dreamed of myself, whether my friends have dreamed of me or whether I have dreamed of others, if the dreams are good, strengthen them and reinforce them like the dreams of Joseph. And if the dreams require healing, heal them like the bitter waters of Mara by Moses our teacher, and like Miriam from her leprosy, and like Hezekiah from his illness, and like the bitter waters of Jericho by Elisha. And just as You transformed the curse of Balaam the wicked into a blessing, so, transform all of my dreams for me for the best.'

And he should complete his prayer together with the priests, so the congregation responds 'amen' both to the blessing of the priests and to his individual request. And if he is not able to recite this entire formula, he should say: 'Majestic One on high, Who dwells in power, You are peace, and Your name is peace. May it be Your will that You bestow upon us peace.'"[253]

Good Dreams and Good People, Bad Dreams and Wicked People

Rav Huna has a rather interesting spin on good dreams and good people, and bad dreams and wicked people. A *"baraita"* is a teaching that comes from outside of the written Jewish tradition in the *Mishnah,* which is part of the Talmud. [As I said before, *Mishnah + Gemara = Talmud].* And Ahitophel was one of David's counselors who left him in order to support the revolt of David's son Absalom. Huna's opinion seems strange to me, and I don't agree with his point of view:

"Rav Huna said: 'A good person is not shown a good dream and a wicked person is not shown a bad dream; rather, a good person is punished for his relatively few transgressions with bad dreams and a wicked person is rewarded for his relatively few merits with good dreams.' That was also taught in a baraita: 'All of King David's life he never saw a good dream, and all of Ahitophel's life he never saw a bad dream.'"[254]

Can You Turn a Bad Dream Into a Good One?

Wouldn't we all like to be able to do that? Bad dreams can literally haunt us and affect the way we think and feel—not just after we wake up from them, but for days or weeks, or even months or years. Three is a significant number of people. A *bet din* (rabbinic court) consists of three rabbis, and they can make a decision about a religious legal matter—such as a divorce or a conversion. I have participated in a number of *bet din* panels throughout my career. In this one, the three advocate for the person with the distraught soul:

"Rav Huna bar Ami said that Rabbi Pedat said that Rabbi Yoḥanan said: 'One who sees a dream from which his soul is distraught, should go and have it interpreted before three.' The Gemara is surprised by this: 'Interpreted? **Didn't Rav Ḥisda say: "A dream not interpreted is like a letter not read?"** [Emphasis added] If one is concerned about a dream, why would he actively promote its fulfillment? Rather, say as follows: "He should better bring it before three." He should bring three people and say to them: 'I saw a good dream.' And they should say to him: 'It is good, and let it be good, may God make it good. May they decree upon you from heaven seven times that it will be good, and it will be good.' Afterwards they recite three verses of transformation from bad to good, three verses of redemption, and three verses which mention peace.'"[255]

No Lack of Dream Interpreters

Notice in this excerpt the chain of tradition that extends through six rabbis. To have twenty-four interpreters seems like an excessive and unreal amount, but the point is well-taken— you can have the same dream and many, many interpretations of it. When they are conflicting, the dreamer has the choice to decide which is the most reasonable or favorable. This can also be applied to contemporary dreams that involve communication from a deceased relative or friend. The same memories of it described by the dreamer can be interpreted in different ways:

"In a long chain of those transmitting this statement, it is said that Rabbi Bizna bar Zavda said that Rabbi Akiva said that Rabbi Panda said that Rav Naḥum said that Rabbi Birayim said in the name of one elder, and who is he, Rabbi Bena'a: 'There were twenty-four interpreters of dreams in Jerusalem. One time, I dreamed a dream and went to each of them to interpret it. What one interpreted for me the other did not interpret for me, and, nevertheless, all of the interpretations were realized in me, to fulfill that which is stated: **All dreams follow the mouth of the interpreter.**'" [Emphasis added][256]

When I began my research, I never expected to find a story like the next one. You can view it as a criticism of dream interpreters in general or of Bar Haddaya in particular. I am surprised that an interpretation of a dream could be influenced by money:

"The Gemara relates: Bar Haddaya was an interpreter of dreams. **For one who gave him a fee, he would interpret the dream favorably, and for one who did not give him a fee, he would interpret the dream unfavorably.** [Emphasis added]

The Gemara relates: There was an incident in which both Abaye and Rava saw an identical dream and they asked bar Haddaya to interpret it. Abaye gave him money and paid his fee, while Rava did not give him money. They said to him: The verse: 'Your ox shall be slain before your eyes and you shall not eat thereof' (Deuteronomy 28:31) was read to us in our dream.

He interpreted their dream and to Rava he said: 'Your business will be lost, and you will derive no pleasure from eating because of the extreme sadness of your heart.' To Abaye he said: 'Your business will profit, and you will be unable to eat due to the joy in your heart.'" [257]

The Symbolism of Parts of the Body

"The Gemara relates a story with regard to a Sage who interpreted dreams, Rabbi Yishmael. Ben Dama, son of Rabbi Yishmael's sister, asked his uncle, Rabbi Yishmael: 'I saw in a dream that **my two cheeks fell off**. [Emphasis added] What does my dream mean?' Rabbi Yishmael said to him: 'Two Roman battalions spoke ill of you, and they died. Cheeks symbolize a mouth that speaks evil.'" [258]

"Similarly, the Gemara relates: Bar Kappara said to Rabbi Yehuda HaNasi: 'I saw in a dream that **my nose fell off,** [Emphasis added] what is the meaning of my dream?' He said to him: 'This is an allusion that anger...that had been directed against you has been removed from you.' Bar Kappara said to him: 'I saw in a dream that **my two hands were cut off.**' [Emphasis added] Rabbi said to him: 'This dream means that you will not require the labor of your hands, as you will be rich, and you will have considerable means without effort.' Bar Kappara said to him: 'I saw **my two legs were cut off.**' [Emphasis added] Rabbi Yehuda HaNasi said: 'You are riding a horse.' He said to him: 'I saw that they were saying to me that in the month of Adar I will die, and I will not see Nisan.' He said to him: 'You will die in glory...and you will not be brought to temptation...'"[259]

Giving Meaning to Dreams

By now, it should be clear that the Rabbis attributed significance to dreams and were not the least bit shy about offering interpretations of what they meant. There is no indication so far that these dreams were conjured up by demons, soothsayers, witches, or pagan priests. Somehow, some way, they seem to have a connection to God. There are in *Berakhot 56b* many examples of and stories about dreams, and they have meaning for the various Rabbis of the Talmud. Rather than reprinting every one of them in full, with texts that support the interpretations given, here is a list of what the dreams are about and what they mean—according to various Rabbis. With each of them, the Talmud says the person who has the dream should "rise early and recite" an appropriate verse from the *Tanakh*:

Ambiguous Interpretations:

- Grapes: sweetness or bitterness
- Mountains: good tidings or weeping and wailing
- A Shofar: ingathering of the exiles or a call to war
- A Dog: no insulting of Israel or greed
- A Lion: fearsomeness or destruction
- Getting a shave: greatness or weakness
- An Ox: sacrificing to God or goring a man

Straightforward Interpretations:

- A Well: peace, Torah, actual life
- A River, a bird, a pot: peace
- A Reed: wisdom;   Several Reeds: understanding
- A Pumpkin, Heart of Palm, Wax, A Reed: reverence for God
- King David: piety; King Solomon: wisdom; King Ahab: calamity
- Book of Kings: greatness/royalty; Book of Ezekiel: wisdom; Book of Isaiah: consolation; Book of Jeremiah: calamity
- Rabbi Yehuda HaNasi: wisdom; Rabbi Elazar ben Azarya: wealth; Rabbi Yishmael ben Elisha: calamity
- Torah scholars who, despite their greatness, were never given the title "Rabbi": Ben Azzai: piety; Ben Zoma: wisdom; Akher (Elisha ben Avuya): calamity

Two Peculiar Interpretations (Provided In Full):

"The Gemara says: '**All types of animals are auspicious signs**

for a dream except for an elephant, a monkey and a long-tailed ape.' [Emphasis added] The Gemara asks: 'Didn't the Master say: "A miracle will be performed for one who sees an elephant in a dream?" The Gemara answers: 'This is not difficult. This statement that a vision of an elephant is a good omen refers to a case where it is saddled, while this statement that it is not a good omen refers to a case where it is not saddled.'"[260]

"With regard to dreams, the Sages taught: **'One who dreams that he sees a corpse** [Emphasis added] in his house, it is a sign of peace in his house. If the corpse ate and drank in the house, it is a good omen for the house. If the corpse removed vessels from the house, it is a bad omen for the house, as it suggests that the corpse is taking someone from the house with him. Rav Pappa explained this only if the dream was with regard to a shoe and a sandal, as that indicates that someone from the house is going to embark on a long journey. As the Sages said: "Everything that a corpse takes in a dream is a good omen except a shoe and a sandal; everything that a corpse gives in a dream is a good omen except dust and mustard, which looks like dust, as they portend burial.'"''[261]

In modern-day interpretations of signs in dreams, animals play a prominent role. Deer, butterflies, dragonflies, and cardinals seem to be the ones most often mentioned. The final quotation about a corpse—eating and drinking, removing vessels, and being linked to a shoe and a sandal—is about as supernatural as you can get. While most people I know don't see "corpses" in dreams, they do relate seeing a much less scary and often peaceful image of someone who has died.

CHAPTER 12: SIGNS FROM OBJECTS, SHAPES, AND PHOTOS

"With You is the fountain of life, by Your light do we see light."[262]

"Many may see it and stand in awe, and trust in the Eternal."[263]

"When death stalks our homes, it brings an end to physical life. The current is cut off. That is all. But the spirit is mightier than the grave. The thoughts and emotions, the ideals and attitudes of the heirs attest to the undying influence of the dead."[264]

Signs that come to people are most often unsolicited and unexpected. Long-lost objects appear out of nowhere, so to speak. Those who are receptive to the possibility of signs regard this phenomenon as a miracle of sorts, as something that was thought to be impossible but is actually occurring, and as a confirmation of their faith in God or the Other Side—rather than being mere coincidence or pure luck. Most of the shapes that recur in stories about signs are hearts. The recipients of these signs regard them as indicative of a love that breaches the wall between life and death. It is this kind of love that I believe is stronger than death, and I speak of it at every funeral I conduct and in every conversation I have with a mourner. The photos could be explained away by skeptics as "trick photography" or as flaws in the camera itself. But those explanations are usually countered by the people who experienced a photo being taken and then see something in the photo that wasn't there at the time. Mostly, it's a light or an orb. Why would such an image appear in a photo of a scene in which it was not obvious to the people standing or sitting right there? I believe that our senses do not always detect and recognize everything around us, and that our being unable to see them does not mean that they don't exist. The experiences conveyed in this chapter relate to what people see without having anticipated that they would see it.

Objects

Maureen L. was one of my Zoom students:

"The Necklace"

"My parents had bought me a beautiful gold Jewish Star necklace in Brazil when I was 12. I wore it day and night and always thought it was my good luck charm.

About 20 years ago, I often slept in my young son's room to comfort him when he could not sleep—until I was divorced later that year. I woke up one morning, and the chain had broken, and the star was gone. I searched for it for years.

After 35 years apart, I reconnected with an old friend, and in September of 2010 he came to Milwaukee to visit. I had new carpet installed the day he was coming, and as I left home that morning, the installer handed me the missing gold star—saying he thought it would be important to me and was something religious, and that he had found it in a baseboard in my son's room. Instead of putting it in my purse, I put it in a small bag in a small purple plastic container that was on a shelf in the garage before getting in my car to go to work. I searched for that star for nine years, going through everything in the garage and in my house. I assumed that the carpenter might have seen me put it in the container and taken it and was really angry at myself.

In May of 2019, I had a routine mammogram in Milwaukee, the day before I was flying back to our London home. On the way to O'Hare Airport, I got a call that I needed a follow-up mammogram. I returned to Milwaukee two weeks later and had multiple tests. In mid-June, while at a restaurant for lunch, I received a confirmation that I had breast cancer. Within an hour of that phone call, I returned home and noticed a purple plastic container on the dresser in my bedroom. It was not there when I had left for lunch. I opened the container, and inside was a zippered pouch with the missing Jewish star from Brazil inside.

I am convinced that my father, Mort, and perhaps a very close friend, Rosie, who had died of cancer a few years earlier, placed it there to tell me that I would be all right. I put the star on a chain and began to wear it daily, and recently had a jeweler create a special chain of gold, silver, and diamonds where the star is part of the necklace, and it can never come off. I wore the star to my surgery and through radiation treatments, and have, thank G-d, had a full recovery and am cancer-free! The necklace will always be on my neck and will hopefully become a family heirloom."

Maureen W.:

"The Candle"

"When my mother-in-law Frances passed away, both of our daughters were living away from home. They decided to stagger their visits during shiva so we would have one of them home with us throughout the week. Stephanie, our oldest, came home from Washington for the first four days. Her sister Tracey flew in from Los Angeles for the last part of the week and remained with us for an extra day. Through all this time, the tall shiva candle burned brightly.

On the eighth day after the funeral, Tracey flew back to California. Her coast-to-coast journey lasted nearly twelve hours. Still, the candle continued to burn. Finally, we received her call, telling us that she had arrived home safely. Minutes later, the shiva candle's flame went out. Her grandma wouldn't leave us until she knew that everyone was safely at home.

In June, on my mother Rosalyn's third yahrzeit, I lit a memorial candle at sunset and prayed for her, as I always do. I fully expected the light to burn out the following evening, but it continued to blaze on my kitchen counter all night long.

The next morning, when I went into the kitchen, the candle was still lit. I ate breakfast, I did some household tasks, I made some phone calls... and the light continued to glow. I went over to the candle and talked to my mother. I had an intense feeling that there was something that she wanted me to do.

I have been estranged from one of my brothers since my mother's passing, and I have always known that she would want us to reconcile. I had reached out to him previously, to no avail. But I told her I would try again. I brought my laptop to the kitchen and composed a letter to my brother, saying what I felt in my heart, offering an apology, and telling him about our mother's yahrzeit candle. I completed the letter and pressed "send." Moments later, Mom's flame finally extinguished. The 24-hour candle had burned for 37 hours."

Christine:

"The Stone"

"While I was going through the aftermath of the loss of both my husband and my mom, the stress was beginning to affect me. I was trying to deal with all the paperwork that comes with the end of a person's life. And not only was I trying to get my life in order, but I was also managing my mom's final wishes.

I decided to do a little gardening, which has always been something that calms me and brings me some peace. I remember not being able to shake off the overwhelming stress of a mountain of paperwork, the endless phone calls, and the responsibility of selling my mom's house back in New York while I was here in Illinois.

I had purchased a new bag of potting soil and decided I was going to re-pot some new plants that I had just bought. I can remember crying while cutting through the plastic bag of soil. I dug the shovel into the dirt and pulled out a small stone with the word "FREEDOM" embossed into it. This took my breath away since this was a new bag that had never been opened. Within a few days, I got an offer on my mom's house and things began to come to some closure.

I really do feel that my mom and my husband were both trying to let me know that everything was going to be just fine."

Dee attended one of my talks:

"The Car"

"Mike was my second husband, and I, his third wife. We had a wonderfully loving relationship based on passion, commitment and respect. When we met, we were in our early 50's. Mike used to tease me mercilessly about wanting to remarry, but I insisted that our relationship would have to be based on want and not need. I wished for us to decide, every day, that we chose to stay together, not because of legal obligation.

Six months into our relationship, I was diagnosed with breast cancer, which was successfully treated at Stony Brook Hospital. Two years after that, Mike, a lifelong heavy smoker, was diagnosed with small cell lung cancer, stage 3B. He was given three weeks to live, but he was no crybaby. He told his doctors to feel free to deliver the most grueling treatments in their repertoire, both in an attempt to extend his life and also to help them learn better ways to treat other patients.

After the immediate shock of his prognosis had passed, Mike flat out insisted that I marry him. He had worked for the Long Island Railroad for over 17 years, and while his illness had forced him to go out on disability, falling short of his 20-year retirement, he still wanted me to have whatever limited benefits were due him. I fought him for days. I did not want to capitulate. I assured him that marriage or no marriage, I was not about to leave him. But he desperately wanted me to enjoy increased financial freedom after he was gone. We headed for Brookhaven Town Hall with five witnesses. It was imperative that we marry before his cancer took him. Stunning all of his doctors, who dubbed him "Miracle Mike," my husband somehow survived for five years and four months.

Mike had a ten-year-old car. He had a great admiration for the latest model Chrysler 300, and whenever we would pass one on the road, he would turn on the charm: "Oh, Dee, I would just love to have one more new car before I die. That's my car, right there, that Chrysler. Can't you go along with me on this one last thing?" Needless to say, I did not support the idea of Mike having a new car. That would only encourage him to drive more than before, plus he was clearly getting weaker. I did not foresee him getting much use out of a new car. And so, I invented a bunch of excuses to keep putting him off. I told him that we should wait until we got our income tax refund. I suggested that it made more sense to buy a new car after the snowy season had ended. I tried every trick in the book, buying time until he was ultimately admitted for what would turn out to be his last hospitalization.

While Mike was confined to Stony Brook Hospital, and I had the opportunity to do so, I gritted my teeth and sold his car to a young college student. Fast-forward to about ten months after Mike's death. I still had the same car I was driving while he was alive. The car was only five years old, and I typically kept my cars for at least seven or eight years. But I had always hated the drab khaki-colored paint on that car, especially after I became widowed. I decided that, once I was ready for a new car, it would have to be a bright color, possibly red. I may be a widow, but surely, I could allow myself a more cheerful-looking vehicle.

One day, I found myself in an angry dispute with the dealership where I had customarily gotten my car serviced. I was infuriated, and I vowed never to set foot inside their establishment again. It was just the excuse I needed to allow myself the frivolity of swapping out my boring tan sedan for a sporty, sparkly new red SUV. My sharp new ride was fun to drive and really lifted my mood. I felt mildly guilty for having used some of Mike's inheritance to buy myself a new set of wheels when I had denied him the very same pleasure.

I thought about his unfulfilled wish for the car of his dreams nearly every time I got behind the wheel during those first couple of weeks. I'd been driving the SUV for less than a month when I decided I'd show it off to my close friend Kathi on our next shopping expedition. She chose the town of Riverhead as our destination. I just about NEVER go to Riverhead, and not once had I ever been inside the particular store she wanted us to visit.

I parked my bright and shiny red car outside the shop, and we did our usual damage, emerging with a cartful of bulging bags. As we were walking down our row in the parking lot, Kathi let out a shriek:

"Dee, did you see that car back there?"

"What car?" I asked. It was a pet peeve of Mike's that I was always lost in space, unaware of my surroundings (and hence, prone to accidental falls). "The one back there. Two cars away from yours."

I doubled back and suddenly felt my knees buckling, but I hadn't tripped or stumbled. I was simply thunderstruck by what I saw, directly in front of me, almost immediately adjacent to my car, in a strange parking lot, in an unfamiliar town, in a place I had never before visited. Staring me straight in the face was the one and only New York State license plate ever to bear the names DEE and MIKE.

'Oh my God!' I screamed. 'I can't believe this! I should have known that Mike wouldn't let me get away with buying myself a new car!' I could just picture him grinning broadly at me, hands on his hips and that gleam in his gorgeous green eyes: 'Very nice, Dee,' I imagined him teasing. 'Very nice that you wouldn't let me have my Chrysler 300, but as soon as I'm gone, you don't waste much time before buying yourself a nice new car.'

I tossed the packages into the back of my SUV and told Kathi I had to take a moment to snap a picture of that license plate. My kids would never believe me unless they saw it for themselves. There had to be at least 10 million vehicles registered in New York State, probably more, and this was the only one with Mike's name and mine. I mean, what are the chances?

I took my photo and then stopped to check out the vehicle itself. It was just entirely too intense to absorb the fact that this vehicle, this DEE MIKE vehicle parked practically adjacent to my own, was a genuine Chrysler 300."

Mindy:

"Hearts"

"I was at a fundraiser for my children's elementary school. There were two psychics named 'The Psychic Sisters.' In a room full of people, they started speaking to me. I asked them what kind of signs my brother left for my niece. I was told he leaves her hearts, which can be in the shape of a spill or a tear.

I called Natalie and asked her if she ever saw hearts. Natalie told me she sees hearts all the time. She sent me a picture of her desk blotter which had a tear in the shape of a heart. She said she had a heart in her beer while she was on a date. In short, she always sees hearts. Now she knows he sends her love all the time."

Jill Sandra:

"The Handprint"

"One day, my husband Jeff and I were bored and looking for something to do. We found out that there was going to be a psychic at a nearby restaurant. We called for a reservation but were told that they were totally booked. After a while, we called back and were told that they had found an open table for us.

After we sat down, the psychic made a beeline for us and we were the first ones he read that night. He knew that we were both teachers, that Jeff's deceased uncle had polio when he was a child, and that everyone in the family had a handprint that our son Ben had done in the first grade. We had put it on the back of the headboard of our bed and it stayed there. The psychic said that we had put it in a strange place and that we see it every night. And…he said that the uncle comes into the room every night and touches the handprints. This gave our family a sense of peace."

Ilene:

"The Missing License Plate"

"My father was involved in the automobile industry most of his adult life after World War II, even in retirement, working part-time at a dealership in Delray Beach, Florida. He had been a salesman initially, and then became sales manager at a Pontiac dealer and then an Oldsmobile dealer through my teen and college years. He was very beloved, had quite a following through recommendations, and was always available to help whenever anyone might have had a problem with their car. He would happily pick up his customers' cars to take to service. I can remember him getting phone calls many a night from customers with questions or concerns, and my mother used to call him 'The Car Doctor!' He was honest, respected greatly, and everyone called Sol, or referred Sol if it had anything to do with a car. He even sold a car to my lifelong friend's father in Brooklyn and taught him how to drive!

My father died in 1993, and subsequently I came home from teaching at Temple Isaiah one very frigid January night, perhaps a year or so after his death. I pulled into the garage, and when my husband Ivan went to take the garbage out after dinner, he noticed that my front license plate was missing off my car. Despite the hour, and despite the absolutely bitter temperature, he suggested that we retrace my steps of everywhere I had been that afternoon before going to Temple, as he was certain that someone would have found my license plate and stood it up in a snowbank.

I thought he was completely out of his mind, but we got in the car and proceeded to go everywhere I had been that afternoon, from Temple Isaiah's parking lot, to any store I might have frequented, to having lunch at Torcello's in Northport with my cousin. That was the very last place we went after being unsuccessful everywhere else we had gone. Lo and behold—there was my license plate stuck upright in the snow mound in the parking lot in front of the restaurant! My immediate comment, with tears in my eyes, was, 'my father put it there!' To this day, I am convinced that my father, who loved all things having to do with automobiles, had a hand in our finding it!"

Ann attended one of my Zoom talks:

"A Newspaper and a Feather"

"I want to tell you my experiences after my husband Lee passed away in 2016. He was ill and in the care of our River Garden Jewish Home here in Jacksonville. He passed on a Monday morning very early about 4 a.m. He had mostly been in a coma and his son, my stepson, had come from California on Sunday morning and was with him all day Sunday. I think Lee waited for him to come so he could go peacefully.

On Tuesday morning, I awoke before my daughter and my sister who were staying with me. The front door was locked, and lying on the sofa was a newspaper folded in half, but not in the plastic bag like always. I thought maybe it was Monday's paper that I had left there. But, no, it was Tuesday's paper, and his obituary was in there with his picture. How did that paper get in the house?

Next, I went into the sun porch, and on the table was a beautiful peacock feather. I do not have any feathers in my house—especially a peacock feather. It was just beautiful, but where did it come from?

A few weeks later, I was asleep, and all of a sudden, something hugged me that took my breath away. It never happened before and never has happened since."

Shapes and Photos

Diane's story about the hawks appeared in Chapter 11. This is about her husband as well:

"From Generation to Generation"

"My eyes are playing tricks on me, maybe because of the poor lighting in my den, or maybe because cataracts are clouding my vision, or maybe because the project I'm tackling is a hard one. I'm guessing it's this last choice—the project. I'm sitting on my couch, reaching into a large paper shopping bag labeled 'Sam's Childhood,' and I'm poring through old photos, mostly black and white, of Sam from infancy to his early-twenties, pictures taken before we met, before we married.

I select about a dozen and spread them out on the floor in front of me: curly-haired toddler Sam holding a fishing rod, a look of intense concentration on his face as his uncle shows him where to place his hands; preschool Sam, sporting a big smile as he plays with a wooden truck; elementary-age Sam learning how to sail and how to row a boat; teenager Sam at Boy Scout camp; college-age Sam navigating the slopes on skis.

My plan is to write a story in verse, using these photos, to create a book for my three young grandchildren. I have the title, 'Grandpa Sam Through the Years,' and now I just have to come up with the words that will convey a sense of who their grandfather was when he was a boy. It's a project I want and need to do, a way for all of us— my children, grandchildren, and me—to remember Sam on the twentieth anniversary of his sudden loss in a plane crash.

So, I'm deep into these thoughts when I hear a truck pull into my driveway, and I see the UPS delivery man placing a package next to my garage door. And I'm still immersed in these thoughts as I open the package and as I discover the large, framed photograph carefully protected in a layer of bubble wrap. What I see, or what I think I see, is a photo of Sam holding a toddler, one of our children, in his arms. His mouth is hidden behind the child, but his eyes convey his serious and reflective mood. His high forehead is framed by a curly head of hair, the same curls that topped his little-boy head. The cloudy sky behind him looks dark, ominous, about to open up and pour. He is standing on a dock, the masts of a dozen sailboats lining the horizon behind him.

Now I'm confused. Why would a photo of Sam as a young father arrive right now, right in the middle of this project? There's no note, no return address. I send a text to my two sons, hoping for an explanation. 'Mom,' comes the immediate reply from the younger of my two boys, 'That's not Dad. It's me.'

My first thought upon reading the text is: how could I confuse my husband and my son, followed by a second thought, that they look so much alike. Sam never made it to his senior years, never saw wrinkles and age spots on his skin, never viewed curly hair turning to grey. While his children grew up and I grew older, my mind's eye retains the memory of his youthful face, the face that I thought I saw in the photo.

Resemblance is a funny thing. Maybe it's the smile, or the hair, or an expression, or the twinkle in the eye that makes the connection from generation to generation. Perhaps it's not so unusual that I became confused when I opened the package, considering the project I'm working on. I examine the photo again, now clearly seeing my child.

When the phone rings, I'm not surprised at the caller: 'You okay, Mom?' says my son. He tells me that the photo was taken a year ago. He'd gone for a sail, his way of remembering and honoring his dad on that anniversary day. I thank him, and we talk a little longer. After hanging up, though, I think about something Sam used to say: 'There are no coincidences. Things happen for a reason.' Why, when the package could have arrived on any day, at any time, does it arrive on the one afternoon I'm devoting to creating a memory book for my family? I could come up with several explanations, but I'm content with just one. Sam, you are lovingly remembered."

Christine:

"The Lighthouse"

"My husband Gary passed away in October of 2018. My children and I decided to have him cremated because, sadly, my mom also passed away just two days before Gary. We live in Illinois and my mom was back in New York. So, my family and I flew to New York for my mom's funeral, and then, three days later, I was back in Illinois, planning my husband's funeral.

The funeral director had asked if I wanted some of Gary's ashes put into a small velvet bag to keep. I thought that was perfect because, even though he loved living in our beautiful little town near the river while he was suffering through dementia, he always wanted to 'go home' to New York.

I found a lovely cemetery plot that he loved—high on a hill overlooking the Fox River—and decided to have his ashes interred there. My plan was to take his remaining ashes back to Long Island, but I had no idea where to scatter them. I struggled for months trying to decide the perfect place. We were both born on Long Island, met, got married, and raised our family there. I remember one day, talking to the air and asking Gary to let me know where he wanted to be. I remember saying out loud, 'Babe, you have to help me, you have to let me know.'

One day, I was working on my computer, and left it to make some lunch. It usually, after a little time, goes to a slide show of photos on the screen, and it's always photos of my daughter's wedding. This time, when I returned to the computer, there was a photo of Gary that I took of him, standing in front of the Fire Island Lighthouse when we made a last visit to the beach before we moved to Illinois. The photo remained on the screen until I turned it off. The next day,

I kept seeing photos of that lighthouse on Facebook, Twitter, and Instagram.

I knew where he wanted to be. So, that following September, when I had to fly back to Long Island to close on my mom's house, I took Gary's ashes to the lighthouse and scattered his ashes there."

Murray is the brother-in-law of my friend Gary:

"The Streak of Light"

"In August of 1997, my wife and I participated in a Rockland County NY UJA-Federation mission to Israel. On Tisha B'Av [the holiday commemorating the anniversary of the destruction of the Temple in Jerusalem], our guide took us to the newly excavated Southern Wall area of the Temple. He told us that this was the exact spot where the Levi'im [Levites] would blow the Shofar during the time of the Great Temple. He asked if anyone was a Levi. I said I was. He then asked if I could blow the Shofar. I told him that I do, at which point he took out a Shofar and handed it to me.

When I blew the shofar, my wife Maureen took two consecutive pictures. When the film was developed, we saw that the second shot had this white light shining through it. What was it? A reflection, a crack in the lens, a tear in the negative? We had professional photographers check everything out, but it was none of the above. All the other pictures on that roll of film were fine—no streaks of light, nothing unusual. If there had been a camera or lens defect, other pictures would have shown up with streaks of light.

The only conclusion we could come up with was a visit from one of my Levi relatives."

Ben is a cousin of my friend Gary:

"Mysterious Photo"

"This is what happened to us in Normandy, France. To be specific, on November 7th, 2019, my wife Rhonda and I were paying a visit to 'Easy Red Sector', the exact area where PFC Tom Horowitz, 16th Regiment, 1st Infantry Division (Big Red One) U.S, Army, came ashore on 06 June 1944. First, as the tour guide stated to us, there were 12 rainbows over Omaha Beach that day, the most she had seen in her many years of leading this tour—double rainbows included.

However, what is even more fascinating, yet comforting, is what happened to us on that day. We were fortunate to find that sector of beach where my father came ashore that morning. We were basically alone, as the balance of the group was about to climb aboard the bus for the trip back to our ship.

We stood close to the water's edge. I asked to stand for a moment by myself and stare out at the channel. Rhonda then joined me, and I decided to snap a photo of the desolate beach where, 75 years earlier, brave men came ashore to literally save the world. Quite the contrast. I intentionally took that photo with our long shadows leading to the water's edge. I saluted my father, who I clearly envisioned, and we walked away.

As we quietly walked away, we were alone. There was not another soul on that beach. There were no trees or monuments nearby. It was a slow, long walk on barren sand to the parking lot. At least 50 yards of sand. I thought of his day on that beach with each step. It took him 12 hours to make that same trek. Although just holding hands with my wife, I felt his presence—vibrant, young, and proud— walking along with me. Later, I found out from Rhonda that she felt the same way. As we made our way back to the ship, I decided to look at the photos I took to capture the day.

When I got to the beach photos, a very cold chill passed through me, something I remember to this day. I stared at one particular photograph. It was the last one I took that day. There was a beautiful shot of the beach, the waves, and our two shadows standing side by side. But my eyes were immediately drawn to the third shadow to the right of ours. I did not notice this shadow when taking the photograph. If another person were nearby, I would have taken it again as

I wanted to capture just our shadows alone being cast upon the beach. Yet, there it was. The photograph showing this moment has not been altered in any way. It is what it is.

In retrospect, Rhonda and I passionately believe that this was indeed my dad with us that day. From the unprecedented multiple rainbows over Omaha Beach to the shadow in this picture, he made sure his presence was unmistakably known."

Gayle sent me a picture after her rabbi told her about my book:

"I was in San Francisco, and my daughter and I were walking in a nature preserve. She took a picture of me and what showed up was quite unbelievable. We both felt that it was my husband Jerry—who died six weeks earlier."

Lisa was described previously as a young widow and podcaster:
"Hearts"

"So, I went out on my patio to cover one of my outdoor couches and I am guided to look at the frozen garden, and what do I see, no

joke …a frozen mushroom. I look at it approximately three times and my eyes just pop out with excitement. It's an Angel! Just can't make it up! SOOO Cool! It's the season to believe!"

Lisa has also received pictures of hearts from some of her friends and followers:

Rabbi Stephen and Donna Karol:

"On Erev Rosh Hashanah, 2020 (the evening of Rosh Hashanah), we said the appropriate blessings to begin the holiday. First came the lighting of the candles, then the Kiddush (wine blessing), then the

Motzi (bread blessing), and later, the blessing for apples and honey. With a round challah representing the shape of the world on the day that is regarded in Jewish tradition as the "Birthday of the World," we decided to tear rather than to cut pieces for ourselves. Donna tore first, and I tore second, and we looked and saw this heart. We have torn many a challah in the years we've been together, but we have never seen a heart!"

A necklace missing for years...a memorial candle burning for a day-and-a-half instead of for a day...a one-of-a-kind license plate...heart shapes...a handprint art project...a lost and found license plate...a newspaper and a feather...a photo arriving on a day devoted to photos...a shadow that wasn't there...a ray of sunlight that wasn't there...heart-shapes of a mushroom, in a cup of coffee, on a tree, as a piece of meat...two pieces of bread randomly torn and forming a heart shape. Taken separately, all of these are random and perhaps subject to a logical explanation. Taken together, this is an incredibly diverse group of signs from a diverse group of individuals who do not know one another. What they have in common as objects, shapes, and photos is that they have brought a sense of comfort, wonder, and gratitude to those who conveyed their experiences to me. And I am sure that there are many more of them out there that I haven't heard yet.

CHAPTER 13: FINDING MEANING
IN NUMBERS, COINS, AND LIGHTS

"The after-life is not a theory to be proven logically or demonstrated by rational analysis. It is axiomatic. It is to the soul what oxygen is to the lungs. There is little meaning to life, to God, to Man's constant strivings, to all of his achievements, unless there is a world beyond the grave."[265]

"The practice of gematria, or the spiritual interpretation of numbers, is one technique for understanding sacred texts."[266]

"Having mentioned the coins of Jerusalem, the Gemara notes: The Sages taught: 'What is the coin of ancient Jerusalem? The names David and Solomon were inscribed on one side, and Jerusalem the Holy City was on the other side. And what is the coin of Abraham our forefather? An old man and an old woman, representing Abraham and Sarah, were inscribed on one side, and a young man and a young woman, representing Isaac and Rebecca, were on the other side.'"[267]

"God said, 'Let there be light'; and there was light. God saw that the light was good, and God separated the light from the darkness. God called the light Day, and the darkness He called Night. And there was evening and there was morning, a first day.[268]

You don't have to be religious or spiritual to want to search for meaning in life. Some of us find it in love, others in achievements, still others in philosophy. Rabbi Maurice Lamm, as stated above in the first quote, believes that we can find it in a belief in the afterlife. In general, it is we who decide to attach meaning to any experience we have. Specifically, people who receive "signs" are giving meaning to what some would call "supernatural phenomena" and others would call "delusions" or "wishful thinking." The meaning of numbers in Judaism is enshrined repeatedly in *gematria* and is prevalent in the Hebrew Bible and in later Jewish sources. The importance of coins in Jewish history dates back some 2,000 years. And, literally from the beginning of time according to the Torah, light is crucial to the world, to God, and to humanity.

Numbers

There are numbers that appear frequently and significantly in the Hebrew Bible and other Jewish writings. Some of these examples are well-known and others may not be known to the average reader. Those that are in italics are taken from Rabbi Geoffrey Dennis's article for *myjewishliving.com*, entitled "Judaism and Numbers":

- 3: sons of Noah, Abraham and Isaac reach Mount Moriah on the third day and the binding of Isaac takes place, patriarchs (Abraham, Isaac, and Jacob), number of rabbis required for a *bet din* (a court to supervise conversion or the granting of a divorce), signatures required on a *ketubah* (marriage contract), *"Three signifies completeness and stability, as represented by the three Patriarchs and the three pilgrimage festivals –Passover, Shavuot, and Sukkot (I Kings 17:21; Daniel 6:10)"*[269]
- 7: days of the week, Shabbat as the seventh day, pairs of clean animals brought to Noah's Ark, number of days in advance God warns Noah about the Flood, the Sabbatical year, 7x7 for the agricultural cycle, *"Seven is one of the greatest power numbers in Judaism, representing Creation, good fortune, and blessing. A Hebrew word for luck, gad, equals seven in gematria. Another Hebrew word for luck, mazal, equals 77. There are seven laws of Noah and seven Patriarchs and Matriarchs. Several Jewish holidays are seven days long, and priestly ordination takes seven days. The Land of Israel was allowed to lie fallow one year in seven. The menorah in the Temple has seven branches. The prophet Zechariah describes a strange celestial stone with seven eyes (Chapter 4)."*[270]

"This emphasis on seven continues post-biblically with seven wedding blessings, seven circuits performed about a groom, and seven days of mourning after the death of a close relative. Events, prayers, and esoteric observances that involve multiples of seven are also common."[271]

"The first verse of the Torah consists of seven words and seven is the recurrent number in Pharaoh's divinatory dreams in Genesis. The walls of Jericho fall after the Israelites encircle it seven times. In the Zohar, the seven lower sefirot are those aspects of God that are present in asiyah, our world of action. Seven is also the preferred number in spells, magic squares, amulets, and the like (Genesis 7:2; I Kings 18:43; Deuteronomy 16:9; Pesahim 54a; Sotah 10b)"[272]

- 10: *"Ten is a symbol of good luck and power,"* [273] the last number of righteous men Abraham presents to God to prevent the destruction of Sodom, Tribes, Commandments, Plagues, Trials of Abraham, Fingers of God [allegorical], *Sefirot* (Spheres in Mystical Judaism)

- 20: the minimum age for a male to be counted in the Israelite census in the Book of Numbers

- 30: the number of days in the mourning period *(Shloshim)*— counted from the day of burial— in which Jewish tradition prescribes that a mourner is forbidden to marry, shave, get a haircut, or attend a festive occasion; *the number of days in five of the twelve months in the Hebrew Calendar (Nisan, Sivan, Av, Tishrei, and Shevat), with the additional month in a leap year making Adar I, bringing the total to six.*[274]

- 40: *"Forty appears many times in the Bible, usually designating a time of radical transition or transformation. Among the most famous examples are these: It rained for 40 days and 40 nights during the Flood (Genesis 7). Exodus records that Moses spent 40 days on Mount Sinai with God. Forty is the number of years the Israelites were required to wander in the wilderness until they were allowed to enter Canaan...Elijah fasted for 40 days prior to receiving his revelation on Mount Horeb. Multiples of 40 are also common: 40,000 men rallied to Barak in the book of Judges. [It is also the] number of days [Israelite] spies were in Canaan, a generation in the desert, Isaac's age when [he] married Rebekah, Esau's age when [he] married two wives, number of days Jonah prophesied would pass before Nineveh is destroyed, [the] number of years in [the] reign[s] of David and Solomon, [the] number of days Moses [was] on Mt. Sinai, [and the] minimum age for a man to join the Sanhedrin."*[275]

"The Talmud also reports wondrous phenomena occurring in units of 40. It also appears in mystical texts, usually as an element of purification. Thus the Book of the Great Name advises its readers to abstain from sleeping in one's own bed for 40 days and nights after using the book, mimicking the time Moses spent away from camp while he received the Ten Commandments (Genesis 7; Exodus 24; I Samuel 17:16; I Kings 19:8; Gittin 39b, 40a;   Sotah 34a)."[276]

- 50: The fiftieth year of an agricultural cycle prescribed in Chapter 25 of the Book of Leviticus in the Hebrew Bible in which the Sabbatical year occurred every seven years. In Hebrew, it is called *Yovel*, which translates as "jubilee." The commandment stipulated that land was to be returned to its original owner and all slaves were to be set free. The Liberty Bell in Philadelphia is inscribed with the words from Leviticus: "Proclaim Liberty Throughout All the Land unto All the Inhabitants thereof."

- 70: *"This number symbolizes the world. There are 70 nations in the world, 70 languages, and 70 princely angels. The Greek translation of the Bible (The Septuagint), the first to make it   available to the gentile, was done by 70 Jewish scholars, who, though working separately, produced 70 identical translations. [There were 70] Members of the Sanhedrin, [the length of the] life of King David, [the number of years between [the] destruction of [the] first temple and construction of [the] second temple, [the] year in which [the] second temple [was] destroyed, [the] number of people who went to Egypt with Jacob."[277]*

- 80: Moses' age when he went to Pharaoh, the length of a life according to Psalm 90:10.

- 120: Moses' age when he died. In Hebrew, *"ad meah v'esrim"* means "(May you/he/she live) to 120"—a wish for a long, full life.

If you are familiar with the significance of Jewish numbers, you may be wondering why I haven't mentioned the number 18 yet. The reason is that, although the word *Chai* (which has the numerical value of 18) appears a few times in the Hebrew Bible and means "live" or "living," it didn't take on its current level of significance until much later. In an article entitled "What Does the Chai Symbol Signify?", Ariela Pelaia wrote on the website of *www.learnreligions.com:*

"Chai as a symbol goes back to medieval Spain, and its use as an amulet originated in 18th century Eastern Europe. Letters were used as symbols in Jewish culture as far back as the earliest Jewish roots. In fact, the Talmud states that the world was created from Hebrew letters that form verses of the Torah."[278]

For most Jews today, 18 or *Chai* is a significant number in regard to giving *tzedakah* (monetary gifts). A donation of $18 or a multiple of 18 is a widespread practice for a Bar Mitzvah or Bat Mitzvah gift, for a wedding gift, for a donation to a synagogue or other Jewish organization in honor or in memory of someone, or for a special, happy occasion. It has become a widespread practice in Jewish life all over the world, and the fact that it emphasizes the concept of life really enhances its significance.

Gematria

There are 22 letters in the Hebrew alphabet, five of which also have an additional "final letter" that is only used at the end of a word. Each letter has a numerical value, starting with the *Aleph,* which is 1. The letters *Bet* through *Yud* are 2 through 10, and then the next 8 letters *Kaf* through *Tzadee* are 20 through 90. The *Koof* is 100, the *Reish* is 200, the *Shin* is 300, and the *Tav* is 400. When you combine different letters, the result will be a certain number. For example, *Chai* is the combination of the letters *Chet* (8) and *Yud* (10). Edward Hoffman, a clinical psychologist and the author of books on Jewish mysticism, spirituality, and psychology, wrote in *The Hebrew Alphabet: A Mystical Journey*:[279]

"Dating back to Talmudic times, the Hebrew letters have not only been celebrated as holy, but also venerated as an actual tool for spiritual mastery...In *gematriyah,* words with dissimilar meanings but equal numerical values...are probed for their hidden linkages...The thirteenth-century *Zohar* (Book of Splendor) is filled with references to the importance of the Hebrew alphabet as a celestial code or blueprint for the cosmos. "

Interestingly, modern science can supply an analogy to clarify this evocative concept: Just as we now regard the DNA molecule as a carrier of incredibly condensed information concerning the development of life, so too have Kabbalists viewed the Hebrew language of Scripture as a cipher describing the universe. The *Zohar* relates that, "God looked into [the letters] of the Torah and created the universe."

Mark Elber writes in *The Everything Kabbalah Book*:

"The *gematria* of a Hebrew word is used to show its connection to another Hebrew word of the same numerical value...the word *gematria*…is a word borrowed directly from Greek…Interpretive tools such as…*gematria*…are outside of the framework of rational thought. Applying the rules of logic to a nonrational system makes the system seem absurd. By remaining open to the message by these nonrational methods, it is possible to see beyond the limitations of rational thoughts."[280]

Keeping in mind the importance of numbers, and being aware that we can find significance in what is not rational, here are four experiences to consider:

Lisa:

"*The number 111 was important in my husband Doug's life. He was a season ticket holder for Hofstra University basketball in Section 111. When he was in hospice care, he was put in Room 111. After he died, I saw that number everywhere, including on a police car. I believe these were signs from him and from God and were intended to help me and my sons heal and feel better. They should be cherished and held dear to our hearts.*"

Kendra:

"*At 19, I always saw the time 12:34. At 21, I discovered a numerology book. After seeing 12:34 AM/PM every day for two years, I wanted to know the signs I was seeing. I found out that the number 12 meant that an angel was watching over me, and the number 34 was the urge to believe in myself. My grandfather, my Poppy was my angel.*
At 29, I lost my grandmother. My Nanny. My rock. We had our calls together once a week. Towards the end, it was always about the same thing—how much she loved me. She was the hardest person I ever had to say goodbye to because she taught me about signs and unconditional love. I sat shiva for her. I remember the sound of Rabbi ripping the shiva ribbon, and I kept it and set it free in the Mississippi River and sang "Oseh Shalom." At 31, I still see 12:34 AM/

PM every day. I wrote her obituary on a fountain stoop in Jackson Square in New Orleans' French Quarter. Every time I pass that area, I see 12:34."

Carol:

"I should preface this with: I NEVER watch morning TV shows, and certain numbers happen with great frequency for me—11:11 and 444 in particular.

So, one morning, I was home with a cold and turned the TV on. I happened on a segment of a show that was an interview with the guy on whom the show "The Ghost Whisperer" was based. Someone had called in and asked about these two numbers! He mentioned that 11:11 and 444 indicate that there are angels present. I had started to see those numbers around the time my dad died. Whether true or not, who knows? But there were many people who called in to the show who said they see the same numbers and no others. I find that oddly comforting. The guest then proceeded to tell the hosts things that he had no way of knowing, totally freaking them out. Could it be real? Is he a charlatan? I have no idea. But it was interesting. Since I NEVER watch morning shows, why did I happen to see THAT one?"

Rabbi Stephen Karol:

"My wife Donna's favorite number is 7. My favorite number is 10. One of the most important numbers in Jewish texts and practice is 3. The numbers of the two apartments in which we have lived together are 37 and 28 (3+7=10 and 2+8=10), and we didn't deliberately choose them.

We got married in September of 2016, and our ketubah contains a line from the traditional text of Pirkei Avot: "Toveem ha'shtayim meen ha-echad" ("Two are better than one") My brother—Rabbi Larry Karol—is a composer of Jewish music and sang his song "Two

Are Better Than One" during our ceremony. A couple of days later, we went to a Sandals resort in Antigua for our honeymoon. When we checked in, we were assigned to a room with a number that can be seen in the picture.

We found significance in this room number: 7 (Donna's favorite), 7+2+1=10 (my favorite), and 7x2=14 (two are better than one)."

Coins

The "coins of Jerusalem" reference from the Talmud is amazing! I doubt that the coins with the names of David and Solomon and the images of Abraham, Sarah, Isaac, and Rebekah on them were ever made. However, the symbolism of them should not be lost on us. We can assume that, in order to have your name and/or image on any coin or paper money in any country in world history, one has to be a significant figure. And, that significance should be long-lasting and impressive. Although coins are becoming less useful in our own time because of credit and "virtual money," they have existed for at least 2,000 years. And they tell us that the person represented by the coin is figuratively linked to us through their image on that coin.

On the website of the Jewish Virtual Library website *(www. jewishvirtuallibrary.com),* there is an article reprinted from the Encyclopedia Judaica about Jewish coins and currency that emphasizes the Jewish connection to coins dating back to the second century B.C.E. Here are some examples of ancient Jewish coins:

- The Hasmonean dynasty (135-37 B.C.E.): established after the victory of the Maccabees: "In accordance with the Second Commandment, no likeness of living beings, men or animals, are found on them...All Hasmonean coins bear Hebrew legends... The Hasmonean rulers are thus styled as high priests."
- The Herodian dynasty (37 B.C.E.-95 C.E.): began with the appointment of Herod the Great by the Romans in 40 B.C.E: "All legends on his coins are in Greek and no Hebrew legends appear."
- The Jewish War (66-70 C.E.): coinage emphasized the assertion of independence and were the first silver coins produced by Jews. "The emblems are as simple as they are beautiful: a chalice with pearl rims and three pomegranates. The legends, which are, of course, only in Hebrew...read *"Yerushalayim ha-*

Kedoshah" ("Jerusalem the Holy") and *"Shekel Yisrael"* ("Shekel of Israel")... The emblems of the bronze coins are the vine leaf, the amphora, the *lulav* [a palm branch], the *etrog* [a citrus fruit], the palm tree, the fruit baskets, and the chalice."

- The *Bar Kokhba* War (132-135): was a Jewish rebellion against the Romans led by a charismatic man born *Shimon ben Kose-vah.* The great Rabbi Akiva viewed him as the Messiah, and gave him the name *"Bar Kokhba,"* meaning "Son of the Star." "The bulk of the coins bear the name Simeon *[Shimon]* and eventually his title 'prince of Israel'...The coins of the first two years are dated, but the formula of the era changed from 'Year one of the redemption of Israel' to 'Year two of the freedom of Israel.' During the third year and until the end of the war, the coins issued were undated and bear the war slogan 'For the freedom of Jerusalem.'"

Examples of modern Jewish coins:
- State of Israel (1948-Present): Most coins have images such as the *menorah,* a palm tree, a lion, a lyre, an ancient gallery, and pomegranates, among others. Paper currency often features images of national leaders, artists, writers, scientists, and Jewish historical figures.

It is apparent to me that the money of a country has more meaning than its monetary value. The image on a coin or paper money is supposed to honor that person's memory and achievements. That honor is independent of the financial value of the coin or paper. Think about American coins—Abraham Lincoln on the penny, Thomas Jefferson on the nickel, Franklin Roosevelt on the dime, and George Washington on the quarter. Think about our paper currency—Washington on the 1, Jefferson on the 2, Lincoln on the 5, Alexander Hamilton on the 10, Andrew Jackson on the 20, Ulysses S. Grant on the 50, Benjamin Franklin on the 100, and Grover Cleveland on the 1000. Through our money, we are meant to be linked with our collective history. And I have found that, through coins, there are people who are linked to their deceased loved ones through their individual history.

Rabbi Steve is a rabbinical school classmate and close friend for almost 50 years:

"About two months after my mother died, I started noticing something odd. Every so often, no more than once a day, but often several days in succession and usually multiple times a week, I'd find a quarter on the floor. Just a quarter. Never loose change. Never a quarter with a nickel or a dime. Just a quarter. This went on for several weeks. At first, I didn't think much of it. 'Oh look, a quarter...,' I'd think to myself, and stick it in my pocket. Then it would be, 'Oh look, another quarter...', but I wouldn't pay too much attention to it. Until, that is, after several weeks turned into two to three months of the quarter thing.

One night I shared this phenomenon while having dinner with friends, whereupon someone said, 'You know, I've heard of such experiences, especially after a death. Maybe it's your mother trying to tell you something?' Of course, I was skeptical. 'Did quarters have any special meaning for your mom?' they asked. I thought about it. 'No, not really. But...one of her classic characteristics was to always try to make things better by giving money. If there ever was an argument or strife, Mom could always be counted on to make up by calling us over, reaching into her purse, and then pushing some money (usually more than quarters) into your hand. She wasn't so good at saying 'I'm sorry,' but money she could give freely.

The quarters went on. And on. Always just a quarter. And always on the floor. Then, after about six months of this, I made the mistake of telling my kids. Hannah, in particular, started then to plant quarters. But even that was just a few times—at least that's what she said. For the next five years, the quarter thing would continue, sometimes with great frequency, sometimes once every two to three weeks. But I'd still find quarters. Until this past May.

Now this is the part of the story where I should tell you about my brother, Larry. He's the spiritualist in the family. He's the one who writes about mysticism and the life of the spirit. So, of course, it would be natural to tell him. And what does he say? 'I only get nickels!' And predictably, after I give him a hard time for being so resistant to such possibilities, he would invariably say (like not remembering that he says this every time the subject comes up), 'When someone comes and tells me where they buried the money, then I'll believe.' He also said, 'I don't think I'd talk about this to your congregation until after you've signed a new contract.'

So, this past May, Larry was in town to speak at our Tikkun Leyl Shavuot, our all-night study session on the eve of Shavuot. Two days before Larry was to speak, I found a dime on the floor in my study. I put it on the mail table in the living room. Later that day, I found another dime—this time in the front hallway—that one I also put on the mail table next to the other dime. I didn't think anything of it. After all, they were dimes. For the next two days, as I'd pass the mail table, I'd see the two dimes sitting next to each other, again not really paying any attention to them. But I distinctly remembered being aware of seeing those two dimes, as if they were a pair. Then, on the morning of Shavuot, as Larry and I were gathering to come to the Temple, we met in the living room – next to the mail table. And then I looked down. The dimes were gone. But, in their stead...were a quarter...and a nickel. When I called its attention to Larry, without saying a word, he threw his arms around me and we hugged. We both believed, whether true or not, that Mom had given us her message (whatever that might be).

I have not found another quarter since that day."

Marilyn is the sister of a rabbinical school classmate and close friend for almost 50 years:

"Our mom passed away on September 11th, 2016, which is 9/11. Immediately following my mom's Shiva in Pittsburgh, we returned home to the Bay Area. I took a walk with a friend on the same

route that I have walked for 28 years.

Once we crossed the street to begin our walk, I happened to look down at my feet, and there were a dime and a penny. I couldn't help but think about my mother possibly showing me a sign. During that same walk, when we got to the top of that hill, (which was a climb), there were another dime and penny on the ground by my feet. I thought about my mom again. And by the way, for all of the years that I have walked this same walk, I don't remember finding money on the trail...

Coincidentally, I was finding dimes and pennies almost every day. There was never a mix of quarters, nickels, or dollars. I called a very good friend of mine who lost her son tragically several years ago. She had told me that she had been to a psychic that she really, really trusted and loved. The psychic had brought a lot of peace to my friend, who then said to me: 'I'm sure that you are getting signs from your mom.' I was trying to figure out why I was getting dimes and pennies.

I remember that, shortly thereafter, I misplaced my special earrings. I was looking frantically everywhere for them. I went into my car thinking that I took them off and put them in my center console. When I opened the console, there were many, many dimes and pennies, but again no quarters or nickels.

We flew back to our home in the desert from the Bay Area and, when I walked to my airplane seat, there were a dime and a penny on it. I started to cry. I knew that my mom was definitely in my presence. When we got back to the desert, we had dinner with some friends. I was telling them what was transpiring, and one friend said: 'Well, of course, you're getting dimes and pennies. A dime minus a penny is nine, and a dime plus a penny is 11. 911!' And, of course, my mother passed away on 9/11!!! I continue to get dimes and pennies, but not as often. I will get them in a grocery store as my change, and of course, it could be nickels and quarters. But, once again, they're all dimes and pennies, and I smile.

On April 6th, 2019, we went back to the Bay Area. The reason why I know this date is because it is on my phone in my photos. We flew back, unpacked, and went to bed, and had not been there for many months. When I woke up in the morning, I went into the kitchen, and on my counter was a pyramid of dimes and pennies. I sent the picture to my kids, and of course asked my husband if he did that, and of course he did not. My daughter had not been in our house since we left—which was months before....

Needless to say, I am thrilled that my mother's presence is in my life!!!"

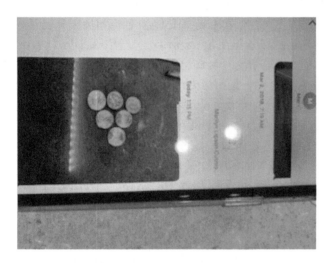

Karen attended one of my Zoom talks:

"When my father was dying and barely conscious, I asked him to look down on the children in the family and protect them. I asked him to send me a sign that he was present, but to send something different so I would know it was him. I asked him to send quarters —not pennies or nickels—so I would know it was him. Here is what happened:

First, after he died, I would find a quarter here and there. Then things became more dramatic. I was helping my son move into an apartment for a college summer internship. The apartment was in a run-down neighborhood, and I was worried. As I was walking through the totally empty apartment before moving him in, there was a quarter in the middle of the kitchen floor. I felt like my father was going to protect my son, and this was a sign.

Another time, I was leaving a very-well-paying job because of an abusive boss. I was so sad the last few weeks, as I knew I was going to leave. One day as I pulled into my designated parking spot, one of my employees came toward me and bent down all of a sudden in front of my car. When I asked her what she was doing, she said there was a pile of quarters in front of my car that someone must have dropped. I then went into my office, and a friend called me to ask if I would take a lucrative consulting job with his company since he heard I was leaving my existing job. I saw that as a sign that my father was helping me.

When my daughter was moving to another city for graduate school and I was helping her move into an apartment, there was a quarter in a totally empty closet in her new apartment.

A number of years ago, my husband and I were traveling through Europe with my son. He was spending the summer in Germany but wanted to see Denmark where my father's family was from. The night before getting to Copenhagen, we spent many hours talking about my father and my son's special relationship with him. Imagine our surprise that, on the first day walking down a street in Copenhagen, we found a Danish quarter in the middle of the street!

I find quarters in other various places and they could all be a coincidence, but it seems that he is looking over my family. I am Christian, but don't believe in organized religion. My father was a very honest and moral person but hated organized religion because he felt it polarized people instead of bringing them together."

Amy is a friend and congregant at Temple Isaiah:

"My mom always taught us to pick up pennies. She called them 'college money.' She also taught her two grandsons to do it. From

the time we were really little, my brother and I had savings accounts. There was not very much in them, and she claimed she was depositing the pennies we found. Of course, we mostly kept them.

People often don't bother with pennies, especially if they've already fallen on the ground. In the months following her death, my dad and I found more than our usual share of pennies. We found a few other coins, too. My brother in Pennsylvania also said that he found more than usual.

At the local Gallery North art show that year, I bought a small glass dish to put the coins in, and I've continued to add coins I found on the ground. It's fairly full. I believe that this is my mom's way of telling us that she's looking out for all of us. Yes, I find that comforting.

It's a small dish, and full of all the coins we've found since April 17th, 2014 when my mom passed away. I bought the dish in September of 2014. When my brother and I were kids, we had a copper enamel set. It took special skill and tools to swirl color in the middle of a piece. The technique on glass is different, but the result reminded me of the homemade copper enamel pieces we presented to both of our parents. At first, I didn't really have a purpose for the dish. By the time I got home, I knew."

Lights

Light plays a role in more than one religion and is prominent in every aspect of our lives. Light or lights can be functional or symbolic, naturally provided or human-powered. For Judaism —and, really, for anyone who believes in the Creation Story in Genesis either literally or figuratively—light is an essential, vital element in the universe in general and in our world in particular. The quotation at the beginning of this chapter ("God said, 'Let there be light'; and there was light'") is indicative of the belief that God created all light. That includes the differentiation between the day and the night, as well as the creation of the sun and the moon and the stars:

"And God said, 'Let there be lights in the vault of the sky to separate the day from the night and let them serve as signs to mark sacred times, and days and years, and let them be lights in the vault of the sky to give light on the earth.' And it was so. God made two great lights—the greater light to govern the day and the lesser light to govern the night. He also made the stars. God set them in the vault of the sky to give light on the earth, to govern the day and the night, and to separate light from darkness. And God saw that it was good. And there was evening, and there was morning—the fourth day."[281]

And please notice that the creation of the various lights is evaluated by God as being "good." Light is so highly regarded in Judaism that the custom developed to kindle two candles on Friday night at the beginning of Shabbat. At the end of Shabbat on Saturday night, a twisted candle with a number of wicks is lit in the Havdalah service—marking the separation between the Sabbath and the six days of the week. Candles are lit as well during the High Holy Days at the beginning of Rosh Hashanah and Yom Kippur, and at the beginning of the Three Festivals of

Sukkot, Passover (*Pesach*), and Shavuot. And, of course, the holiday of Chanukah is referred to as the "Festival of Lights." When we light the candles on all of these holidays, we say a blessing in which we praise God for making us holy with commandments and commanding us to light the candles. In terms of mourning practices, a candle is lit to begin the initial period of *shiva*, and it is intended to burn for seven days. On the anniversary of a loved one's death, we light a *yahrzeit* candle that is designed to burn for twenty-four hours. Some families observe the custom of *Yizkor* four times during the year and will light a *yahrzeit* candle then as well. In synagogues, members will make a donation for a *yahrzeit* plaque, and its light bulbs will be turned on for the anniversary of their loved one's death. In many synagogues, all of the light bulbs on the *yahrzeit* boards may be turned on for *Yizkor* services. None of these occasions for lighting have a functional, utilitarian purpose; you are not supposed to read by the light of the candles or the bulbs. Instead, they represent an undying link between us and our loved ones who have died.

The importance of light in the Hebrew Bible goes far beyond its creation in the Book of Genesis:

- Exodus 10: The three-day plague of darkness in Egypt did not affect the Israelites, who had light in their homes.
- Exodus 13: In addition to a pillar of cloud by day, God provides a pillar of fire as a source of light at night for the Israelites to travel through the desert.
- Exodus 35: The lampstand *[menorah]* is in the Tabernacle and oil is used for lighting it.
- Leviticus 24: God commands that the people should bring pure olive oil to the Tabernacle for lighting the *menorah.*
- Numbers 6: The second line of the Priestly Blessing asks that the light of God's countenance should shine on the people.
- Isaiah 2: This verse is in the service for the Reading of the Torah and urges us to walk in God's light.
- Isaiah 42: The prophet speaks of the covenant between God

and the Jewish people, and of them being a light to others.
- Isaiah 60: The people are urged to rise because they have received light from God's presence and will be radiant and shining for the rest of the world.
- Psalm 27: God gives light and is the Source of salvation, and the Psalmist has no reason to be afraid.
- Psalm 97: Light is for the righteous.
- Proverbs 6: The Torah and commandments provide light.
- Proverbs 20: Human life is God's lamp.
- The Book of Job: The word "light" appears 29 times.
- Esther 8: In a verse that is also said during the Havdalah service, we recall that the Jews enjoyed light, joy and honor.

It should be obvious by now that light is extremely important in the Hebrew Bible, and that it is regarded as positive in both the writings and customs of Judaism. Those who receive "signs" report unusual experiences with lights appearing out of nowhere, working or not working for no apparent reason, and taking on shapes that are inexplicable to those who see them. I have provided three experiences here on this subject—each one different from the other, but each one having to do with light or lights. Two photos follow the third story.

Gary is one of my best friends and a congregant at Temple Isaiah:

"My aunt, who was my godmother, had passed away. That night, as I lay asleep beside my wife, I awoke suddenly. My eyes opened wide and I beheld a beautiful, intricately detailed, geometric orb floating above our bed. Instinctively, my hand shot out toward it, and the orb disappeared.

I had never heard of orbs or similar phenomena before this instance. It may have been a vision, but it was certainly not a dream, as I was fully awake and cognizant at the moment it occurred. To this day, it instills me with wonder and a sense that something awaits us beyond this familiar, earthly existence."

Fred is a friend and a former congregant in Hingham:

"Something weird happened at my mom's funeral at the temple. As the service was starting, all the power in the building went out— sort of like my mom telling us she was there and was getting the last word. But, as we rolled her casket out to the hearse, when we reached the front doors, all the power came back on. It was like 'Leila has left the building!'"

Jill Sandra:

"I have been seeing signs for a while, but I could never convince my mother that they were real. One night, on my kitchen ceiling, I saw three lights "dancing." I took a video of it and showed my mom when she came over. Three is a huge sign, a significant number. When she saw the video, neither one of us could come up with a logical explanation as to where the lights came from, why they were dancing, and why there were three of them."

The first photo shows a light, reflecting off of nothing. The second photo shows the same light, spinning around.

CHAPTER 14: I CAN HEAR MUSIC

*"And the name of his brother was Jubal; he was the ancestor of all who play the **lyre and pipe**."*[282]

Hallelujah.
Praise God in His sanctuary; praise Him in the sky, His stronghold.
Praise Him for His mighty acts; praise Him for His exceeding greatness.
Praise Him with blast of the horn [shofar]; praise Him with harp and lyre.
Praise him with timbrel and dance; praise Him with lute and pipe.
Praise Him with resounding cymbals; praise Him with loud-clashing cymbals.
Let all that breathes praise the Lord. Hallelujah.[283]

"We can learn from the robust piety of the psalmists that it is all right to release your feelings in worship; to sing and clap your hands and even dance, as a happy response to God's presence."[284]

"October 12, 2018 was Gary's funeral memorial. I decided I wanted to drive myself the short way to the funeral home since I had lots of photo displays to bring. I decided to listen to songs by Peter, Paul, and Mary on Pandora, which had always been Gary's favorite music to listen to. As I was pulling into the parking lot, with my kids and their families following behind me, our wedding song "Longer" by Dan Fogelberg began to play. I had never heard that song on the Peter, Paul, and Mary playlist all the times I listened with Gary. To this day, I still have not heard that song again in that mix of old folk songs."

Christine

In the Introduction, I shared with you an occurrence that my wife and I had with music that played all of a sudden—which was a surprise, and for which we had no logical explanation. Donna has been a music teacher at a private school in our area for 25 years and has taught piano students in her studio for more than 30 years. She also was the music teacher in our temple's Religious School for 20 years and an occasional accompanist for Friday night services. As for me, I have always enjoyed music. In fact, one of my hopes for the World-to-Come is that there will be music. Having been a congregational rabbi for 37 years, I felt that the music provided for services by the cantor or cantorial soloist was integral to the content and mood of the prayer experience. Some of it was a cappella, some was with piano accompaniment or guitar, and—in my first congregation in Buffalo—the role of the cantor was supplemented with an organist, a magnificent pipe organ, and a choir consisting of well-trained singers. This is what I had grown up with in Kansas City, and it was typical for a Reform temple to present the liturgical music in that way. My parents were choir members in the small congregation we belonged to before that, when I was much younger. So, music for temple services is what I have been accustomed to for many, many years.

People talk about the changing trends and tastes in music in general, and I have witnessed that in regard to music for services. Although that big Reform temple had an organ and a choir, we also had a cantor who eventually learned to play a guitar in response to the changing tastes in music. For me, singing along with a guitar is my preferred manner of musical worship —with the exception of certain melodies for the High Holy Days. And, I have learned that people who come to services have their favorites. They could listen to the same melody for a prayer over and over again and resist even the suggestion of replacing that melody with a new one. I remember asking my senior rabbi in Buffalo if we could replace the final hymn that we sang each and every week at Saturday morning services with a different one. He said that we couldn't do that because our service regulars *loved* that particular song. Summoning up all of the *chutzpah* I could, I suggested that maybe this much-loved song had been a new melody at one point and replaced the previous old favorite because someone decided it was worth trying. He smiled, shook his head, chuckled, and told me not to bring it up again.

No matter whether you are a trained musician or not, you probably *love* certain types of music or particular songs. The stories you will read later on in this chapter are about favorite songs that played without having been programmed, requested, or planned. Those who heard them were surprised and heartened and attached tremendous significance to the music. That is what we do with music—couples have what they call "our song," individuals remember when they first heard a melody that still touches them, sports arenas and stadiums blast certain songs to get fans charged up, and the National Anthem is a staple at public events. It is hard to imagine a wedding without music during the processional and recessional, a Jewish funeral without the *El Malei Rachamim*, or a meal at a Jewish summer camp without the chanting of the *Motzi* and the *Birkat Hamazon*. And it all got started a long time ago.

If you read the first quotation at the beginning of this chapter, you may have been as surprised as I was. While I have read that section of the Torah more times than I can count, I look at that verse differently now. Have you ever heard of "Jubal?" I wouldn't think so. Having consulted seven different commentators to see if they had anything to say about Jubal (*Yuval* in Hebrew), I came up with nothing. But two of them commented about the instruments. In *Pentateuchs and Haftorahs* (known as the *Hertz Commentary*), the author translates the instruments as "harp and pipe," and states: "Music, according to Hebrew tradition, is thus the most ancient art, dating from the beginnings of the human race."[285] *The JPS Torah Commentary: Genesis—*authored by Nahum M. Sarna— says: "The two [lyre and pipe]

...represent stringed and wind instruments, respectively. The term testifies to the important role of music in ancient Israelite culture."[286]

Other than the solitary reference to Jubal near the beginning of Genesis, there are only a few instances of singing or instruments in the Torah. After Jacob and his wives Rebekah and Leah leave their father Laban to journey to Canaan, he chases after them—mostly because he wants to get his household idols back. Typically, he is dishonest and accusatory:

"Why did you flee secretly and trick me, and did not tell me, so that I might have sent you away with mirth and songs, with tambourine and lyre?"[287]

In the Book of Exodus, when the Israelites race out of Egypt and reach the Sea of Reeds, they celebrate with music (and dancing):

"Then Moses and the people of Israel sang this song to the Lord, saying, 'I will sing to the Lord, for He has triumphed gloriously; the horse and his rider he has thrown into the sea'...'Then Miriam the prophetess, the sister of Aaron, took a tambourine in her hand, and all the women went out after her with tambourines and dancing'..."[288]

And, in connection with the Tabernacle, we have this from the Book of Numbers:

"The Eternal One spoke to Moses, saying: 'Have two silver trumpets made; make them of hammered work. They shall serve you to summon [military bodies of] the community and to set the divisions in motion...The trumpets shall be blown by Aaron's sons, the priests; they shall be for you an institution for all time throughout the ages...And on your joyous occasions—your fixed festivals and new moon days—you shall sound the trumpets over your burnt offerings and your sacrifices of well-being. They shall be a reminder of you before your God: I, the Eternal, am your God.'"[289]

Rabbi W. Gunther Plaut wrote in *The Torah: A Modern Commentary* about the amazing significance of these trumpets:

"Their sound supplemented the visible sign of the cloud. They were about three to four feet long, straight, with flaring ends. A reproduction may be seen on the Arch of Titus in Rome and on a coin from Bar Kochba's time. (Such trumpets were for centuries used in St. Peter's Basilica at papal masses)."[290]

They appear again twice in the Book of Numbers—in Chapter 29, Verse 1, where the word *"teruah"* is substituted for the word *"shofar"* that is being sounded on the first day of the seventh month for a sacred assembly, and in Chapter 31, Verse 6, where they are carried by one of the priests who will blow them as a campaign against the Midianites begins.

There are 21 books in the second section of the *Tanakh*—known as the *Nevi'im* (Prophets), and only one *explicit* mention of trumpets. It is from the Book of Second Kings, Chapter 11, in which there is an episode of palace intrigue in the 9th century B.C.E. in the Kingdom of Judah, and the new king is revealed by the blowing of trumpets *(hatzotzrot)*. Then, in the Book of Ezekiel, Chapter 7, the prophet known for his many visions speaks of doom and disaster to those who were exiled to Babylonia. He refers to the blowing of a horn to call people to battle, but they are unable to respond. In this case, the word for "horn" is not *hatzotzrot; takoah* is used, and the blowing or sounding of the horn is *tak'u*—like the *shofar* sound *t'keeyah*. Is sounding a horn to call soldiers to battle an example of music? It's certainly different than a leader whistling or yelling to get everyone's attention. The trumpets seem to have been for religious and royal use, and the *shofar* can also be blown for a military purpose, as we will see later.

But, in The Writings, the trumpets are much more prominent, used only for religious purposes, and are played by the priests. That is made clear in Psalm 98:6, Ezra 3:10, First Chronicles 13:8 and 16:42, and in Second Chronicles 5:12-13 and 7:6. The quotation from Psalm 150 at the beginning of this chapter reveals what is, essentially, an orchestra. Dr. A. Cohen—author of The Soncino Press's edition of the psalms—quotes another scholar in describing this psalm:

"The Psalm is evidently meant for liturgic use, and one may imagine that each instrument began to take part in the concert as it was named, til at last all blended in a mighty torrent of praiseful sound, to which the whirling dancers kept time."[291]

For at least the last 40 years, many synagogues have brought instrumental music into their services. Guitars have been the most popular, and so have other string instruments, pianos, woodwind instruments, and even brass instruments. The Reform movement, of course, introduced the organ some 200 years ago in Western Europe—mostly to duplicate the formality and grandeur of Christian churches—and, as I mentioned in my own experience, the presence of choirs whose members did not have to be Jewish. And, it has been the Reform movement that has led the way in musical innovation during the last few decades by having guitars as an alternative to the organ and by encouraging the creation of new melodies for old prayers.

The fact is that attaching significance to music, singing, and instruments has its origins in the Hebrew Bible. Without listing every mention of singing or a musical instrument, and without listing the *shofar* (which I talk about later), consider this:

In The Prophets:

- Judges: tambourines and dancing
- 1st Samuel: harp, tambourine, flute, lyre, singing, and dancing
- 2nd Samuel: songs, lyre, harp, tambourine, castanets, cymbals
- 1st Kings: lyre, harp, singers, flutes
- 2nd Kings: trumpets
- Isaiah: lyre, harp, tambourine, flute, songs, strings
- Jeremiah: tambourine, dancing
- Ezekiel: lyre
- Amos: songs, harp, other instruments
- Habakkuk: choirmaster, strings

In The Writings:

-     Psalms: lyre; harp; tambourines/timbrels; lute; dancing; strings; pipe; cymbals; flute; trumpets; psaltery [a string instrument like a zither]; *nehiloth* [wind instruments]; *sheminith* [strings]; choristers; *Jeduthun* [the Temple Choirmaster]; *Heman* [the Temple music director]; Levites [singers at the Temple]
- Job: tambourine, lyre, pipe
-   Daniel: horn, pipe, lyre, trigon [a triangular stringed instrument], harp, bagpipe
- Ezra: trumpets, cymbals
- Nehemiah: singing, cymbals, harps, lyres
-   I Chronicles: singers, lyres, harps, tambourines, cymbals, trumpets, the sons of *Asaph, Heman, Jeduthun*
-   II Chronicles: Levitical singers, *Asaph, Heman, Jeduthun,* cymbals, harps, lyres, priests sounding trumpets

So, in approximately half of the books in the Hebrew Bible, singing and instruments are mentioned—more than once in many cases and in close to half of the 150 psalms. There is a tremendous musical heritage that dates back more than 3,000 years from a religious standpoint, and it is still reflected in the liturgy of synagogues and churches all over the world.

The second section of the Jewish daily morning liturgy—following the *Birkhot Hashachar* (Morning Blessings) and preceding the *Sh'ma* and Its Blessings—is called *P'sukei D'zimrah* (Verses of Song). There is an opening blessing, six psalms, and a concluding blessing. Rabbi Lawrence A. Hoffman has referred to this section as "'the prayer before the prayer.' It functions as the warm-up for the morning service, a recognition that prayerfulness cannot be summoned on demand.'"[292] He also provides this excellent insight about these prayers:

"As praise of God, these psalms were intended all along to be sung, not just read. Though we have no way of knowing what melodies accompanied them early on, we have every reason to believe that such melodies existed. Psalms 145-150 all begin with 'Hallelujah,' a shout of joy to God. Their mood and subject matter almost demand music for a full appreciation of what they are about. The last line (the *chatimah*) of the concluding Blessing of Song is explicit: Blessed is God 'who chooses songs.'"[293]

When the Temple in Jerusalem stood and its sacrificial system was fully operative, the priests and Levites had various musical roles, which I referred to above. Rabbi Hoffman continues:

"...there rose the sound of a variety of instruments and a levitical choir. The psalms formed the repertoire for the choir. We no longer know the entirety of what was sung when, but the Mishnah provides some recollections and so too (whether accurately or not) do other later rabbinic works."[294]

But the Temple didn't last forever, with its second destruction occurring in the year 70 C.E. When the rabbinic period started, Judaism's idealization of the Temple and the hopes and prayers for its rebuilding changed the role of music. And that has been the case for almost 2,000 years in synagogues all over the world that follow the rules of Jewish tradition strictly. One final observation from Rabbi Hoffman:

"In the early synagogue, however, the psalms were not accompanied by instruments because the Rabbis banned instrumental music as part of the prayer service. They were probably reacting to the continued use of instrumentation in pagan temples, hoping to mark off the synagogue as a different kind of sacred venture. It would be without the entertainment aspect that had been central even to the Temple in Jerusalem...

Eventually, other reasons for dispensing with instruments were offered. Instrumental music was inappropriate in an era of mourning for the Temple, it was said. Also, fixing broken instruments on Shabbat constituted a breach of Shabbat work regulations. It was feared that if a musician's instrument broke while it was being used, the temptation to fix it would be too overwhelming to refuse."[295]

The *Shofar* is first mentioned in the verse right after the Ten Commandments in the Book of Exodus when the people see lightning and smoke above Mount Sinai and hear the sound of the *Shofar*. This is quite a debut, and there is no indication in the text that anyone is actually blowing the *Shofar*. We shouldn't be surprised that the Israelites step back and keep what they think is a safe distance from this scene. They promise Moses that they will obey the commandments. In Chapter 23 of Leviticus, the *Shofar* is blown on the first day of the seventh month—"a sacred occasion commemorated with loud blasts."[296] Two chapters later, for the Day of Atonement on the tenth day of the seventh month, the text says that "you shall sound the horn loud... throughout your land and you shall hallow the fiftieth year."[297]

That is immediately followed by the words that are also on the Liberty Bell in Philadelphia: "Proclaim liberty throughout the land unto all the inhabitants thereof." The commandment from Chapter 23 is reiterated in Numbers 29 in the midst of a list of burnt offerings to be made to God. Both Leviticus 23 and Numbers 29 use the word *"teruah"* for the instrument instead of *"shofar,"* and that is one of the notes blown on the *shofar* today.

In contrast to the trumpets, the *shofar* "plays" an important role in the books of the Prophets—beginning with the noise from the ram's horns being responsible for the walls of Jericho collapsing in the Book of Joshua. In the following books, its purpose varies:

- Judges 3 and 6, 1st Samuel 13, and 2nd Samuel 2: Blown for military purposes
- 2nd Samuel 6: David brings the Ark to the City of David
- 1st Kings 1: Solomon's coronation and anointing
- Isaiah 18 and 27: The prophet tells of the downfall of the Assyrians and a return to Jerusalem
- Isaiah 58: God tells the prophet to be as loud as a *shofar* on behalf of the oppressed and hungry and poor
- Jeremiah 4, 6, 42, 51; Ezekiel 33; Hosea 5 and 8; Joel 2; Amos 2 and 3; Zephaniah 1: The blowing of the horn is a warning about an invasion and suffering
- Zechariah 9: God will sound the *shofar* and will protect Jerusalem
- In the Writings, including Psalms 47, 98, and 150; First Chronicles 15; and Second Chronicles 15: the predominant reason for the *shofar* is religious.

The *shofar* was also used to announce gatherings. In this example, the prophet Nehemiah
supervised the reconstruction of Jerusalem after the return from the Babylonian Exile:
- Nehemiah 4: The prophet goes out to inspect the walls of Jerusalem and has a *shofar*-blower with him. He tells the leaders and workers to listen for the sound of the *shofar* as a time to

gather together.

The *shofar* today is, of course, prominent and essential during the High Holy Days. The notes that are played—*t'keeyah, t'ruah, sh'varim,* and *t'keeyah g'dolah*—do not combine to form what most people would call a melody. Yet, the sounds are familiar, and the playing of their notes is eagerly anticipated on Rosh Hashanah and at the end of Yom Kippur. *Shofar*-blowers are held in high esteem. I know some people for whom the Rosh Hashanah morning service is not complete until they've heard the blowing of the *shofar.*

There is a certain amount of fear that is associated with the sound of the *shofar* in the Torah and in some of the prophetic books. But, in The Writings, we find a definite sense of celebration associated with hearing those notes, and that is what we experience now. The *Shofar* Service has three different sub-sections: *Malchuyot* (sovereignty), *Zichronot* (remembrances), and *Shofarot.* In the Central Conference of American Rabbis High Holy Day prayer book *Mishkan Hanefesh: Machzor for the Days of Awe,* we learn: "Each motif for the sounding of the *shofar* is an opportunity to reflect on a different dimension of our thoughts and beliefs about God."[298] And, there is another purpose for the *shofar,* which I quoted above from the Book of Isaiah, and which is at the end of the *Shofar* Service, coupled with a quotation from Rabbi Dov Baer of Mezeritch:

The prophet said: "Cry aloud: Lift up your voice like a shofar!"
"This is the meaning of the verse: See yourself as a shofar, an instrument of the Divine. Do not take pride in your virtue or the power of your deeds. With every mitzvah you do—every act of intellect, goodness, and love—God's spirit breathes through you."[299]

Music is significant for us and is meaningful to us—emotionally, intellectually, and spiritually. We love the comfort of an old familiar tune and the excitement of a new one. Whether it is chanted or sung a cappella, played with one instrument or an entire band or orchestra, music can evoke feelings of joy and sadness, respect and defiance, reverence and insubordination, optimism and pessimism, hope and despair. Some music can be linked with a particular occasion or time of the year, other music connects us with memories of experiences and people. The stories that follow fit into that last category and, like most of the experiences in this book, they brought a smile to the faces of the people who wrote about them. Music continued to connect them with their deceased family.

Stacey is a former student from my congregation in Hingham:

"My father's mother, whom we all referred to as 'Ema', passed a few years back. She was and remains one of the classiest, strongest and fiercest women I've ever known. She put up with absolutely nothing and taught us about respect, family as a priority, and knowing who you are in the world. She slowly fell ill over her later years, with tremors and difficulties walking. Her hearing was terrible, but she could read lips better than anyone.

Despite her maladies, I always saw her as the dazzling gem from Woodmere, Long Island. Everyone knew her and respected her. She and my grandfather were country club, social butterflies. They went out all the time to dinners and dances. They told grand stories of their earlier years. They loved jazz and the music of the 30's and 40's. In fact, at nearly all of our bar and bat mitzvah parties, my Ema and grandfather walked in the room to the swells of "In the Mood" by Glenn Miller. It was 100% her signature song, and she wagged her little pointer fingers in the dance style of those times.

When she really fell ill, it was shortly before Thanksgiving 2017. Nearly our entire family had flown to Boca, to her home, for the holiday. Though we cooked and tried to keep things as "normal" as we could, my Ema was in and out of consciousness, and her home nurses were really there in lieu of hospice. As always, Ema held up and held us all together until after the holiday. We stuffed ourselves full of turkey and brisket, as she would have insisted. We then cleaned up, we hugged and consoled my grandfather, and we said our goodbyes to the woman who raised us all.

My family then flew home. That very afternoon, after walking through our door and putting some bags away, the phone rang. It was my father, with the news that my Ema had left us. We all expected it, but now it was real. I began to cry. I sat down on our living room couch and little Ben—3 at the time—climbed up into my lap. I told him Ema was in heaven, and we blew her kisses. I didn't want him to continue seeing me cry, and so I turned on the TV.

I don't know why, but for some reason, the last channel on had been PBS. This was so unlikely; we were usually subjected to cartoons and lots of Disney Jr. Before any images even registered on the screen, I began to hear familiar music notes playing. When the picture eventually showed up, I saw that they were airing an advertisement for "Big Band" music and were going through a variety of songs sampled on the CD collection. Perhaps you've guessed it—the notes that were playing, just seconds after the phone call, were those from "In the Mood." Her song. 100%.

Just writing this, I'm tearing up. It was as if she was speaking directly to me or wrapping me in a giant embrace from so far away. I've never had an experience quite like it—I had chills and felt so completely connected to her. I was speechless. It was a message of love, one last time. I'll tell the story until the day I die. When/if we one day reunite in heaven, I'll return the hug."

Christine:

"This past December, more than a year after Gary's passing, my sister flew out here to Illinois from New York to enjoy the holidays with me and my family. During that week, I suggested that she and I treat ourselves to a night out. I chose a special restaurant that Gary and I had once gone to at Christmastime and remembered that it was beautifully decorated. We were seated at (of all tables) the same

table Gary and I shared nine years ago. When I mentioned that to my sister as we were sitting down, she reassuringly said that Gary was with us.

After dinner, I thought it would be fun to show my sister around town and have an after-dinner drink at an old historic hotel in the area. We got in my car and I started to drive. I always have Pandora playing on my radio. And most of the time, it's a random collection of songs. A song started to play, but my sister pointed out to me that the song that was playing was not the song that was identified on the screen. So, I asked her what was on the screen and she told me that it was 'Just the Two of Us' by Grover Washington, even though that was not the song playing.

I was a little surprised by that because, as I explained to her, that was one of my favorite songs while Gary and I were dating. And, when we were planning our wedding, I suggested this song as our first dance song. Gary told me that it really wasn't 'just the two of us' since he had the two boys, and I agreed that it really was the four of us. But I remember him telling me that, when the kids were grown and in their own lives, then it would be 'just the two of us' and we would have our 'us' time. That song title remained on my screen all the way to the hotel, even though the songs played were different. And my sister and I both agreed that Gary really was with us.

I shared with my sister that, while Gary and I were dating, he had put together a cassette tape of songs that he felt told a story of our courtship. And he added 'Just the Two of Us' on the tape because he knew how much I liked it. We reached the hotel, went into the lounge area, sat at a table far from the little stage, and ordered drinks as a jazz quartet was setting up. They welcomed everyone in the room and, to our surprise, began to play 'ust the Two of Us!' We could not believe what we were hearing!

While the band was playing that song, my sister wanted to know more about the other songs on that tape. I told her that there were just a few that stuck out in my mind—one being Neil Diamond's "Forever in Blue Jeans.' I told her that Gary loved this song and always told me he couldn't promise me fancy things, but he could promise me happiness and blue jeans. To our shock, the very next *song the band played was 'Forever in Blue Jeans.' That made it certain to us that Gary really was trying to get our attention!*

Gary and I would have celebrated our 39th anniversary this past June. Ever since that date, 'Just the Two of Us' is almost always the first song that comes up in my car. I take it as a 'Hello"'from Gary."

Lisa attended one of my Zoom talks:

"Yesterday I went for my morning walk. I put in my iPod earbuds, started Sibelius Symphony #5, put the iPod in my front pants pocket and started walking—the same routine that I've done for about a month. As I walked, I thought about Darrell's memorial service, the priest, and what I could have done differently.

About twenty minutes later and well into the third movement, the Sibelius suddenly changed to Vivaldi's Gloria in D, "Et in Terra Pax"! That was the piece of music chosen by Darrell to start his service! I have no explanation of how the music changed. That's never happened to me before. I hadn't listened to Vivaldi for many months.

Even if someone could give me a technical reason why the music changed, could they explain why it changed to that particular piece? Darrell had picked out 8 recordings of Vivaldi's Gloria. We had sat together and listened to them all. Then he picked the one that he wanted played at his memorial service. And it was.

I wrote about this sign when it happened because I didn't want to forget it. I felt it was important to have the experience and not miss the point. This was breathtaking. Stunning.

We connected through the music. The sign was a beautiful reminder."

CHAPTER 15: SIGNS: FEELING BLESSED AND RECOGNIZING OUR BLESSINGS FROM GOD

"The conception of an after-life is fundamental to the Jewish religion; it is an article of faith in the Jews' creed. The denial of the after-life constitutes a denial of the cornerstone of the faith. This concept is not merely an added detail that may lose its significance in some advanced age. It is an essential and enduring principle." [300]

"The measure of your blessing is the measure of your loss. We focus on the end of life, but each life is filled with days of accomplishment, beauty, wonder and love. When someone we love passes away, remember the blessing. If we could go back, we would choose to love all over again, even knowing it cannot last forever." [301]

"For love is fierce as death." [302]

"Our ability to receive God's blessings with thanksgiving will never exceed God's ability to bless us. For those who have cultivated the habit of gratitude, no matter how large a bowl we set out to receive God's blessings, it will always overflow." [303]

"Faith is a place of mystery, where we find the courage to believe in what we cannot see and the strength to let go of our fear of uncertainty." [304]

"Most of us who are searching for spiritual connection spend too much time looking up at the sky and wondering why God lives so far away. God lives within us, not above us. Sharing our gifts and talents with the world is the most powerful source of connection with

God."[305]

A fundamental concept...blessings...gratitude...love... faith. What a powerful and meaningful combination to have in your life! If we were to be guided by a fundamental concept, to appreciate the blessings of life, to be habitually grateful, to feel that love is as strong as death (or stronger), to be courageous enough to have faith, wouldn't our lives be richer and happier? Of course, I would respond with a "yes." For me, the answers are easy. They weren't always "yes", but they have become "yes" over the years, and that is because of the important influence of certain people and experiences. I have come to see the existence of "signs" as blessings, as gifts from a loving God, and as the opportunity to maintain contact with the people we loved who have died. Furthermore, the crucial role of signs as mostly positive phenomena has deep and significant roots in the Hebrew Bible and in Jewish tradition.

The Hebrew word for "sign" is *"oht."* As I have done in previous chapters, I want to make you aware of how frequently we read about signs in the Hebrew Bible:

- Genesis 1: God sets the lights in the sky to be signs for the times of the days
- Genesis 9: The rainbow will be a sign that God will honor a covenant with humanity and will never again send a flood to destroy the earth
- Genesis 17: Circumcision will be a sign of the covenant
- Exodus 3: When a reluctant Moses asks God why he should go to Pharaoh, God assures him that God's presence will be a sign for him
- Exodus 4: A still-reluctant Moses is assured by God that the Egyptians will pay attention to the signs given by God
- Exodus 4: God provides a rod to Moses and Aaron, with which the signs will be performed
- Exodus 4: Moses tells Aaron about all of God's commitments and signs
- Exodus 7: God says to Moses that Pharaoh's heart will be

hardened in order to multiply signs and marvels
- Exodus 10: God commands Moses to go to Pharaoh so that signs can be displayed and to recount how signs have appeared
- Exodus 13: As a reminder of God freeing the people from Egypt, they are supposed to have a "sign" on the hand and the forehead—which became the basis for *tefillin* [phylacteries]
- Exodus 31: Observing the Sabbath will be a sign of the eternal covenant between the people of Israel and God (this became the third verse of the *Shabbat* song *V'shamru)*
- Numbers 14: God wants to know how long the people will continue to have no faith despite all of the signs that have been performed
- Deuteronomy 4: Moses reminds the people how unique it was that God chose them and provided signs and other means to rescue them
- Deuteronomy 11: God's words should be a sign on the hand
- Deuteronomy 13: Do not trust signs from prophets of another god
- Deuteronomy 28: Curses will be a sign for the people and their offspring for not having obeyed God's commandments
- Deuteronomy 34: Moses is unique for God having chosen him to show signs sent by God
- Joshua 4: Joshua selects twelve men and has each of them lift a stone onto his shoulder as a "symbol" [the same Hebrew word for "sign" is used here]
- Joshua 6: Gideon asks God for a sign that it is God speaking to him
- 1st Samuel 2: The death of the priest Eli's two sons on the same day will be a sign to him how much he has failed God
- 1st Samuel 14: Jonathan says that what the Philistine soldiers say will be a sign about what God is doing for him and his soldiers
- Isaiah 7: God will provide a sign that will be a young woman giving birth to a son (this is the basis for the Christian belief in "virgin birth")
- Isaiah 55: A cypress and a myrtle will be an everlasting sign of

God
- Isaiah 66: God will set a sign among nations and gather them together
- Jeremiah 32: The prophet praises God for displaying signs and marvels in Egypt and freeing the people Israel with signs and marvels
- Psalm 105: Moses and Aaron performed God's signs in Egypt
- Daniel 6: King Darius praises God performing signs and wonders

Most of these Biblical references promote a link between God and human beings and are generally positive in nature. Some of them—such as the lights in the Creation Story, the rainbow from the Flood Story, the reassuring presence and support of God for Moses, the wearing of *tefillin,* the observance of Shabbat, the gathering together of many nations, and the signs performed in Egypt—are among the most significant beliefs and practices in Judaism. In the Hebrew Bible, the signs are proof of God's love and concern, which are inherent in the covenant relationship. And, they are initiated by God, not solicited by humans, and are regarded as having an undeniable link to God. Every one of these signs has a tremendous impact on Jewish identity and continuity. Even if someone chooses not to affirm one of them—such as *tefillin*—that doesn't negate being aware of God's constant presence, or the commandments. Someone who identifies as "spiritual" rather than "religious" can still derive meaning from and an appreciation for the sun and the moon and rainbows, a sense of divine support, a special time to relax and to focus on our inner selves, the ideal of unifying the international community, and the pursuit of freedom for all who are enslaved in ways that are similar to the Israelites' oppression in Egypt.

But the affirmation of signs doesn't stop with the Hebrew Bible. In 1990, Paul Cohen wrote his rabbinical thesis for the Hebrew Union College-Jewish Institute of Religion in Cincinnati. It was entitled: *Modes of Divine Communication: Aspects of the Rabbinic Views.* He has given me permission to quote him, and I am doing so because his focus was on the rabbinic emphasis on perceived signs. Rabbi Cohen—who was a rabbinical school student when he wrote the thesis—reached several conclusions:

1) "The Mishnah, Tosefta and the Babylonian Talmud each contain a significant amount of information concerning the interpreting of signs and omens as communication from God."[306]

2) "The references to signs and omens, again in contrast to verbal communication, are quite ubiquitous...This is to say, the rabbis do not draw undue attention to the phenomena of signs and omens, because they are taken for granted (and are thus, in principle, non-controversial)...God works through the natural order and through history in its unfolding and communicates with the people through signs and omens."[307]

3) "Signs and omens, that is to say, portentous phenomena both natural and human, were understood to contain information or instruction of divine origin."[308]

4) "God wishes to maintain contact with creation and makes such contact possible through signs and omens built into the natural order. The concept of randomness has no place in the world of the rabbis, for God created the world carefully and with a plan in mind."[309]

5) "God remains in close touch with creation through the manipulation or control of these phenomena which thereby become purposeful and not merely random."[310]

6) "By the very fact that we are alive and possess certain senses we can all see the natural face of signs and omens. That is to say, no special qualities are necessary to see the sign. All can experience the natural events, but all do not necessarily construe them as signs and omens."[311]

7) "The rabbis depicted have not actively sought out the sign. They reacted to an event or an object as they happened into or upon it."[312]

8) "Signs and omens are implanted and are therefore very intimate, existing in the world around us and even at times em-

anating from within us. Yet, the signs are seen as the work of God."[313]

9) "In a practical way, the sign enhanced the rabbi's understanding of the world and history. The sign could be used to trace the sequence of events leading to the present condition of the Jewish people. For the rabbis, it was axiomatic that there was an order and purpose to the world; all one needed to do was to read the signs correctly to see this."[314]

To sum up these conclusions:

First, signs are communication from God, ubiquitous, taken for granted, and part of the natural order. Second, signs are natural and human phenomena, God's way of maintaining purposeful (not random) contact with us. Third, you don't have to be special in order to see a sign. Nor do you have to actively seek out a sign, but it is your reaction that determines whether you recognize it or not. Fourth, signs are viewed as the work of God. The rabbis learned to read them and attach significance to them so that they could understand the world better.

I am well aware that the signs people believe they are receiving from deceased loved ones would not be regarded by some people as being on the same level or in the same class as the sun and the moon, rainbows, circumcision, a "face-to-face" with God, tefillin, Shabbat, unifying the world's nations, and The Ten Plagues. But they have a common thread, and that is the belief that God is behind them. Cohen provides a large number of textual citations, but I am sharing just two of them with you:

"Aher's daughter came before Rabbi and said to him: 'O master, support me!' He asked her: 'Whose daughter are you?' She replied: 'I am Aher's daughter.' He said: 'Are any of his children left in the world? ...' She answered: 'Remember his Torah and not his deeds.' Immediately, a fire came down and enveloped Rabbi's bench. Rabbi wept and said: 'If it be so on account of those who dishonor her, how much the more so on account of those who honor her!'

The verdict in heaven seems to be in favor of Aher. This is revealed in the sign that appears during the conversation between his daughter and Rabbi. The merit of Aher is proclaimed through the sign given to Rabbi...Here Rabbi is prevented from acting callously towards this woman. The merit which Aher achieved through the study of Torah is highlighted as well as, implicitly, the _zekhut_ of Rabbi who merited such an intervention. BT Haggigah 15b[315]

In another story of a confrontation with a Sadducee, Rabban Jonathan b. Zakkai's legal opinion is divinely vindicated by the death of that same Sadducee. The Sadducee had come to offer a sacrifice and, through a bit of deception, R. Jonathan b. Zakkai renders him unfit to perform the ritual. The Sadducee threatens revenge but dies before he can make good on his threat. His death occurs only three days after this incident. (Tosefta Parah 3: 8) This sign comes to validate the superiority of the sages over the Sadducees.[316]

A fire comes down and envelops the bench of the man who has dishonored the daughter of a colleague, albeit a colleague who was not approved of by others. How do you explain that logically? Where did the fire come from? How do you explain it scientifically? Is all of this made up just to prove a point and it really didn't happen at all? And, if this story is judged to be far-fetched and unrealistic, why include it in the Talmud? I believe it is included because it is a story about showing respect—even for the children of those for whom you have no respect. It is about merit; "Rabbi" merited this sign because he was basically a decent man who said something terrible. The second story is about attributing death to God, and about the conflict between the Pharisees and the Sadducees. Does the Sadducee die because he threatened revenge? Does God choose sides by causing the death of the Sadducee? Or is this just pure coincidence, luck, or Fate? Or is it totally disconnected from the interaction between Rabban Jonathan and the nameless Sadducee? In each case, both of the actions are viewed as being sent by God.

Just as the Rabbis could decide what the reason was for something happening, so can we. Just as they could think that God was behind what happened to them, and especially the phenomena and events that couldn't be explained logically, so can we. It may just be a matter of semantics that the significant word *oht* in Hebrew is translated as "sign" in English, and that the word describing the supernatural occurrences and experiences presented in this book is "signs." For the most part, the signs in the Hebrew Bible are positive, impactful, and connective. So are the signs that have been related in the close to 75 stories in this book.

One thing more, and this is really important. I believe that the signs are blessings provided for us by God. Most of the time, when we think of the word "blessing," we think of a series of words that are said before or after we do something—like eating or studying or beginning a holiday. Based on a *gematria* interpretation [numerology] of Deuteronomy 10:12, the Talmud mandates the recitation of 100 blessings each day.[317] The first time we encounter the word "blessing" in the Torah is in God's promise to Abram:

I will make of you a great nation, and I will bless you: I will make your name great, and you shall be a blessing. I will bless those who bless you and curse him that curses you; And all the families of the earth shall bless themselves by you."[318]

In the Hertz Edition of Torah commentary, we read:

These words contain the ideal which Abram was to set himself, to become a blessing to humanity by the beneficent influence of his godly life and by turning others to a knowledge of God...And such has indeed been the role played by the children of Abraham on the stage of human history.[319]

Other references in the Torah include:

- God's promise to make Abraham's descendants numerous (Genesis 22)
- Isaac's blessing in Genesis, Chapter 27 (mentioned in verses 4, 11, 28, and 41)
- Moses' mention of it in Deuteronomy 11 and 29 (paired with a curse)
- Moses' extended blessing of the tribes in Deuteronomy 31—in the Torah portion that is called *V'zot Hab'rachah,* "(and)This is the Blessing."

With these citations, we have the word "blessing" meaning an elevated and esteemed position worthy of a role model, a hope for many descendants, a status (that, unfortunately, becomes a source of conflict for Esau and Jacob), a clear choice between good and evil, and a farewell speech from the great leader Moses. From all of these examples, I find the most meaning in the first one, which emphasizes being a blessing and having others influenced by the example you set.

Furthermore, there is an entire tractate of the Talmud called *Berachot* or *Berachos.* It presents in meticulous detail the occasions on which blessings should be said and the formulaic wording which is to be used. In the Introduction, Hersh Goldwurm— General Editor of the Schottenstein Edition of the *Talmud Bavli* —writes in Volume 1 of Tractate *Berachos:*

"In essence, a blessing (which invariably begins and/or ends with the formula Blessed are You, Hashem), is an **acknowledgment of God as the Creator of the phenomenon beheld** [Emphasis added], the Commander of the mitzvah performed, or Provider of the benefit enjoyed. Sometimes, a blessing simply acknowledges; at times it also implores. Always, it serves to heighten **our awareness of our Heavenly Father and His intimate closeness to us.**" [Emphasis added][320]

He goes on to comment about the interpretation of the Sages

that a hundred blessings should be recited every day:

"By thoughtfully blessing and acknowledging God on one hundred occasions throughout the day, one cultivates **a profound awareness and awe of the Creator**, [Emphasis added] and learns to go in His ways and love and serve Him with the totality of heart and soul."[321]

That is especially pertinent to what this book has covered. The stories and experiences of the people whom I have quoted are a blessing to them and can be a blessing for others. Contrary to what my original thoughts were, there are many Jewish traditional sources that attribute value to what I labeled in the beginning of this book as "supernatural." Just as our reciting of blessings shows that we are not taking for granted what we have or what we are doing, so the reciting of stories and experiences is indicative of not taking for granted a connection to our deceased loved ones. Just as feeling blessed with good health or love or friends is positive, so is the feeling of receiving signs that lead to joy and hope and faith. Just as there is an affirmative connection with God through the reciting of blessings and the attributing to God of what we have, so is there an affirmative connection with God through the experience of signs. There are no witches or magic, no delusions or illusions, no fakery or tricks, no strangeness or psychosis.

Two more quotations—from Rabbi Jules Harlow and Rabbi Harvey J. Fields—are relevant here, followed by a personal reflection on blessings:

"The Hebrew *brakhah* formally articulates our gratitude and praise. It provides us with a way of saying 'thank you' to our Creator... When we recite a *brakhah*, we express not only **our gratitude for a specific gift.** [emphasis added] Reciting a *brakhah* reflects our awareness of the bounty the world holds for us... Since reciting a *brakhah* reflects an awareness of what has been given to us, we could call a *b'rakhah* a **not-taking-for-granted.**

[Emphasis added]"[322]

"The religious Jew sees God in every aspect of existence. God is in the beauty of the sunset, in the morning dawn, in the love we feel for another person, in the desire we have to provide for the poor, in the help we experience in times of trouble, in the gratefulness we sense in satisfying our hunger, and in our struggles to overcome evil and suffering. The *brakhah* is a means through which Jews give thanks and praise to God and remind themselves that **life is a sacred opportunity.** [Emphasis added]"[323]

I say a *b'rakhah* every morning when I wake up because I want to thank God that I am alive and ready to start the day. I say the *Sh'ma* before I go to sleep every night because I want to affirm my faith in God. These rituals aren't new for me and I didn't start them as the result of a terrible crisis that led to a sudden change in belief. They have come to mean more to me in the last 27 years since I had a heart attack, and they are representative of the depth and strength of my faith that have both increased as I have gotten older. I still recall my parents telling me to say "thank you" to people because it was the polite thing to do. And, whether I did so or not, and whether I did so reluctantly or sincerely, it was always the *right* thing to do.

God and I have a very close relationship that is not simply confined to formal prayers and formal times for praying—at least, I think it's close. My God loves me, cares about me, listens to me, guides me, and responds to me. When my sense of logic can't provide answers that I'm seeking, my sense of faith does. When there is no logical explanation for what has happened, my faith helps me to understand that some things just can't be explained logically. I take nothing for granted anymore—love, health, success, prosperity, kindness, generosity, time, technology, faith, or belief. They are all blessings. And I know that I can be, and have been, a blessing for other people just as they have been a blessing for me.

No matter how you may define "religious," I fit into Rabbi Fields' description because I see God everywhere, and that includes in the signs about which I have written and in the vivid experiences I and others have provided. I believe that, if God is everywhere, then God is above us, beyond us, and within us. And I believe that God makes it possible for our connections to our deceased loved ones and friends to never die. All we need to do is to be receptive, accepting, faithful, and grateful—not blindly or without thinking, but with joy and hope and love. That adds up to a wonderful life as far as I'm concerned—a sacred opportunity that we shouldn't take for granted. Life is a blessing ... and so are signs.

FOOTNOTES

[1] Dictionary.com—supernatural:
of, relating to, or being **above or beyond what is natural**; unexplainable by natural law or phenomena; abnormal.
of, pertaining to, characteristic of, or **attributed to God** or a deity.

[2] Dr. Mark Pitstick, soulproof.com

[3] Talmud, Sotah 2a, sefaria.org.

[4] JPS Hebrew-English Tanakh, The Jewish Publication Society, Philadelphia, 1999, Genesis 24:44, p. 45.

[5] Sforno on Genesis 24:44-45, sefaria.org.

[6] JPS Hebrew-English Tanakh, Genesis 24:50, p. 46.

[7] Sforno on Genesis 24:50, sefaria.org.

[8] JPS Hebrew-English Tanakh, Genesis 24:51, ibid.

[9] Sforno on Genesis 24:51, sefaria.org.

[10] The Jewish Way in Death and Mourning, Maurice Lamm, Jonathan David Publishers, New York, 1969, p. 221.

[11] What Happens After I Die? Jewish Views of Life After Death, Rifat Sonsino and Daniel B. Syme, UAHC Press, New York, 1990, pp. 11-12.

[12] A History of the Jewish Experience: Eternal Faith, Eternal People, Leo Trepp, Behrman House Publishers, New York, 1962, pp. 431-432.

[13] What Happens After I Die?, p. 15.

[14] "Heaven and Hell in Jewish Tradition," Rabbi Or N. Rose, MyJewishLearning.com.

[15] The Torah: A Modern Commentary (Revised Edition), W. Gunther Plaut, General Editor, Union for Reform Judaism, New York, p. 802.

[16] op.cit., p. 803.

[17] op.cit., pp. 1298-1299.

[18] op.cit., p. 798.

[19] The Five Books of Moses: Genesis, Exodus, Leviticus, Numbers, and Deuteronomy, A New Translation with Introductions, Commentary, and Notes by Everett Fox, Schocken Books, New York, 1995, p. 605.

[20] The JPS Torah Commentary: Leviticus—The Traditional Hebrew Text with the New JPS Translation Commentary, Baruch A. Levine, Nahum M. Sarna, General Editor, Jewish Publication Society, Philadelphia, 1989, p. 133.

[21] The Pentateuch and Haftorahs, Dr. J. H. Hertz, ed., Soncino Press, London, 1978, p. 503.

[22] The Torah: A Modern Commentary, p. 802.

[23] op.cit., pp. 802-803.

[24] Commentary on the Torah: With a New English Translation and the Hebrew Text, Richard Elliott Friedman, HarperSanFrancisco (A Division of HarperCollinsPublishers), New York, 2001, p. 384.

[25] The Pentateuch and Haftorahs, p. 504.

[26] JPS Hebrew-English Tanakh, Jewish Publication Society, Philadelphia, 1999, p. 587.

[27] The Torah: A Modern Commentary, pp. 1298-1299.

[28] The JPS Torah Commentary: Deuteronomy, Jeffrey H. Tigay, 1996, p. 172.

[29] The Torah: A Women's Commentary, Tamara Cohn Eskenazi and Andrea L. Weiss, eds., URJ Press, New York, 2008, pp. 1148-1149.

[30] The Five Books of Moses: A Translation with Commentary, Robert Alter, W. W. Norton & Company, New York and London, 2004, p. 969.

[31] What Happens After I Die?, p. 23.

[32] The Jewish Way in Death and Mourning, p. 222.

[33] Mishnah Peah, 1:1, sefaria.org.

[34] Mishnah Sanhedrin, 10:1, sefaria.org.

[35] Pirke Avot: A Modern Commentary on Jewish Ethics, Rabbi Leonard Kravitz and Rabbi Kerry M. Olitzky, eds., UAHC Press, New York, 1993, p. vii.

[36] op.cit., pp. xi-xii.

[37] Talmud Berachot, 10a, sefaria.org.

[38] Pirke Avot, p. 8.

[39] op,cit, p. 22.

[40] op.cit., p. 29-30.

[41] op.cit., p. 30.

[42] Ibid.

[43] op.cit., p. 43

[44] op.cit., p. 56.

[45] op.cit., p. 65.

[46] op.cit., p. 66.

[47] op.cit., pp. 68-69.

[48] op. cit., p. 98.

[49] op.cit., p. 100.

[50] op.cit., pp. 102-103.

[51] op.cit., pp. 104-105.

[52] Swimming in the Sea of Talmud: Lessons for Everyday Living, Michael Katz and Gershon Schwartz, Jewish Publication Society, Philadelphia, 1998, p. 311.

[53] Mishnah Peah 1:1, sefaria.org.

[54] ibid.

[55] Mishnah Sanhedrin 10:1, sefaria.org.

[56] The Death of Death: Resurrection and Immortality in Jewish Thought, Neil Gillman, Jewish Lights Publishing, Woodstock, VT, 1997, pp. 59-60.

[57] Swimming in the Sea of Talmud, p. 27.

[58] Talmud Ketubot 104a, sefaria.org.

[59] ibid.

[60] ibid.

[61] Talmud Berakhot 34b, sefaria.org.

[62] Talmud Shabbat 63a, sefaria.org.

[63] Talmud Menachot 43b, sefaria.org.

[64] Talmud Pesachim 50a, sefaria.org.

[65] Talmud Berakhot 17a, sefaria.org.

[66] Talmud Pesachim 50a, sefaria.org.

[67] Talmud Niddah 73a, sefaria.org.

[68] Talmud Avodah Zarah, 5a

[69] Talmud Berachot 46a

[70] Talmud Sanhedrin 91b, sefaria.org.

[71] Talmud Berachot 28b, sefaria.org.

[72] *Talmud Berakhot* 18b, sefaria.org.

[73] ibid., sefaria.org.

[74] ibid., sefaria.org.

[75] ibid., sefaria.org.

[76] ibid., sefaria.org.

[77] ibid., sefaria.org.

[78] ibid., sefaria.org.

[79] ibid., sefaria.org.

[80] ibid., sefaria.org.

[81] ibid., sefaria.org.

[82] ibid., sefaria.org.

[83] ibid., sefaria.org.

[84] ibid., sefaria.org.

[85] The Talmud for Beginners, Judith Z. Abrams, Jason Aronson Inc., Northvale, New Jersey, 1993, p. 41.

[86] dictionary.com

[87] The Death of Death, p. 31.

[88] JPS Hebrew-English*Tanakh*, Daniel 12:2, p. 1834.

[89] op.cit., Isaiah 25:8, p. 899.

[90] *Mishkan T'filah*: A Reform *Siddur*, Central Conference of American Rabbis, CCAR Press, New York, 2007, p. 78.

[91] JPS Hebrew-English *Tanakh*, II Kings 2:11, p. 777.

[92] op.cit., Malachi 3:24, p. 1410.

[93] Everyman's Talmud, A. Cohen, Schocken Books, New York, 1978, p. 45.

[94] JPS Hebrew-English *Tanakh*, p. 1088.

[95] *Mishkan T'filah*: A Reform Siddur, p.24.

[96] op.cit., p. 142.

[97] op.cit., p. 138.

[98] A Passover Haggadah: Revised Edition, Central Conference of American Rabbis, New York, Herbert Bronstein, ed., 1994, p. 88.

[99] Everyman's Talmud, p. 270.

[100] The Death of Death, pp. 96-97.

[101] JPS Hebrew-English *Tanakh*, Ezekiel 37:12, p. 1240.

[102] The Death of Death, p. 75.

[103] JPS Hebrew-English *Tanakh*, Daniel 12:1-3, p. 1834.

[104] Sabbath and Festival Prayer Book, The Rabbinical Assembly of America and the United Synagogue of America, Rabbi Morris Silverman, ed., 1946, p. 29.

[105] *Mishkan T'filah*, p. 168.

[106] *Talmud Ketubot*, 111b, sefaria.org.

[107] "Jewish Resurrection of the Dead: When and how will the dead be brought back to life?", myjewishlearning.com. by MJL.

[108] The Death of Death, pp. 273-274.

[109] JPS Hebrew-English *Tanakh*, II Kings 2: 1, 3, 11, pp. 776-777.

[110] Tales of Elijah the Prophet, Peninnah Schram, Jason Aronson Inc., Northvale, New Jersey and London, 1997, p. xxiii.

[111] A Passover Haggadah, p. 68.

[112] op.cit., p. 70.

[113] Gates of Shabbat: A Guide for Observing Shabbat, Mark Dov Shapiro, CCAR Press, New York, 1991, p. 70.

[114] JPS Hebrew-English *Tanakh*, p. 1410.

[115] The Jewish Home: A Guide for Jewish Living, (Updated Edition), Rabbi Daniel B. Syme, Behrman House, Inc., Millburn, New Jersey, 2017, p. 97.

[116] Tales of Elijah the Prophet, pp. xxiii-xxiv.

[117] *Tosifta Sot.* XIII.2, sefaria.org.

[118] *Talmud Yoma* 9b, sefaria.org.

[119] *Talmud Eruvin* 13b, sefaria.org.

[120] *Talmud Avodah Zarah* 10b, 18a, sefaria.org.

[121] *Talmud Sotah*, 2a, sefaria.org.

[122] *Talmud Pesachim*, 94a, sefaria.org.

[123] *Talmud Megillah*, 29a, sefaria.org.

[124] *Talmud Menachot* 53b, sefaria.org.

[125] *Talmud Shabbat* 33b, sefaria.org.

[126] *Talmud Shabbat* 88a, sefaria.org.

[127] *Talmud Sotah* 48b, sefaria.org.

[128] *Talmud Sotah* 33a, sefaria.org.

[129] *Talmud Bava Metzia,* 86a, sefaria.org.

[130] JPS Hebrew-English *Tanakh*, Genesis 29:10-12, 17-18, 20), pp. 57-58.

[131] op.cit., Genesis 35:19-20, p. 74.

[132] op.cit., Jeremiah 31:15-17, p. 1088.

[133] "Why Rachel's Tomb Occupies So Remarkable a Place in the Physical and Spiritual Geography of Judaism, mosaicmagazine.com, Sarah Rindner, December 13, 2019.

[134] ibid.

[135] *Talmud Berakhot* 57b, sefaria.org.

[136] *Kitzur Shulchan Aruch,* "Olat Reiyah, Modeh Ani 1," sefaria.org.

[137] To Pray As A Jew, Rabbi Hayim Halevy Donin, Basic Books, New York, 1980, p. 200.

[138] *Mishkan T'filah*, p. 625.

[139] op.cit., p. 142.

[140] ibid.

[141] *Talmud Shabbat* 119b, sefaria.org.

[142] *Talmud Shabbat* 119a, sefaria.org.

[143] The Legends of the Jews, Volume I, Louis Ginzberg, Jewish Publication Society of America, Philadelphia, 1968, p. 241.

[144] A Gathering of Angels: Angels in Jewish Life and Literature, Morris B. Margolies, Jason Aronson, Inc., Northvale, New Jersey, 2000, pp. 101-102.

[145] Authorised Daily Prayer Book: Revised Edition, Dr. Joseph H. Hertz, Bloch Publishing Company, New York, 1971, pp. 312-313.

[146] The Jewish Book of Why, Alfred Kolatch, Jonathan David Publishers, Middle Village, New York, 1981, p. 245.

[147] JPS Hebrew-English *Tanakh*, Job 1:8, p. 1657.

[148] *Talmud Bava Batra*, 16a:8, sefaria.org.

[149] The Jewish Home, pp. 105-106.

[150] The Book of Why, p. 65.

[151] The Jewish Home, p. 189.

[152] The Second Jewish Book of Why, Alfred J. Kolatch, Jonathan David Publishers, Inc., Middle Village, New York, 1985, p. 177.

[153] "Who's Afraid of the Evil Eye?", moment magazine.org., George E. Johnson, 2014.

[154] *Pirke Avot*: A Modern Commentary on Jewish Ethics, Leonard

Kravitz and Kerry M. Olitzky, eds., UAHC Press, New York, 1993, p. 24.

[155] op.cit., p. 25.

[156] op.cit., p. 26.

[157] op.cit., p. 27.

[158] ibid.

[159] sefaria.org.

[160] ibid.

[161] ibid.

[162] ibid.

[163] *Talmud Berakhot* 55b, sefaria.org.

[164] *Talmud Bava Metzia*, 85a, sefaria.org.

[165] *Talmud Bava Metzia* 107b, sefaria.org.

[166] *Midrash Tanchuma, Emor*, sefaria.org.

[167] moment magazine.org.

[168] *Pirke Avot*, p. 31.

[169] *Rabbeinu Bahya, Bamidbar* 12, sefaria.org.

[170] Major Trends in Jewish Mysticism, Gershom G. Scholem, Schocken Books, New York, 1978, pp. 10-11.

[171] The Everything Kabbalah Book, Mark Elber, Adams Media, F+W Publications, Inc., Avon, Massachusetts, 2006, p. xi.

[172] Tales of the Hasidim, Martin Buber, Schocken Books, New York, 1991, p. xvii.

[173] op.cit., pp. 1-2.

[174] The Everything Kabbalah Book, p. 5.

[175] The Grief Journey and the Afterlife: Jewish Pastoral Care for Bereavement, Simcha Paull Raphael, Albion-Andalus Books, Boulder, Colorado, 2015, pp. 61-62.

[176] op.cit., pp. 63, 62

[177] JPS Hebrew-English Tanakh, Jeremiah 7:30-31, p. 1026.

[178] op. cit., Jeremiah 19:4-5, p. 1057.

[179] The Grief Journey, p. 66.

[180] ibid.

[181] op.cit., p. 68.

[182] op.cit., pp. 69-70.

[183] The Everything Kabbalah Book, p. 234.

[184] JPS Hebrew-English Tanakh, Exodus 34:7, p. 188.

[185] The Everything Kabbalah Book, p. 234.

[186] Jews: The Essence and Character of a People, Arthur Hertzberg and Aron Hirt-Manheimer, HarperCollins Publishers, New York, 1999, pp. 155-156.

[187] Tales of the Hasidim, Martin Buber, Schocken Books, New York, 1991, Book One, pp. 84-85.

[188] op.cit., p. 85.

[189] op.cit., Book Two, p. 121.

[190] op.cit., Book Two, p. 122.

[191] op.cit., Book One p. 112.

[192] op.cit., Book One, Page 115.

[193] ibid.

[194] op.cit., p. 117

[195] op.cit., Book One, p. 157.

[196] op.cit., Book Two, pp. 271-272.

[197] op.cit., Book One, p. 158.

[198] op.cit., Book One, p. 296.

[199] op.cit., Book Two, p. 182.

[200] op.cit., Book Two, p. 197.

[201] The Essential Kabbalah: The Heart of Jewish Mysticism, Daniel C. Matt, HarperOne, HarperCollins Publishers, New York, 1994, p. 1.

[202] Tales of the Hasidim, p. 6.

[203] Merriam-Webster Online Dictionary

[204] Saul McLeod, "Attribution Theory," simply psychology.org., 2012.

[205] David Spiegelhalter, in "Coincidences and the Meaning of Life," Julie Beck, theatlantic.com, February 23, 2016.

[206] SQuire Rushnell, When God Winks: How the Power of Coincidence Guides Your Life, Howard Books, New York, 2001.

[207] Laura Lynne Jackson, Signs: The Secret Language of the Universe, Spiegel & Grau, New York, 2019, p. xviii.

[208] David Emery, "What Is Superstition? How Does It Differ from Religion?," liveabout.com, December 27, 2019.

[209] Neil Dagnall and Ken Drinkwater, "The science of superstition —and why people believe in the unbelievable," the-conversation.com, July 2, 2018.

[210] Corey Nachman, "The 30 Strangest Superstitions in Sports History," Business Insider Online, August 9, 2011.

[211] Jewish Federation of Baltimore, associated.org, October 27, 2019.

[212] Saul McLeod, "Attribution Theory."

[213] Julie Beck, "Coincidences and the Meaning of Life."

[214] Yitta Halberstam and Judith Leventhal, Small Miracles for the Jewish Heart: Extraordinary Coincidences from Yesterday and Today, Sterling Ethos, New York, 2014, pp. 11,13.

[215] op.cit., p. 43.

[216] SQuire Rushnell, When God Winks: How the Power of Coincidence Guides Your Life, pp. xix-xx.

[217] op.cit., pp. 112-113.

[218] Laura Lynne Jackson, Signs: The Secret Language of the Universe, p. xviii.

[219] Mitch Albom, www.jewelsofelul.com, September 1, 2020.

[220] Anita Diamant, Saying Kaddish, Schocken Books, New York, 1998, p. 23.

[221] Alfred J. Kolatch, The Jewish Mourner's Book of Why, Jonathan David Publishers, Middle Village, New York, 1993, p. 135.

[222] Hillel Halkin, After One-Hundred-and-Twenty: Reflecting on Death, Mourning, and the Afterlife in Jewish Tradition, Princeton University Press, Princeton, New Jersey, 2016, p. 138.

[223] The Authorised Daily Prayer Book, Joseph H. Hertz, Bloch Publishing Company, New York, 1971, p. 270.

[224] Mishkan HaNefesh: Yom Kippur: Machzor for the Days of Awe, CCAR Press, New York, Kindle Edition, 2015, p. 123.

[225] Alfred J. Kolatch, The Jewish Mourner's Book of Why, pp. 123-124.

[226] The Jewish Way in Death and Mourning, pp. 160-161.

[227] After One-Hundred-and-Twenty, pp. 143-144.

[228] The Grief Journey and the Afterlife, p. 33.

[229] Hadassah Magazine, July/August 2020, p. 31.

[230] Rabbi Elie Kaunfer, "Saying Kaddish Without A Minyan?", myjewishlearning.com, April 23, 2020, p. 1.

[231] The Jewish Mourner's Book of Why, p. 234.

[232] Talmud Bava Metzia 86b, sefaria.org.

[233] Talmud Taanit 9a, sefaria.org.

[234]The Jewish Mourner's Book of Why, op.cit.

[235]After One-Hundred-and-Twenty, pp. 150, 152.

[236] Kitzur Shulchan Aruch, 128, sefaria.org.

[237]After One-Hundred-and-Twenty, 169, 170, 171.

[238]The Jewish Mourner's Book of Why, p. 135.

[239] Leon Wieseltier, Kaddish, Albert A. Knopf, New York, 1998, pp. 301, 302, 305.

[240]op.cit., pp. 386-387.

[241] "Shared ADC's (After Death Communications), soulproof.com

[242] The Hand on the Mirror: A True Story of Life Beyond Death, Janis Heaphy Durham, Grand Central Publishing, New York and Boston, 2015, p. 1.

[243] "The Experience of God," Kenneth D. Roseman, CCAR Journal: The Reform Jewish Quarterly, Winter 2020, Central Conference of American Rabbis, New York, p. 54.

[244]Talmud Berakhot, 55b, sefaria.org.

[245] ibid.

[246] Talmud Berakhot, 56b, sefaria.org.

[247] JPS Hebrew-English Tanakh, Genesis 37:19, p. 78.

[248] op.cit., Genesis 41:33, p. 87.

[249] op.cit., Daniel 7:27, p. 1823.

[250] op.cit., p. 1772.

[251] The Jewish Study Bible, Adele Berlin and Marc Zvi Brettler, eds., Oxford University Press, New York, 2004, p. 1612.

[252] Talmud Berakhot 55a, sefaria.org.

[253] op.cit., 55b.

[254] ibid.

[255] ibid.

[256] ibid.

[257] Talmud Berakhot, 56a, sefaria.org.

[258] op.cit., 56b, sefaria.org.

[259] ibid.

[260] op.cit., 57b.

[261] ibid.

[262]JPS Hebrew-English Tanakh, Psalms 36:10, p. 1454.

[263] op.cit., Psalms 40:4, p. 1459.

[264] The Jewish Way in Death and Mourning, p. 161.

[265] The Jewish Way in Death and Mourning, Maurice Lamm, p. 221.

[266] "Judaism and Numbers," Rabbi Geoffrey Dennis, myjewishlearning.com, Sukkot 2020, Reprinted with permission from The Encyclopedia of Jewish Magic, Myth, and Mysticism (Llewellyn Worldwide)

[267] Talmud Bava Kamma 97b, sefaria.org.

[268] JPS Hebrew-English Tanakh, Genesis 1:3-5, p. 1.

[269] ibid.

[270] ibid.

[271] ibid.

[272] ibid.

[273] ibid.

[274] ibid.

[275] ibid.

[276] ibid.

[277] ibid.

[278] "What Does the Chai Symbol Signify?", Ariela Pelaia, www.learnreligions.com, April 17, 2019.

[279] Edward Hoffman, The Hebrew Alphabet: A Mystical Journey, Chronicle Books, San Francisco, 1998, pp. 12-13.

[280] Mark Elber, The Everything Kabbalah Book, pp. 30, 71, 122.

[281] JPS Hebrew-English Tanakh, Genesis 1: 14-19, pp. 1-2.

[282] JPS Hebrew-English Tanakh, Genesis 4:21, p. 8.

[283] The Jewish Study Bible (iBook), Second Edition, Adele Berlin and Marc Zvi Brettler, editors, Oxford University Press, New York, 2014, p. 4530.

[284] Healing Psalms That Help You Cope with Life, Rabbi Joshua O. Haberman, John Wiley & Sons, Hoboken, New Jersey, 2003, p. 146.

[285] The Pentateuch & Haftorahs, J.H. Hertz, ed., Soncino Press, London, 1978, p. 16.

[286] The JPS Torah Commentary: Genesis, Nahum M. Sarna, Jewish Publication Society, Philadelphia, 1989, p. 37.

[287] JPS Hebrew-English Tanakh, Genesis 31:27, p. 64.

[288] op.cit., Exodus 15: 1, 20, p. 145, 146.

[289] op.cit., Numbers 10: 1, 2, 8-10, pp. 304-305.

[290] The Torah: A Modern Commentary (Revised Edition), URJ Press, New York, 2005, p. 957.

[291] A. Maclaren quoted in The Psalms: Hebrew Text & English Translation With an Introduction and Commentary, A. Cohen, The Soncino Press, London, 1950, p. 479.

[292] Traditional Prayers, Modern Commentaries, Volume 3, P'sukei D'zimrah (Morning Psalms), Rabbi Lawrence A. Hoffman, ed., Jewish Lights Publishing, Woodstock, Vermont, 1999, p. 5.

[293] op.cit., p. 9.

[294] op.cit., p. 11.

[295] op.cit., p. 12.

[296] JPS Hebrew-English Tanakh, Leviticus 23:34, p. 262.

[297] op.cit., Leviticus 25:9-10, p. 265.

[298] Mishkan Hanefesh: Machzor for the Days of Awe, CCAR Press, New York, 2015, p. 262.

[299] op.cit., p. 268.

[300] Rabbi Maurice Lamm, The Jewish Way in Death and Mourning, p. 224.

[301] Rabbi David Wolpe, Jewels of Elul, August 29, 2020.

[302] JPS Hebrew-English Tanakh, The Song of Songs 8:6, p. 1739.

[303] Rabbi Harold Kushner, Mishkan HaNefesh: Machzor for the Days of Awe, CCAR Press, New York, 2015, p. 589.

[304] Brene Brown, The Gifts of Imperfection: Let Go of Who You Think You're Supposed to Be and Embrace Who You Are, Hazelden Publishing, Center City, Minnesota, 2010, p. 90.

[305] op.cit., p. 112.

[306] Paul Cohen, Modes of Divine Communication: Aspects of the Rabbinic Views, Hebrew Union College-Jewish Institute of Religion, Cincinnati, Ohio, 1990, p. 150.

[307] op.cit., p. 154.

[308] op.cit., p. 123.

[309] op.cit., p. 124.

[310] op.cit., p. 126.

[311] op.cit., p. 137.

[312] op. cit., p. 139.

[313] op.cit., p. 144.

[314] op.cit., p. 146.

[315] op.cit., pp. 132-133.

[316] op.cit., p. 133.

[317] *Talmud Menachot 43b, Orach Chaim* 46:13, sefaria.org.

[318] JPS Hebrew-English *Tanakh,* Genesis 12: 2-3, p. 21.

[319] The Pentateuch and Haftorahs, J. H. Hertz, Ed., Soncino Press, London, 1978, p. 45.

[320] The Schottenstein Edition of the *Talmud Bavli,* The ArtScroll Series: Tractate *Berachos,* Vol. 1, Hersh Goldwurm, General Editor, Mesorah Publications, ltd, 1997, (First Edition), p. lv.

[321] ibid,

[322] Pray Tell: A Hadassah Guide to Jewish Prayer, by Rabbi Jules Harlow, with Tamara Cohen, Rochelle Furstenberg, Rabbi Daniel Gordis & Leora Tanenbaum, Jewish Lights Publishing, Woodstock, Vermont, 2003, p. 5.

[323] *Bechol Levavcha*: With all your heart, Harvey J. Fields, Union of American Hebrew Congregations, New York, 1976, p. 11.

BIBLIOGRAPHY

Abrams, Judith Z., The Talmud for Beginners, Judith Z. Abrams, Jason Aronson Inc., Northvale, New Jersey, 1993.

Albom, Mitch, www.jewelsofelul.com, September 1, 2020.

Alter, Robert, The Five Books of Moses: A Translation with Commentary, W. W. Norton & Company, New York and London, 2004.

Baltimore, Jewish Federation of, associated.org, October 27, 2019.

Beck, Julie, "Coincidences and the Meaning of Life," theatlantic.com, February 23, 2016.

Berlin, Adele, and Brettler, Marc Zvi, eds., The Jewish Study Bible, Oxford University Press, New York, 2004.

_____The Jewish Study Bible (iBook), Second Edition, Oxford University Press, New York, 2014.

Bronstein, Herbert, ed., A Passover Haggadah: Revised Edition, Central Conference of American Rabbis, New York, 1994.

Brown, Brene, The Gifts of Imperfection: Let Go of Who You Think You're Supposed to Be and Embrace Who You Are, Hazelden Publishing, Center City, Minnesota, 2010.

Buber, Martin, Tales of the Hasidim, Schocken Books, New York, 1991.

Cohen, A., Everyman's Talmud, Schocken Books, New York, 1978.

_____, The Psalms: Hebrew Text & English Translation With an Introduction and Commentary, The Soncino Press, London, 1950.

Cohen, Paul, Modes of Divine Communication: Aspects of the Rabbinic Views, Hebrew Union College-Jewish Institute of Religion, Cincinnati, Ohio, 1990.

Dagnall, Neil, and Drinkwater, Ken, "The science of superstition —and why people believe in the unbelievable," the-conversation.com, July 2, 2018.

Dennis, Rabbi Geoffrey, "Judaism and Numbers," myjewish-learning.com, Sukkot 2020, Reprinted with permission from The Encyclopedia of Jewish Magic, Myth, and Mysticism (Llewellyn Worldwide).

Diamant, Anita, Saying Kaddish, Schocken Books, New York, 1998.

Donin, Rabbi Hayim Halevy, To Pray As A Jew, Basic Books, New York, 1980.

Durham, Janis Heaphy, The Hand on the Mirror: A True Story of Life Beyond Death, Grand Central Publishing, New York and Boston, 2015.

Elber, Mark, The Everything Kabbalah Book, Adams Media, F+W Publications, Inc., Avon, Massachusetts, 2006.

Emery, David, "What Is Superstition? How Does It Differ from Religion?", www.liveabout.com, December 27, 2019.

Eskenazi, Tamara Cohn, and Weiss, Andrea L., eds., The Torah: A Women's Commentary, URJ Press, New York, 2008.

Fields, Harvey J., Bechol Levavcha: With all your heart, Union of American Hebrew Congregations, New York, 1976.

Fox, Everett, The Five Books of Moses: Genesis, Exodus, Leviticus, Numbers, and Deuteronomy, A New Translation with Introductions, Commentary, and Notes by Everett Fox, Schocken Books, New York, 1995.

Friedman, Richard Elliott, Commentary on the Torah: With a

New English Translation and the Hebrew Text, HarperSanFrancisco (A Division of HarperCollinsPublishers), New York, 2001.

Frishman, Rabbi Elyse D., Mishkan T'filah: A Reform Siddur, Central Conference of American Rabbis, CCAR Press, New York, 2007.

Gillman, Neil, The Death of Death: Resurrection and Immortality in Jewish Thought, Jewish Lights Publishing, Woodstock, VT, 1997.

Ginzberg, Louis, The Legends of the Jews, Volume I, Jewish Publication Society of America, Philadelphia, 1968.

Goldberg, Rabbi Edwin, Marder, Rabbi Janet, Marder, Rabbi Sheldon, Morris, Rabbi Leon, Mishkan HaNefesh: Yom Kippur: Machzor for the Days of Awe, CCAR Press, New York, Kindle Edition, 2015.

_____, Mishkan Hanefesh: Yom Kippur: Machzor for the Days of Awe, CCAR Press, New York, 2015.

Goldwurm, Hersh, General Editor, The Schottenstein Edition of the Talmud Bavli, The ArtScroll Series: Tractate Berachos, Vol. 1, Mesorah Publications, ltd., 1997, (First Edition).

Haberman, Rabbi Joshua O., Healing Psalms That Help You Cope with Life, John Wiley & Sons, Hoboken, New Jersey, 2003.

Hadassah Magazine, July/August 2020.

Halberstam, Yitta, and Leventhal, Judith, Small Miracles for the Jewish Heart: Extraordinary Coincidences from Yesterday and Today, Sterling Ethos, New York, 2014.

Halkin, Hillel, After One-Hundred-and-Twenty: Reflecting on Death, Mourning, and the Afterlife in Jewish Tradition, Princeton University Press, Princeton, New Jersey, 2016.

Harlow, Rabbi Jules, with Tamara Cohen, Rochelle Furstenberg, Rabbi Daniel Gordis & Leora Tanenbaum, Pray Tell: A Hadassah Guide to Jewish Prayer, Jewish Lights Publishing, Woodstock, Vermont, 2003.

Hertz, Arthur, and Hirt-Mannheimer, Aron, Jews: The Essence and Character of a People, HarperCollins Publishers, New York, 1999.

Hertz, Dr. J. H., The Pentateuch and Haftorahs, Soncino Press, London, 1978.

_____, Authorised Daily Prayer Book: Revised Edition, Bloch Publishing Company, New York, 1971.

Hoffman, Edward, The Hebrew Alphabet: A Mystical Journey, Chronicle Books, San Francisco, 1998.

Hoffman, Rabbi Lawrence A., Ed., Traditional Prayers, Modern Commentaries, Volume 3, P'sukei D'zimrah (Morning Psalms), Jewish Lights Publishing, Woodstock, Vermont, 1999.

Jackson, Laura Lynne, Signs: The Secret Language of the Universe, Spiegel & Grau, New York, 2019.

Katz, Michael, and Schwartz, Gershon, Swimming in the Sea of Talmud: Lessons for Everyday Living, Jewish Publication Society, Philadelphia, 1998.

Kaunfer, Rabbi Elie, "Saying Kaddish Without A Minyan?", myjewishlearning.com, April 23, 2020.

Kolatch, Alfred J., The Jewish Book of Why, Jonathan David Publishers, Inc., Middle Village, New York, 1981.

_____, The Second Jewish Book of Why, Jonathan David Publishers, Inc., Middle Village, New York, 1985.

_____, The Jewish Mourner's Book of Why, Jonathan David Publishers, Inc., Middle Village, New York, 1993.

Kravitz, Rabbi Leonard, and Olitzky, Rabbi Kerry M., eds., Pirke Avot: A Modern Commentary on Jewish Ethics, UAHC Press, New York, 1993.

Lamm, Maurice, The Jewish Way in Death and Mourning, Jonathan David Publishers, Inc., New York, 1969.

Levine, Baruch A., and Sarna, Nahum M., The JPS Torah Commentary: Leviticus—The Traditional Hebrew Text with the New JPS Translation Commentary, Jewish Publication Society, Philadelphia, 1989.

Margolies, Morris B., A Gathering of Angels: Angels in Jewish Life and Literature, Jason Aronson, Inc., Northvale, New Jersey, 2000.

Matt, Daniel C., The Essential Kabbalah: The Heart of Jewish Mysticism, HarperOne, HarperCollins Publishers, New York, 1994.

McLeod, Saul, "Attribution Theory," simply psychology.org., 2012.

MJL, "Jewish Resurrection of the Dead: When and how will the dead be brought back to life?", myjewishlearning.com.

Nachman, Corey, "The 30 Strangest Superstitions in Sports History," Business Insider Online, August 9, 2011.

Pelaia, Ariela, "What Does the Chai Symbol Signify?", www.learnreligions.com, April 17, 2019.

Plaut, W. Gunther, General Editor, The Torah: A Modern Commentary (Revised Edition), Union for Reform Judaism, New

York, 2005.

Raphael, Simcha Paull, The Grief Journey and the Afterlife: Jewish Pastoral Care for Bereavement, Albion-Andalus Books, Boulder, Colorado, 2015.

Rindner, Sarah, "Why Rachel's Tomb Occupies So Remarkable a Place in the Physical and Spiritual Geography of Judaism," mosaicmagazine.com, December 13, 2019.

Rose, Rabbi Or N., "Heaven and Hell in Jewish Tradition," MyJewishLearning.com.

Roseman, Kenneth D., "The Experience of God," CCAR Journal: The Reform Jewish Quarterly, Winter 2020, Central Conference of American Rabbis, New York.

RUshnell, Squire, When God Winks: How the Power of Coincidence Guides Your Life, Howard Books, New York, 2001.

Sarna, Nahum M., The JPS Torah Commentary: Genesis, Jewish Publication Society, Philadelphia, 1989.

Scholem, Gershom, Major Trends in Jewish Mysticism, Schocken Books, New York, 1978.

Schramm, Peninnah, Tales of Elijah the Prophet, Jason Aronson Inc., Northvale, New Jersey and London, 1997.

Shapiro, Mark Dov, Gates of Shabbat: A Guide for Observing Shabbat, CCAR Press, New York, 1991.

"Shared ADC's (After Death Communications), www.soul-proof.com.

Silverman, Rabbi Morris, ed., Sabbath and Festival Prayer Book, The Rabbinical Assembly of America and the United Synagogue of America, 1946.

Sonsino, Rifat, and Syme, Daniel B., What Happens After I Die? Jewish Views of Life After Death, UAHC Press, New York, 1990.

Stein, Rabbi David Sulomm, JPS Hebrew-English Tanakh, The Jewish Publication Society, Philadelphia, 1999.

Syme, Rabbi Daniel B., The Jewish Home: A Guide for Jewish Living, (Updated Edition), Behrman House, Inc., Millburn, New Jersey, 2017.

Tigay, Jeffrey H., The JPS Torah Commentary: Deuteronomy, The Jewish Publication Society, Philadelphia, 1996.

Trepp, Leo, A History of the Jewish Experience: Eternal Faith, Eternal People, Behrman House Publishers, New York, 1962.

Wieseltier, Leon, Kaddish, Albert A. Knopf, New York, 1998.

Wolpe, Rabbi David, Jewels of Elul, August 29, 2020.

ACKNOWLEDGEMENTS

Pirke Avot, A Modern Commentary on Jewish Ethics, 1993, Leonard Kravitz and Kerry M. Olitzky, © Behrman House, Inc., included with permission www.behrmanhouse.com

What Happens After I Die: Jewish Views of Life After Death, 1990, Rifat Sonsino and Daniel B. Syme, Behrman House, Inc.--© Behrman House, Inc., included with permission www.behrmanhouse.com

A History of the Jewish Experience: Eternal Faith, Eternal People, 1962, Leo Trepp, Behrman House, Inc.--© Behrman House, Inc., included with permission www.behrmanhouse.com

The Jewish Home: A Guide for Jewish Living (Updated Edition), 2017, Rabbi Daniel B. Syme, Behrman House, Inc.--© Behrman House, Inc., included with permission www.behrmanhouse.com

The Hebrew Alphabet: A Mystical Journey, 1998, Edward Hoff-

ABOUT THE AUTHOR

Stephen A. Karol

Rabbi Stephen A. Karol is a native of Kansas City, Missouri, and Rabbi Emeritus of Temple Isaiah in Stony Brook, New York. He was ordained at the Hebrew Union College in Cincinnati in 1977, and has served at Temple Beth Zion in Buffalo, New York, Congregation Sha'aray Shalom in Hingham, Massachusetts, and Temple Isaiah.

He teaches for Temple Isaiah and for the Osher Lifelong Learning Institute (OLLI) at Stony Brook University. He has been a blogger for www.JewishSacredAging.com and for www.jewish-funerals.org.

His book FINDING HOPE AND FAITH IN THE FACE OF DEATH: INSIGHTS OF A RABBI AND MOURNER was given to the newly-ordained rabbis at the Cincinnati campus of the Hebrew Union College in 2019 and was on the reading list for a doctoral program course at HUC in New York for the Spring 2021 semester.

In addition, he has developed 40 talks (Zoom or in-person) about a variety of subjects for synagogues, Jewish Community Centers, Hadassah meetings, and churches.

Rabbi Karol lives in Port Jefferson Station, New York with his wife Donna.

Made in the USA
Coppell, TX
22 May 2022